Quests

Quests

Design, Theory, and History in Games and Narratives

Jeff Howard

A K Peters
Wellesley, Massachusetts

Editorial, Sales, and Customer Service Office

A K Peters, Ltd.
888 Worcester Street, Suite 230
Wellesley, MA 02482
www.akpeters.com

Library of Congress Cataloging-in-Publication Data

Howard, Jeff, 1978-
  Quests : design, theory, and history in games and narratives / Jeff Howard.
     p. cm.
  Includes bibliographical references and index.
  ISBN-13: 978-1-56881-347-9 (alk. paper)
  1. Video games--Authorship. 2. Quests (Expeditions) 3. Quests (Expeditions) in
literature. I. Title.
  GV1469.34.A97H69 2008
  794.8--dc22

                            2007043883

Printed in the United States of America

12 11 10 09 08   10 9 8 7 6 5 4 3 2 1

To my parents, Lamar and Melissa Howard

Contents

It is often modest beginnings that lead to something important. It certainly seems like a little thing, a quest. Everybody has an idea of what a quest is. And yet going deeper into its meaning can serve to bridge some of the deeper gaps in the study of new media. As Howard is aware, quests are a way to "play" literature that can combine the interpretive and configurative functions (in Aarseth's terms) and avoid exclusionist and often unproductive debates. Howard goes beyond the utilitarian and most common view of quests, dwelling instead on their symbolic and meaning-charged possibilities, thus offering a way to teach both literature and new media to those who move effortlessly between print and digital worlds.

This is one of those uncommon books that build bridges between alien disciplines. Howard is a true Renaissance man in these electronic times. He merges his knowledge and love of literature with his enthusiasm for computer games and the unexplored possibilities of the new medium. Human intellectual activity has a common base, be it expressed in the form of poems or computer games, and Howard shows us some of the most stunning connections between the old form of quest literature and the new challenges of games.

This is a book for humanists, who will find a refreshing new relevance to their field. It is also a book for digital theorists, who will be interested in how the old can tell us something about the new. Computer game designers will learn how to make better use of symbolism and allegory to improve the emotional impact of, and give a deeper meaning to, their quests. Other quest theorists have talked of "meaning" in general, but Howard analyzes just what "meaning" could be, what kinds of meaning there are, and how these kinds of meaning are valuable in different ways.

This book's achievements include a history of quest computer games and quest narratives, as well as a summary of classic literary theories about quests; an analysis of newer games with more challenging structures than the ones studied up to now; a convincing discussion of the importance of space in relation to quests; and descriptions of the different kinds of quests. Especially valuable are the book's practical applications, in which quest components are carefully described and then tested in the accompanying exercises. The book also reprints portions of old texts, *Sir Gawain and the Green Knight* and *The Faerie Queen*, which will help the reader understand the historical legacy of quest literature.

I am convinced that the study of the theories proposed and the completion of the exercises in this book (try to make your own Holy Grail!) will fulfil Howard's goal of giving teachers and students "a set of strategies for designing meaningful action," a worthy aim in these times of bad design and drought of the imagination.

Dr. Susana Tosca
Associate Professor
IT University of Copenhagen

This is a book about quests. A quest is a journey across a symbolic, fantastic landscape in which a protagonist or player collects objects and talks to characters in order to overcome challenges and achieve a meaningful goal. This definition draws upon the work of both new media theorists like Espen Aarseth and Susana Tosca and literary critics like Joseph Campbell and Northrop Frye. However, my definition is unique because it seeks to bring together literary and new media theorizations of the quest in a way that can allow designers to create better games. A quest is a middle term, a conceptual bridge that can help to join together many two-part or "binary" pairs that are often considered separately in new media and literary studies. These include:

- game and narrative
- gaming and literature
- technology and mythology
- and meaning and action.

In terms of games and narratives, quests are one way of resolving the debate between "narratologists," who see games as stories, and "ludologists," who see games as rule-based simulations. But this debate is starting to wind down, with some factions suggesting that the argument never actually took place because it was always the product of misunderstanding and vague terminology.[1] This book joins the growing consensus that games and narratives are not fundamentally in conflict and can complement each other.

When we view games and narratives as complementary, we will find three related terms in the discussion of quests:

- quests
- quest games
- and quest narratives.

Quests take place in between games and narratives, as well as within games and narratives. Stories about quests, known as quest narratives, constitute an ancient and well-known literary genre. In these narratives, a quest is a structure in which a hero embarks on a journey to attain a meaningful goal. Quest narratives include heroic epics like *The Odyssey,* medieval romances like *Parzival* or *The Quest for the Holy Grail,* and Renaissance allegories like *The Faerie Queene.* Well-known critics of myth and literature have theorized quest narratives as a universal or "archetypal" structure, such as Joseph Campbell's "monomyth" of the hero's journey or Northrop Frye's idea of the quest as the defining structure of romance. More recent narratologists and literary critics, such as Wayne Erickson in *Mapping the Faerie Queen: Quest Structures and the World of the Poem* and Piotr Sadowski in *The Knight on His*

Quest, have extended understandings of the spatial and temporal patterns of the quest through sophisticated readings of particular narratives.

There is also a shorter but heavily influential history of games that feature quests, or "quest games," extending from early adventure games like the *King's Quest* series up until role-playing games like *The Elder Scrolls IV: Oblivion* and *World of Warcraft.* In these games, a quest is an activity in which players must overcome challenges in order to reach a goal. When players successfully surmount the challenges of a quest and achieve its goal, the players' actions bring about a series of events that may comprise a narrative in the process. But quest games and quest narratives are not entirely separate. Because readers of literature have to work to actively interpret a story, there are game-like elements to quest narratives.

Because game designers sometimes draw upon the conventions of quest narratives, elements of quest narratives have also influenced quest games. For example, the early history of tabletop role-playing games and computer role-playing games drew substantially on the work of J. R. R. Tolkien, a professor of medieval literature and languages who modeled his own quest narratives on the medieval literature that he studied. Game designers often cite Joseph Campbell's "hero's journey" as a pattern for their games. The relationship between quests, quest games, and quest narratives can be visualized as the Venn diagram below, with "quest games" and "quest narratives" forming two circles with one overlapping portion in the middle that stands for "quests."

In addition to the usefulness of these three terms in connecting games and narratives, quests have even more theoretical and practical potential to help reconcile meaning and action. So far, the theoretical literature on quests has revolved around a supposed conflict between meaning and action, but I argue this conflict is illusory. In my theory, quests can be used to unify both

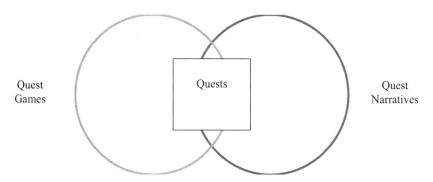

Figure 1. The overlapping relationship of quests, quest games, and quest narratives.

meaning and action. Meaning is at the heart of quest games, and it is a form of meaning that is much closer to literary traditions than other game genres. Quests are about action that is meaningful to a player on the level of ideas, personal ambitions, benefit to society, spiritual authenticity. This is what sets them apart as an especially rich and important gaming activity. Gamers and theorists do not talk about a "quest" to gobble all the white dots in *Pac-Man* or to take out the trash in *The Sims*, just as literary critic W. H. Auden insists that the search for a lost button is not a quest. Instead, designers and players discuss quests to save Princess Zelda, achieve all the virtues of the Avatar in the *Ultima* games, or close the gates to the hellish plane of Oblivion in *The Elder Scrolls IV: Oblivion*.

The meanings of quest games emerge from strategic actions, but these actions have thematic, narrative, and personal implications. Salen and Zimmerman have eloquently called for "meaningful play" as the primary goal of game design, but their definition of meaning involves receiving feedback from a system that makes the outcome of one's choices strategically intelligible (37). In addition to this discernible feedback, I argue that designers can produce meaningful action, as well as helping to bridge the gap between games and narratives, by drawing upon strategies derived from quest narratives, such as medieval romance and Renaissance allegory. In particular, designers can benefit from the tradition of symbolic correspondences that operates in these narratives, in which every space, character, object, and action stands for another idea in a complex array of interrelationships. To function in games, these correspondences should emerge from fun gameplay, discovered through the player's strategic actions undertaken to overcome challenges and achieve goals.

These principles have educational implications, both for how we teach literature through games and how we teach aspiring game designers to design quests. As an exercise, I advocate transforming quest narratives into quest games through the construction of design documents and the use of construction sets, such as the *Aurora Toolset* and *The Neverwinter Nights 2 Toolset*. Many of the exercises in this book challenge readers to do precisely this. While such exercises are useful in pedagogical terms, this does not mean that all quest games must or should be based on works of literature. Literary quest narratives primarily offer a set of strategies for making more meaningful quest games, and quest games present an array of tools for making literary interpretation both interactive and goal-oriented.

Transforming narratives into quest games allows students to see that meaning is produced by cognitive and imaginative activity rather than passively consumed. In other words, readers shape the meaning of a text in the way that both designers and players shape the outcome of a game. This goes slightly against the position of many game theorists and game designers such as Zimmerman, who argues that the interactivity of readers who interpret a book differently is distinct from the interactivity that allows a player to change a game (158). This book seeks to bridge the gap between these two types of interactivity, or what Espen Aarseth calls the "interpretative" and "configurative" functions (64–65). At the same time, I want to allow individual players and readers the right to choose the interpretative goals that they pursue according to their own sense of belief and value, rather than suggesting that a book can mean anything or that a game has to be pure simulation without meaning.

In terms of bridging interpretative and game-like interactivity, the closest ancestor to my own project in literary theory is Jerome McGann's "Ivanhoe Game," as theorized in *Radiant Textuality*. McGann is an accomplished Romanticist and textual studies scholar who invented this exercise, dedicated to showing students how they can "transform" or "deform" the interpretation of a literary work within the rules provided by the author. McGann's work is brilliant, but he does not talk much about the actual historical tradition of video games, which means that he has to reinvent the wheel of game scholarship. He also is not interested primarily in having students design games and has instead designed a predominantly text-based game for them. Without working video games and game design theory as models, the Ivanhoe Game does not have particularly goal-oriented gameplay. It is primarily a metaphor—a highly intelligent application of the concept of games that has little relationship to any particular genre of existing digital games. Somewhere in the middle of Salen and Zimmerman's meaningful play and Jerome McGann's creative "transformation," there is a gap between game design and literary history that remains to be filled. Quests are one way of filling it.

Who Is This Book For?

This book is intended for a broad range of audiences, all of whom can take something useful from each of its sections.

- As a bridge-building text, it belongs in the toolkits of both humanities scholars and independent designers.
- New media researchers can benefit from the analysis and modification of the theories of quest narratives.
- Humanities scholars and professors, such as literature teachers wanting to bring computer-assisted instruction into their classroom in an innovative way, can benefit from the book's combi-

nation of literature, games, and practical classroom exercises. Such professors might consider using this book in a class on the relationship between narratives and games, where it would work well as a practical and accessible textbook. This book includes many tutorials and excercises for use with the Aurora Toolset, which can be purchased with the role-playing game *Neverwinter Nights* for fifteen dollars or less.

- Independent designers seeking to create new, innovative quest games can benefit from the theoretical arguments and tutorials, which present useful skills in the accessible, user-friendly Aurora toolset.

Because the audiences for the book are varied, I have tried to keep overly obscure theory to a minimum, relegating postmodern ideas about language and interpretation primarily to footnotes. Similarly, I have provided historical background on both quest games and quest narratives, assuming that a reader who knows the acronyms for role-playing terminology may not know the plot of *Sir Gawain and the Green Knight* and vice versa. When designers, scholars, and students share knowledge of their respective disciplines and collaborate on focused, unified projects, the results are likely to help everyone involved.

This Book's Structure

After a general introduction to the theory and history of quests, this book contains four chapters about four aspects of quests, each consisting of two subsections. The chapters discuss four theoretical components of quests:

- spaces;
- objects;
- actors;
- challenges.

For each theoretical subsection, there is a corresponding section describing a practical skill associated with this aspect of the quest, with accompanying exercises and suggestions for the use of particular technologies for designing aspects of quests. These four practical sections are:

- level design;
- quest-item creation;
- NPC and dialogue construction;
- event-based programming, or "scripting."

Understanding the theory of the spaces of the quest can improve the practice of level design, and understanding the role of objects in quest narratives and games can help one to craft interesting treasures as goals or rewards of one's quests. Studying NPCs leads to better quest dialogue, and knowing the central challenges of quests leads to better gameplay in the form of scripting.

These correspondences are deliberate, since a key purpose of the book is to build bridges between the theory of literature and games and the practice of game design, both independently and commercially. There is a tendency on the part of many game designers to view theory skeptically because they consider it to be divorced from practice, like Chris Crawford's diagram of a fractured pyramid in which a base of "Interactive Storytelling" is separated from a broken-off tip contemptuously labeled "AArseth [sic] et all [sic]" (74). Crawford's argument is that game designers often do not think that theory can help them to make a better product—an accusation that is frequently leveled against theorists of the ludology/narratology debate. Yet I would respond that designers do not benefit from ignoring the theory or history of quest games or quest narratives, and they may even lose out significantly by being forced to reinvent the wheel of quest design, struggling with a design problem that has already been solved in the history of quest games or quest narratives.

Some game designers might suggest that understanding the "meaning" of quests is not important to design, but this objection overlooks a fundamental aspect of quest design: the audience of role-playing games and adventure games. A player who goes to a game store and selects a role-playing game or an adventure game over a shooter or a simulation is likely to already have an investment in an epic experience. Supporting this idea, Chris Bateman in *21st Century Game Design* offers an audience-centered approach to game design that draws upon extensive quantitative research of audience preferences to classify marketable games, including three overall genres categories of "quest," "strategy," and "simulation." "Quest" games include the genres of adventure and role-playing games, suggesting that these two genres are linked by a shared central activity. As Bateman argues,

> the term quest accurately describes the core value of the games grouped here. All tell stories, and, due to the nature of the medium, these stories tend towards the epic (with more intimate stories better suiting action games). Players expect their quest games to last many hours of play, so stories are often wide in scope. (264)

From Bateman's perspective as a successful designer who has done substantial research into self-reported audience preferences, many gamers prefer a sweeping, epic experience that can best be described as a "quest game," which includes a variety of more commonly used genre labels such as "adventure game" or "RPG." One example of a quest-based RPG that has benefited from its designers' consideration of the meaning of quests is *Neverwinter Nights 2*. The tagline "everything you do has a meaning" points toward the relevance of meaningful action in a commercially successful RPG. This is a deliberate marketing strategy geared toward the idea that players of quest games buy their games on the basis of meaningful quests.[2] Such players want a game to give them a sense that their play is part of an epic storyline with consequences that will affect a simulated world positively or adversely. These players will continue to appreciate their favorite quest forms, whether kill quests or fetch quests, but they will also gravitate toward games that use these forms or others in new and interesting ways.

Notes

[1] Gonzalo Frasca makes this argument in "Ludologists Love Stories, Too: Notes from a Debate That Never Took Place" (Frasca, 2003).

[2] Moreover, reviews of *Neverwinter Nights 2* have suggested that the variety and ingenuity of quests as well as their integration into an engaging storyline is a selling point of the game. For example, the Gamespot review argues that "The quest design is interesting and usually fits well within the context of the story. There are some quests that just require you to find or deliver a certain item, but the required quests are usually much more involved than that. You'll be asked to do everything from saving damsels in distress to answering riddles and even acting as a trial attorney."

Quests as a Bridge Between Games and Narratives

As Jesper Juul explains in *Half-Real: Video Games between Real Rules and Fictional Worlds*, some scholars of video games have written about the concept of the quest as one attempt to resolve a long and bitter conflict between "narratologists" and "ludologists." In game studies, narratologists argue that games can be analyzed as narratives, whereas ludologists (from the Latin *ludare*: "to play") insist that games should be studied for the features that are distinctively related to play, such as rules and simulation. While the definitions of both narrative and game are highly contested by both camps, these theorists tend to define a narrative as a sequence of causally and dramatically connected events that a reader follows in time. In contrast, a game is a set of rules for interactive play. Juul writes:

> As an attempt at bridge-building between the open structure of games and the closed structure of stories, the concept of *quests* has been proposed by Ragnhild Tronstad, Espen Aarseth, and Susan Tosca. Quests in games can actually provide an interesting type of bridge between game rules and game fiction in that the games can contain predefined sequences of events that the player then has to actualize or effect. (17)

Juul concisely defines the difference between a quest and a narrative by focusing on the issue of performative activity, which requires the player of a game to cause events to occur through effort rather than passively observing as these events unfold.

Rather than dispensing with the events of narrative altogether, as many radical ludologists propose, Juul suggests that a game can be interactive and contain a strong story if the player must enact its events. This quality of quests can be more accurately referred to as "enactment" rather than "interactivity." Interactivity means that a player can change aspects of a simulated world, which responds to her actions. Interactivity can result in what Henry Jenkins calls "emergent narratives," such as the conversations that a character has with another character in *The Sims* (128–29). Interactivity is a prerequisite of enactment but is not sufficient to produce it, because enactment refers not just to random changes created by the player in a simulated world but rather to the overcoming of specific challenges that results in particular events. Enactment requires active, goal-directed effort, often in the form of balancing long-term and short-term goals.

In "Quest Games as Post-Narrative Discourse," Aarseth defines a quest in a way that highlights enactment as well as the movement through space and the identification of a player with a virtual identity, or "avatar." He writes that "a player-avatar must move through a landscape in order to fulfill a goal while mastering a series of challenges. This phenomenon is called a quest" (368). Aarseth is one of the leading proponents of ludology and is famous for having vehemently opposed the use of "narratology" to analyze games as stories. Believing that massively multiplayer online role-playing games such as *Everquest* cannot be understood as stories, yet faced with the popularity of some action-adventure games that do seem to have a strong story, Aarseth opts for the intermediary activity of the quest.

Literary Definitions of Quests

In contrast to many but not all ludologists, I argue that a search for meaning is not analogous but rather intrinsic to the design of quests because of the literary history of quest narratives and their associations with religion and mythology. As Tosca acknowledges, "The idea of [the] quest as a search with a transcendent meaning (as in "quest for the Holy Grail") is part of the everyday use of the word and no doubt has some influence in the way players and designers look at them" (sec. 4.1). The word *quest* etymologically comes from the Latin word *questare,* meaning "to seek." This definition suggests a goal-oriented search for something of value. *The Oxford English Dictionary* corroborates this explanation in one of its definitions of "quest": a "search or pursuit, made in order to find or obtain something." A related definition of quest gestures back toward its origins in "mediæval romance," in which a quest is "an expedition or adventure undertaken by a knight to procure some thing or achieve some exploit."

As these definitions suggest, quests in games were influenced by a long tradition of quest narratives, ranging from Homer's *The Odyssey* to the medieval romances of the Holy Grail, formalized in Joseph Campbell's "hero's journey" and Northrop Frye's anatomy of the "quest romance." Susana Tosca observes the relevance of the genres of epic and romance as well as that of Joseph Campbell's hero's journey to the "background" of quest games, though she brackets the question of how closely the literary and gaming traditions can be related, arguing primarily that such theories are "not pointless" to the study of games. However, she views Campbell's pattern as either "too general" to be analytically useful or as incidental to the main thread of her inquiry. Yet I would argue that these patterns must have explanatory usefulness specifically relevant to games because they are part of the historical origins of games, and game designers themselves acknowledge their influence. Tosca's claim is insightful but deserves further development, since a more detailed and forceful statement of the relationship between the literary tradition of quests and their operation as a gaming activity would allow the quest concept to fulfill its bridge-building function more effectively.

Moving Past the Ludology and Narratology Debate

Quests take their place in an increasing consensus that games and narratives can work productively together, allowing us to move beyond the debate between ludologists and narratologists. Theorists and designers alike agree that there can be transformations back and forth between games and narratives as well as many intermediate forms in between the two categories. The idea of adapting material from narrative to game and back again is rapidly becoming well-accepted in the academic study of new media and literature, as can be seen in the transition from the anthology *First Person* to its sequel *Second Person*. Moving past the contentious ludology versus narratology debate that characterized the first volume and the first wave of game studies, many of the essays in the second volume discuss ways that designers have based games upon stories (including *The Name of the Rose*, Lovecraft's Cthulhu mythos, and many other franchises). The title of James Wallis's essay, "Making Games That Make Stories," sums up just how closely intertwined these two forms are currently understood to be. There are many strategies for adaptation represented in *Second Person*, in which computer games become collectible card games and novels become board games.

Perhaps especially intriguing is the editors' decision to single out two writers of narratives on the various types of games and adaptation in the book: Tolkien (for his "quest structure") and H. P. Lovecraft (for his Cthulhu mythos). The fictional worlds of Tolkien and Lovecraft can accommodate both quest games and quest narratives, offering examples of transformations in both directions. We do not have to speculate on whether quest narratives can be transformed into quest games strictly as a pedagogical exercise, because this transformation has been successfully achieved many times in both directions.

For example, the fictional universe of H. P. Lovecraft's "Cthulhu mythos" has generated many narratives written by other authors as well as many games. Authors and designers have transformed several of the tales (some of them, like "The Dream Quest of Unknown Kadath," themselves quest narratives) into games. Lovecraft's fiction forms the basis for the rules of the tabletop role-playing game *Call of Cthulhu*, which gives rise to many possible quests, including scenarios/modules and computer games like *Call of Cthulhu: Dark Corners of the Earth*. Similarly, the quest narratives of fantasy writers J. R. R. Tolkien and Fritz Leiber influenced the rules and worlds of

Dungeons and Dragons; later, Margaret Weiss and Tracey Hickman adapted several play sessions of *Dungeons and Dragons* into the *Dragonlance* trilogy. This trilogy in turn became a rule-book, which was part of the inspiration for the Dragonlance Adventures modding group to create mods in the Dragonlance universe using the Aurora Toolset.

Quests, Games, and Interpretation

As the debate between the ludologists and the narratologists dies down, many game theorists and game designers increasingly focus on meaning and interpretation as central to game design and narrative. Salen and Zimmerman call for "meaningful play" as the overarching and central goal of successful game design. In *Unit Operations,* Ian Bogost incisively challenges Aarseth's longstanding claim that readers and game players engage in two distinct cognitive activities, or "functions." Aarseth argues in *Cybertext* that the dominant function of non-cybertextual literature is interpretative, in which readers determine implied meanings of a book or imagine its events and characters differently. Aarseth suggests that the dominant function of cybertexts, including games, is configurative. Users reconfigure the elements of a simulation, as when they make strategic decisions about the deployment of resources within a set of rules (64).

In contrast to Aarseth, Bogost suggests that literary texts and video games (as well as a variety of other art forms, including film) are both comprised of discrete "units" that can be configured by users (ix). As Bogost argues, "any medium—poetic, literary, cinematic, and computational—can be read as a configurative system, an arrangement of discrete, interlocking units of expressive meaning. I call these general instances of procedural expression *unit operations*" (ix). Bogost asserts that these "unit operations" can be studied and interpreted critically in terms of the ideas about society that they express, consciously or unconsciously, and that an awareness of these operations can in turn encourage more expressive game design. Bogost tends to focus on modern and contemporary texts, in part because he is interested in ways that games can comment on contemporary political ideology rather than in ancient mythology or the Western canon of quest narratives. Nevertheless, he eloquently argues that "we must also make room for interpretative strategies that remain faithful to the configurative properties of games" (108). His point remains that games and literature can meet at the issue of interpretation.

In contrast to Bogost's discrete "units," the quest is a feature of gameplay and narrative that is both "progressive" and "systematic," two qualities that he denies to units (3). The configuration of a reader in a quest narrative and a quest game is defined by being "goal-oriented." This emphasis on goals often includes sequences of objectives in which there is some choice, such as the order of certain optional quests or whether to undertake a side quest. The portions of the game engine and interface that keep track of quests are often called the game's "quest system." This system frequently consists of a main quest as well as many side quests, yet the variety of localized actions that players can perform while completing quests might still be regarded as "unit operations."

The History and Theory of Quest Narratives

The argument about the intersection of interpretative and configurative meaning in games and narrative is not just a theoretical one. Indeed, understanding the theory of quest games and quest narratives is closely intertwined with issues of design and history. By studying the history of both quest narratives and quest games, designers can benefit from "paradigmatic" examples of quests—especially well-constructed, innovative quests that can inspire their own designs. This inspiration is more than emotional encouragement that such achievements are possible. Examples of excellent games and narratives in this genre provide designers with a set of strategies for building meaningful quests. There are four classic theorists whose work can help designers to understand the history of quest narratives:

- Joseph Campbell;
- Northrop Frye;
- W. H. Auden;
- Vladimir Propp.

Campbell, the Hero's Journey, and Quests

The designers who work with the quest note its resemblance to the "Hero's Journey" as described by Joseph Campbell in *The Hero with a Thousand Faces* and popularized by Christopher Vogler in *The Writer's Journey.* Many game designers embrace the hero's journey as a potential structure for games because it is effective in creating a compelling storyline that will motivate ongoing play. Authors of books on game design who are also practicing game designers have praised Campbell's structure in detail as a model for constructing games. These authors include Glassner in *Interactive Storytelling*, Rollings and Adams in *Game Design*, Novak in *Game Development Essentials*, and Dunniway in "Using the Hero's Journey in Games" (Glassner 59–66, Novak

116–17, Rollings and Adams 93–111).   For Campbell, this journey constitutes a protagonist's quest to overcome various obstacles and enemies with the help of mentors in order to gain a mystical reward which she can then bring back to benefit her society.

Campbell's 1949 book *The Hero with a Thousand Faces* contains a schematic outline of a "monomyth" of the "hero's journey," consisting of a threefold structure of "separation, initiation, and return." Campbell writes, "A hero ventures forth from the world of common day into a region of supernatural wonder: fabulous forces are there encountered and a decisive victory is won: the hero comes back from this mysterious adventure with the power to bestow boons on his fellow man" (30).   While Campbell's formula is useful in understanding the stages that many questing heroes pass through, a "journey" is not synonymous with a quest.   Rather, a "journey" is the spatial movement and temporal duration entailed by a quest.[1]

As a student of mythology and spirituality as well as a devoted Jungian, Campbell regards this narrative as archetypal, underlying all cultures because it expresses a transcendent psychological and spiritual truth.   The usefulness of the quest structure often exists in tension with the postmodern theoretical assumptions of many game researchers, who are skeptical toward transcendence and the "grand narratives" that symbolize it.   For example, Tosca acknowledges the practical association of the quest with narratives about transcendence and mythic apocalyptic epics about "saving the world" while expressing theoretical distrust of this association.   She writes that "the word quest evokes the dreaded great narratives, and maybe that is why we should be careful when using it, although it seems that, at least in the game design field, it has come to stay" (sec. 4.1).

While many game designers and theorists cite Campbell's "hero's journey" to discuss the literary origins of the quest, Campbell actually addresses this concept more directly in his late writings and lectures on the quest for the Holy Grail. The roots of the hero's journey are in Campbell's study of the Arthurian cycles and grail legends, which were the topic of his master's thesis. While he persuasively argues that the hero's journey is a cross-cultural, archetypal pattern running through the myths of many countries, the Grail legend offers a particularly complete and rich template for heroic deeds that Campbell returns to in his late work *Creative Mythology*, the last volume of his *The Masks of God* series. For Campbell, the Grail quest emblematizes the Western search for an individual path in life that manifests itself in the purposive striving of the free will (564).

This capability of each player to make choices about the unfolding of a narrative in accord with her own sense of self is only literally possible in a quest game, but it is the value that is most deeply at the heart of quest narratives. Campbell discusses the "quest" as exemplified in the Grail cycle most directly in his book *Creative Mythology.* For Campbell, the quest for the Grail is ultimately a symbolic narrative of a deeply individualistic search to follow the promptings of one's innermost self, exercised through constant striving within society. He sees the stories of the Grail as "the first sheerly individualistic mythology in the history of the human race: a mythology of quest inwardly motivated—directed from within" (553).

At the deepest level, these are the aspects of players that can also be encouraged through quest games, which allow individual players to strive toward the goals that are most relevant to their own values and beliefs as readers and players. As Campbell explains, "The Grail here, as in the later *Queste,* is the symbol of supreme spiritual value. It is attained, however, not by renouncing the world or even current social custom, but, on the contrary, by participation with every ounce of one's force in the century's order of life in the way or ways dictated by one's own uncorrupted heart: what the mystics call the Inner Voice." "Participation with every ounce of one's force" suggests unswerving effort to reach a goal of self-expression and self-improvement. This is an enterprise that we can only admire in one of the knights searching for the Holy Grail but which we can cultivate in ourselves through gaming.

It is important for designers to understand the distinction between the hero's journey and Campbell's late work on quests in order to avoid using Campbell in rigid, mechanical, and monotonous ways. The "hero's journey" as Campbell theorized it in 1949 was a "monomyth"—a single three-part pattern that Campbell believed to extend across the most diverse myths from different cultures. When Campbell speaks of a "quest" in his late work, he is referring to a specifically Western emphasis on different individuals' search to realize their own unique selves. The "hero's journey" is always the same, but every quest is different—a shift in emphasis that Campbell illustrates through the moment in *The Quest for the Holy Grail* at which each knight deliberately sets off alone into the forest at a point where there is no path. When some designers express weariness with the hero's journey as a model for narratives in games, they are responding to a popular misconception of Campbell's theories that emphasizes the monomyth over the individual multiplicity of creative quests. If the hero's journey is applied unimaginatively, every game will follow the pattern of *Star Wars* and *The Lord of the Rings.* If quests are created with an eye toward the emphasis on individuality found in Western medieval romances, then they can be as idiosyncratic and original as the players who embark on them.

Northrop Frye

Just as Campbell's writings help to establish a historical relationship between the journey and the quest through its roots in medieval romance, Northrop Frye's *Anatomy of Criticism* offers a rigorous terminological distinction among the related terms of "romance," "quest," and "adventure." For Frye, the "romance" is the genre, or "mythos," that both contains the quest and is contained by it in its overall structure. Frye writes that "the essential element of plot in romance is adventure, which means that romance is naturally a sequential and processional form, hence we know it better from fiction than from drama" (186). Adventure is not synonymous with romance but rather supplies its content, and this content takes the form of a sequence.

For Frye, the quest is the climactic episode in a series of adventures, distinguished from minor events by its size and centrality. At the same time, the quest is also the formal principle by which the romance is structured, without which it would only be a sequence of adventures. Frye concisely summarizes, "We may call this major adventure, the element that gives literary form to the romance, the quest" (187). Frye explains, "The complete form of the romance is clearly the successful quest, and such a completed form has three main stages: the stage of the perilous journey and the preliminary minor adventures; the crucial struggle, usually some kind of battle in which either the hero or his foe, or both, must die; and the exaltation of the hero" (187). Frye's structure, like Campbell's, has three parts, but Frye collapses the second of Campbell's stages ("initiation") into the first stage of his schema. Frye also ends the quest at the conclusion of Campbell's second stage, directly after what Campbell would call the hero's greatest battle, or "ordeal," and his subsequent "apotheosis," or elevation to divinity.

W. H. Auden

A third theorist of quest narratives worth considering in conjunction with Campbell and Frye is W. H. Auden, the famous modernist poet and critic whose 1961 essay "The Quest Hero" is both a literary analysis of quest narratives and a review of J. R. R. Tolkien's *The Lord of the Rings*. Auden argues that the enduring popularity of quest narratives is due to their "validity as a symbolic description of our subjective personal experience of existence as historical" (82). While this definition can sound intimidating, Auden is simply arguing that human lives closely resemble the pattern of a quest because of the way that we experience our day-to-day existence as a sequence of major and minor goals with an uncertain outcome in which we struggle with good and evil impulses.

Auden concedes that in terms of our "objective" lives, most of us are not heroes on long journeys through space because our jobs keep us in one place, but the ways that we change over time make our lives seem like epic journeys. Auden does not rely on Jungian archetypes but on an appeal to an imaginative way of looking at everyday life in a way that helps us to make sense out of it through the epic storytelling of a story such as *The Lord of the Rings*. Auden's argument would therefore be a useful answer to skeptics who might doubt the worth of computer games because of their connections to fantasy worlds like that of Tolkien. Auden's argument might imply (though he wrote long before the advent of computer games) that such games can be relevant to human life precisely because they are delving into a long literary tradition that reaches a peak of modern popularity in Tolkien, where it is then taken up by designers of tabletop role-playing games.

Vladimir Propp

Vladimir Propp's 1928 *Morphology of the Folk Tale* is one of the first rigorous analyses of narratives involving quests. Using Russian formalist theories of narratology, Propp breaks down the component parts of folktales and their possible combinations. For Propp, a tale is a sequence of rigorously defined transformations by which elements are recombined according to strict rules of substitution and linkage, much like the grammar of a language. The elements combined in a folktale are a set of recurrent characters, or "dramatis personae," who perform "functions," or prototypical actions, such as giving a talisman or testing the hero. In particular, Propp discusses one type of main character that he calls the "questing hero," who engages in a quest in order to fulfill a perceived lack in his life or that of his family. The character fulfills this lack by seeking out a wondrous "object." Propp's tone and method are scientifically detached, focusing on patterns found objectively in the data of a vast collection of folk tales. His strength as a theorist is his awareness of the many possible recombinations of functions in a dizzying array of tales. Although his version of quest narratives anticipates that of Joseph Campbell and Frye, his description of these tales is less philosophical and more concrete.

Narrative Structures Become Activities in Games

What Campbell and Frye understood as a structure operates as an activity in quest games. Campbell's unified "monomyth" becomes the "main quest" in a complex quest system of intersecting, forking, and shifting "side quests." The balance of main quest and side quests resolves potential tension between the multiplicity valorized by postmodern theories of new media and the unity implied by an ancient "monomyth" or "grand narrative." Tosca's wariness regarding "grand narratives" that associate quests with transcendent meaning stems from this tension between postmodern media and ancient source material, which can be surmounted by a close examination of the ways that game designers themselves address the issue.

Designers of quest systems extend Campbell's middle phase of "initiation" and Frye's "minor adventures" in order to put the primary focus on player action, and they repeat the "separation-initiation-return" pattern iteratively to allow for prolonged, varied gameplay. In this respect, quest systems differ from Vogler's *The Writer's Journey,* which simplifies Campbell's pattern into a relatively rigid three-part structure that describes and generates uninventive Hollywood films. Instead, designers of quest systems complicate and enrich Campbell's structure, awakening the latent potential for variety and activity in Campbell's source material. [2] By understanding how quest games function, literary critics can also reexamine narratives, from ancient epic to medieval romance, as potential "quest systems" because they have always implied the possibility of goal-oriented imaginative action.

Authors of quest narratives always sought to encourage these activities but were limited by the oral and written media available to them. These authors could create only the potential for activity, since readers or listeners might or might not imagine themselves acting within the authors' fictional world or changing everyday actions in response to quest narratives. Digital games require players to actualize this potential through goal-oriented actions in simulated space. Quest narratives and quest games are not identical (as Barry Atkins suggests in his chapter on "Tomb Raider as Quest Narrative" in *More Than a Game*), nor are they irreconcilably different (as Aarseth implies in his antinarratological analysis of "Quest Games as Post-Narrative Discourse"). Rather, quest narratives and quest games clarify and illuminate each other, so that the most contemporary, technologically sophisticated games offer insights into the most ancient narratives and vice versa.

The History of Quest Games

The history and theory of quest games takes up where the work of Joseph Campbell and Northrop Frye leaves off, making literal a potential for interactivity that was always present in quest narratives. The work of J. R. R. Tolkien, an accomplished medievalist who produced the first modern translation of the romance *Sir Gawain and the Green Knight,* converges with the early tabletop role-playing to produce quests in adventure games, the first and second generation of computer role-playing games, and MMORPGs. Moreover, a shift away from random puzzles and hack-and-slash gameplay toward an increasing emphasis on the underlying meaning of quests appears in the evolving careers of pioneering designers like Richard Garriott and Roberta Williams.

Designers' concern with the meaning of quests does not sell copies of the earliest quest games, like *King's Quest I* or *Ultima I,* but it does help in marketing the later installments in these series, as well as recent innovative quest games like *Neverwinter Nights 2.* Educational game designers as well as independent designers with an emphasis on innovative gameplay could learn from these historical patterns by foregrounding meaningful quests from the beginning of the design process. Moreover, designers can follow the examples of Garriott and Williams by deliberately drawing on literary source material that is at the root of quest games but easy to forget when narratives and games are seen as in conflict rather than complementary. As in most fields, an awareness of the history of game design keeps practitioners of this craft from having to reinvent the wheel, saving them both time and money.

Tabletop Role-Playing Games: Dungeons and Dragons

As Tosca argues, the history of quest games is strongly rooted in "tabletop" or "pen-and-paper" role-playing games, in which referees called "dungeon masters" or "game masters" guided players through adventures using rulebooks, dice, and imagination to calculate the outcomes of players' actions. With this background in mind, the history of quests in games might be said to begin in 1974 with the publication by Gary Gygax and David Arneson of *Dungeons and Dragons,* the first massively popular pen-and-paper role-playing game. The precursor to *Dungeons and Dragons* was the war strategy game *Chainmail,* whose large-scale battles were closer to a real-time strategy video game than the dungeon crawls that we associate with the game today. As Schick argues in *Heroic Worlds* and Erik Mona clarifies in "From the Basement to the Basic Set: The Early Years of *Dungeons & Dragons,*" David Arneson expanded on Gygax's rules for group combat by creating a campaign organized around single players exploring a dungeon beneath a castle (Schick 18–20, Mona 26).

The idea of the quest recurred in *Dungeons and Dragons* as a unit of gaming activity around which role-playing sessions could be based, although the word "scenario" or "module" was often used to refer to the paper books that contained stories and guidelines for game masters to use in these sessions. However, the module writer David Emigh did write a resource for game masters called *The Quest,* billed as "a design guide book for the imaginative fantasy game referee" that draws on "themes common to ancient myth, medieval romance and modern fantasy" and "guides the referee toward designing more exciting role playing scenarios." Emigh provides a bibliography of mythological and literary sources for constructing engaging quests, advocating Campbell's *Masks of God* series over *The Hero with a Thousand Faces* and presenting a rich variety of quest types from Celtic, Arthurian, and Norse mythology (55–59).

The reference to "modern fantasy" highlights the undeniable influence of J. R. R. Tolkien on tabletop role-playing, along with that of many other fantasy authors cited by Daniel Mackay as evidence of his historical "equation" for the genesis of the games: "Fantasy Literature + Wargames = Role-Playing Games" (17). However, the awareness of the literary sources of "myth" and "medieval romance" suggests that there was some awareness of a broader tradition of quest narratives among game masters. Indeed, Gary Gygax himself acknowledges the inspirational value of a variety of literary sources, including mythology, in the appendix of *Master of the Game*, where he includes several such works in his ideal list of a "Master's Library" (172–73). Gygax also cites Joseph Campbell's *The Hero with a Thousand Faces* as a useful text for game masters, because this text summarizes the structures of heroic adventure underlying *Dungeons and Dragons*. Gygax explains that "although I was totally unaware of it at the time," most of the elements of the hero's journey were "included in the thesis of the DUNGEONS & DRAGONS work, the first role-playing game created" (166).

Text-Based Interactive Fictions: Adventure and Zork

Building upon *Dungeons and Dragons*, the second step toward quests in video games was the text-based interactive fiction called *Adventure*, whose history has been chronicled in detail in Nick Montfort's *Twisty Little Passages: An Approach to Interactive Fiction* and in Dennis Jerz's "Somewhere Nearby is Colossal Cave: Examining Will Crowther's Original 'Adventure' in Code and in Kentucky." Crowther completed his first version of *Adventure* in 1975, based on his sessions playing the pen-and-paper *Dungeons and Dragons* as well as on his real-life explorations of Mammoth Cave. Players explored a simulation of this cave, collecting treasures and solving puzzles by typing two-word commands, such as "go north" and "examine rock." In 1977, Don Woods expanded upon Crowther's version, combining it with fantasy elements derived from Tolkien to produce a larger game called *Colossal Cave Adventure*, which in turn gave rise to many variant games on the networks that preceded the Internet.

In the article "Interactive Fiction," Anthony Niesz and Norman Holland argue that the quest is the central underlying motif of most interactive fiction. They argue:

> In general, the structure is the Quest. The reader-hero sets out along a series of roads or passageways or rooms (one has to sketch a map to have any success at all with these games). She meets various helpers or adversaries; encounters obstacles, aids, or treasures; and finds dead ends, or, more likely, that she has left something several stages back that she now needs. (115)

Niesz and Holland's generalization about IF originates in part from the early date of their article, written in 1984 when classic IF like the *Adventure* variants and the *Zork* series drew heavily on the quest motif. High fantasy, swords-and-sorcery settings were very common in early interactive fiction, which eventually branched out into many other genres as well as the genre-bending experimentations of today's independent interactive fiction. One might also argue that the earliest interactive fictions tended to be "scavenger hunts" as much as quests, in which players often collected items and solved puzzles with little sense of an ultimate goal contextualized in narrative.

Nevertheless, Niesz and Holland's focus on the quest as a primary motif in IF is valid in that many classic and contemporary interactive fictions, from *Zork* to Graham Nelson's *Curses,* are structured on a player's movement through a symbolic environment in order to achieve a meaningful goal. Of particular note is *Brimstone: The Dream of Sir Gawain,* which was based on Arthurian legend. Writer James Paul creatively transforms elements of *Sir Gawain and the Green Knight* as well as other Arthurian narratives into a quest game, using strategies to increase the immersion and interactivity of this narrative such as setting the game within a dream and allowing for the exploration of different paths and locations not included in the story-cycle (such as the inclusion of Ulro, the hell of poet William Blake's writings). Similarly, Robert Pinsky locates the worlds of interactive fiction in the "standard Gothic furniture of dwarfs, swords, torches, and dungeons," suggesting his awareness of the literary origins of interactive fiction in the Gothic representation of the middle ages as a fairy-tale realm of swords and sorcery. Interactive fiction passed this motif on to the early graphical adventure games, action-adventure games, and role-playing games that it influenced (3).

Graphical Adventure Games: King's Quest

Graphical adventure games then arose out of interactive fiction, including the *King's Quest* series, created by Roberta Williams for Sierra Online, the company founded by her and her husband, Ken Williams. As the annotated timeline in the official manual to the *King's Quest* collection explains, the first *King's Quest,* subtitled *Quest for the Crown,* was produced in 1983 for the IBM PCjr, followed by a re-release in 1984 for the IBM PC and the Tandy 1000. A series of seven sequels, *King's Quest II–VIII,* followed the original, spanning 1985–1994. For the sake of comparing the evolution of *King's Quest* with other quest games, the dates of these sequels are as follows: *King's Quest II: Romancing the Throne* (1985), *King's Quest III: To Heir is Human* (1986), *King's Quest IV: The Perils of Rosella* (1988), *King's Quest V: Absence Makes the Heart Go Yonder* (1990), *King's Quest VI: To Heir Is Human* (1992), *King's Quest VII: The Princeless Bride* (1994), and *King's Quest VIII: Mask of Eternity* (1998). As Roberta Williams acknowledges, Woods and Crowther's *Colossal Cave Adventure* was a key influence on the original *King's Quest* game. In Rusel Demaria's *High Score: The Illustrated History of Electronic Games,* Williams explains, "Colossal Cave changed my life. I owe a lot to Will Crowther" (134). Like *Adventure, King's Quest* required the player to manipulate the avatar of a knight, Sir Graham, through a simulated fairy-tale environment, solving puzzles in order to collect three treasures to save the fairy-tale kingdom of Daventry.

King's Quest foregrounds the role of the quest in this game, since it contextualizes Sir Graham's actions within an overarching set of goals motivated by honorable service to an aging king and knightly protection of the kingdom. The tone of the visuals and action in *King's Quest* is playful rather than solemn, yet a chivalric, fairy-tale narrative motivates Sir Graham's adventure. Indeed, Roberta Williams was quite consciously mining the same folk tales that Vladimir Propp studied, as she suggests when she explains, "I was thinking about a fairy tale adventure with lost treasures, giants, leprechauns, a gingerbread house, a troll bridge, guessing a gnome's name" (7). As in Propp's folk tales, *King's Quest* and its sequels revolve around a game character motivated to embark on a quest by the lack of desired object or person, including both magical items and, in *King's Quest II* and *V,* a bride. Just as Propp argued that this "lack" drives "seeker-heroes" toward an adventure that will fill this lack, so Roberta Williams punningly entitled the fifth game in the series *Absence Makes the Heart Go Yonder* (Propp 34–35).

In a pattern that later repeated itself in Richard Garriott's design of the *Ultima* games, the sequels increase the degree of coherent narrative backstory and meaningful action. As Williams herself emphasizes in her introduction to *King's Quest VI* in the manual to the collection, "I wanted to get away from just putting together a jumble of puzzles in some sort of meaningless quest; you should have a clear sense of what you're doing and why, with some emotion behind it" (30). Williams created this meaningful action in *King's Quest VI* by using cut-scenes and music to give specificity and poignancy to a fairy-tale romance in which the protagonist must rescue a princess in a tower. The gameplay of *King's Quest VI* was enriched rather than slowed down by these narrative elements, resulting in a richly immersive story that motivated players to explore the game's multiple endings, optional puzzles, and side-narratives.

Action-Adventure Games: Adventure (Atari 2600) and The Legend of Zelda

At the same time that quests were becoming a staple of CRPGs, some early console action-adventure games began to incorporate quest activity, either concurrently or in response to earlier RPGs. *The Game Design Reader* explains that Warren Robinett, the designer of the 1978 Atari 2600 game *Adventure,* originally intended it to be an adaptation of the text-based interactive fiction *Adventure.* Robinett contrasts the treasure hunt of this game with the quest of his graphical *Adventure* when he writes that "whereas the goal of the original text game Adventure was treasure gathering, the video game Adventure is defined as a quest. One single treasure, the Enchanted Chalice, must be located and brought home. Thus, the tool objects must contribute somehow to the overall goal of the quest" (699). Robinett sees that the difference between a treasure hunt and a quest is that each barrier to an overall goal requires an object to surmount it, which can in turn require another object, creating a proliferation of "sub-goals." In Robinett's design, the relationship between main quest and side quest was beginning to solidify. As *The Game Design Reader* suggests, *Adventure* was an influence on both the *Legend of Zelda* and the *Ultima* games.

After the Atari 2600 version of *Adventure,* the *Legend of Zelda* series brought the quest into the genre of action-adventure games. This franchise began in 1986 with the original *The Legend of Zelda*, which Bateman identifies as the "nucleating game" of the "action adventure genre." This series increased the amount of fast-paced action associated with the quest, requiring that players be as adept in wielding Link's sword as in the navigational abilities to move through dungeons. While many of the Zelda games feature an overarching main quest to save Princess Zelda, defeat Gannon or Ganondorft, and recover the pieces of the Triforce, they also break this quest up into manageable parts. The most celebrated installment in the Zelda series, the 1998 *Ocarina of Time,* features a "quest status" screen that registers one's progress in the quest through the collection of "spiritual medallions."

Computer Role-Playing Games

A pattern of evolution similar to that in adventure game appears in the history of early computer role-playing games, which began as technical reproductions of hack-and-slash dungeon exploration from *Dungeons and Dragons,* out of which some examples of meaningful action could appear. As Matt Barton argues in his article "The History of Early Computer Role-Playing Games Part I: The Early Years (1980–1983)," one of the earliest CRPGs was a direct adaptation of *Dungeons and Dragons* for the computer mainframe called *dnd.* Barton sees the emergence of a quest with a narrative framework as central to the development of the genre, since "Perhaps most important, *dnd* featured a story and a quest—kill the dragon and fetch the Orb."

Following the scattered appearance of this genre on mainframes, the computer role-playing game began to develop in several competing series, including *Ultima* and *Wizardry.* These games often adapted the mechanics of *Dungeons and Dragons,* sometimes as a strict "dungeon crawl" and at other times in conjunction with the exploration of a larger outside world. Garriott explains that the confluence of *Dungeons and Dragons,* J. R. R. Tolkien, and the computer inspired his game, combining the same set of influences as William Crowther and Don Woods with a graphical interface and more character and story intensive gameplay. Garriott deliberately marketed the first commercial precursor to *Ultima,* entitled *Akalabeth,* as both inspired by and surpassing *Adventure,* as the tagline on its cover suggested: "Beyond adventure lies *Akalabeth.*" *Akalabeth* was published in 1980, followed by the first *Ultima* in the same year.

The first *Ultima* trilogy was composed of standard battles with monsters, dungeon crawls, and treasure seeking derived from *Dungeons and Dragons,* but *Ultima IV: Quest of the Avatar* combined the concept of the "quest" with a complex "virtue system," a coherent backstory, and ethical and spiritual implications to the gameplay. In Demaria's *High Score,* Garriott himself makes the distinction between the early *Ultimas* and *Ultima IV* based on a shift from his early development of programming skills to an interest in an underlying narrative: "*Ultima IV* is special also, because, if you think of the first three as 'Richard learns to program,' *Ultima IV* was where I learned to tell a story" (122). The *Ultima* games grew in sophistication, introducing the dilemmas of fundamentalism and cultural intolerance that complicate any "virtue system." The nine installments in the single-player *Ultima* series (not counting numerous expansion packs) and the intermediary series of *Ultima Underworld* lasted from 1980 until 1999.

Concurrently with the *Ultima* series, Andrew Greenberg and Robert Woodhead developed the *Wizardry* series, whose first installment was also published in 1981 as *Wizardry I: Proving Grounds of the Mad Overlord.* The eight official *Wizardry* games and multiple spin-offs were produced between 1981 and 2001. The original dungeon crawls in this series featured standard fetch quests for the magical amulet of Werdna and, later, the pieces of the armor of the Knight of Diamonds. Later installments in this series began to introduce slightly more complicated scenarios, involving the assembly of two adventuring parties of opposing ethical alignments to restore a cosmic balance.

A second generation of single-player role-playing games featured more open-ended worlds as well as multiple interrelated side quests managed through a "journal" of pending and completed tasks given by NPCs. *Baldur's Gate* (1998) and *Neverwinter Nights* (2002) both took place in the Forgotten Realms section of the *Dungeons and Dragons* universe, while the *Elder Scrolls* games, produced by Bethesda, allowed players to explore an original RPG universe called Tamriel. Based on the highlights of Barton's "History of Computer Role-Playing Games Part 3," the games that garner the highest praise from critics and the most vehement fan popularity as "cult classics" integrate the immersive gameplay of a well-designed engine with the narrative context that increases the meaning of player's actions. In a bold move, Barton pronounces *Baldur's Gate II* "the finest CRPG ever designed" and backs up this evaluation with the criteria of "good stories, fun characters, meaningful quests, high-stakes combat, and an intuitive interface." The culmination of Barton's three-part history thus revolves around a game with "meaningful quests" seamlessly woven into its gameplay and storyline. Barton reemphasizes that the most high-quality games, regardless of the time period in which they were produced, conjoin solid gameplay with a narrative that gives this action meaning. As he eloquently puts it,

> Getting it right involves more than just having an outstanding engine; significant craft is involved in creating a compelling story that makes the player's actions meaningful. The best games (*Curse of the Azure Bonds, Baldur's Gate II, Planescape: Torment*) offer far better rewards than just experience points and gold coins.

One crucial feature of this time period of game development is that the most meaningful games are not always the highest sellers.

As with any art form, there is a divergence between what Barton identifies as the dumbed-down action gameplay of the hugely popular *Diablo* and what he dubs the "cult classic" of *Planescape: Torment* (1999). Barton argues that the metaphysical and moral thematic implications of this game are precisely what makes it beloved by a core fanbase, delighted by a game that "really get the player thinking deeply about morality" through the creation of "an interactive *Inferno.*" As quest games matured, they began to split slightly into vastly popular hack-and-slash games and more sophisticated games that garner critical praise and enough of a fanbase to be classics. This division might well resemble the current split between commercial blockbuster MMOs and experimental action-adventure titles like *Too Human* and *Assassin's Creed.* While the more complex games are still quite commercially viable, an independent or educational designer is well advised to know her audience and market accordingly, finding a niche similar to those of *Planescape: Torment.* These games increasingly complicated the model of a single quest found in the scenarios of *Wizardry* and moved toward a complex interrelationship of multiple side quests. This shift paved the way for massively multiplayer online role-playing games (MMORPGs), composed of thousands of collaborative quests.

Massively Multiplayer Online Role-Playing Games

The late nineties witnessed the decline of the graphical adventure game, the continuance of single-player role-playing games in fewer quantities but greater sophistication, and the rebirth of quests as an inexhaustible gaming activity in massively multiplayer online role-playing games; one of the earliest and most popular ones was entitled *Everquest.* There is a continuity between single-player role-playing games and MMORPGs in that one of the first of this genre was *Ultima Online,* created by Garriott and set in the same world where his single-player games had taken place. However, the concept of the quest occurs most prominently in the title of the highly popular game *Everquest,* published in 1999 and designed by Brad McQuaid, Steve Clover, and Bill Trost. The ability of multiple players to play at once for an indefinite period of time reduced the emphasis on a single "main quest" with an underlying storyline in favor of multiple proliferating tasks that would have been "side quests" in a large single-player RPG. The online aspect of the game also encouraged the design of quests which required teams of players to complete, shifting away from the solo play (or a single player's control over a party) that had characterized single-player RPGs.

While Espen Aarseth argues that *Everquest* is the paradigmatic example of "post-narrative" discourse and a game that emphasizes simulation over narrative, the historical origins of the MMORPG genre suggest that this may be something of a generalization. Quests in contemporary MMORPGs, such as the hugely popular *World of Warcraft,* sometimes do culminate in vast "raids" comprised of hundreds of players hacking and slashing their way into an enemy castle. On the other hand, *World of Warcraft* and *Everquest II* do contain "quest lines" of related quests, often enriched by underlying narrative content and sometimes by meaning. For example, the shaman quest line in *World of Warcraft* involves "rites" of each of the four elements designed to initiate a prospective shaman into the mysteries of his natural environment, while helping him to accumulate experience points and the "totems" that will give him his shamanic spells. Hence, the structures of initiation found in Campbell, which involve a transitional rite of passage associated with mythological quest narratives, can reappear in the most popular of MMORPGs, depending upon a player's choice of class and imaginary race. In addition, as R. V. Kelly argues, some quests in MMOs are "lore quests," whose primary motivation is to uncover the mythologies and political intrigues that constitute the backstory of a the game's simulated world (32). Because of the frequency of such lore quests, many MMORPG players cited by Kelly regard their experience as a form of collaborative and interactive storytelling (70–71). Historically speaking, while MMORPGs tend to eschew a single epic "main quest" and to emphasize constant, cooperative action, there is no predefined reason why they could not integrate meaning and action.

Enacted Meaning, Meaningful Action

The critical studies of the "quest" are increasingly becoming more than just a middle ground between game and narrative, but rather a focus on the relationship between meaning and action, revolving around the issue of significant gameplay. Theoretical and pedagogical understandings of the quest will increase if we examine further the issue of meaning in quests, extending the idea of meaning beyond semiotic indications of function to thematic implications. For Tronstad, "to do a quest is to search for the meaning of it" (Tronstad 2001). However, Tronstad's use of "meaning" is primarily functional rather than thematic in that it is concerned with signs as indicators of a game object's function rather than with the ideas associated with it. Hence, she argues that when a player finds a new object, she must "decode its significance in relation to the quest, to come closer to the quest's solution." In other words, if a player discovers a key, the "meaning" of this key is that there will be something for it to open, such as a chest. If the player then discovers a sword in the chest upon opening it, this sword might have the "meaning" that a dragon must be fought and slain.

This concept of meaning ignores the possibility of deeper thematic significance, in which the player must enact not only events, but also ideas and insights. Tronstad does argue that the motivation for the quest is the "promise of meaning," but she also argues that quests must withhold this meaning if they are to keep their status as quests. She explains that "quests are promising their solution, promising meaning. But as meaning is also the death of the quest, it is frequently breaking this promise, in order to prolong the questing experience." By setting up a false binary between meaning and action, Tronstad overlooks the idea that players can enact meaning if the elements of the quest have thematic implications that are revealed through play.

Because Tronstad's focus on meaning is strictly functional, she views the movement from quest to narrative as unidirectional and unrepeatable. Thus, she argues that "the paradox of questing is that as soon as meaning is reached, the quest stops functioning as *quest*. When meaning is found, the quest is *history*. It cannot be done again, as it is simply not the same experience to solve a puzzle quest for the second time." This analysis is true only if meaning is conceived of in the utilitarian manner that Tronstad suggests. It is true that once a player has determined what chest a key unlocks, the meaning of the key ceases to be interesting in subsequent playing sessions. However, if the key has greater, multivalent allegorical and symbolic connotations, then these might be productively and enjoyably enacted multiple times by different players, as they deepen their understanding of this meaning or seek a different interpretation.

The performance of the quest multiple times would result in the production of more richly developed or different constatives. Conversely, the constatives of literary narratives can be transformed into quests, which has the advantage both of making literature interactive and of bringing deeper symbolic meaning to the actions of the quest. Tosca raises the possibility that literary narratives can inspire quests but temporarily brackets the issue, noting that "this is more a question of adaptation from one medium to another, and as such is beyond the limits of this paper." At the same time, she does raise a series of interesting questions about to what extent such an adaptation would recreate the book's "story-world," its events, or be a "thematic adaptation" of the work.

The "thematic adaptation" possibility highlights the importance of meaning in quests, the feature that Tosca explores least in her criticisms of existing quests and her suggestions for new ones. Tosca's students criticized many existing quests in games for being "too linear, boring, repetitive, and unrelated to the character's 'physical' and emotional development." In response to these critiques, they created quests that were nonlinear and emotionally involving and had surprising plot twists. While these are positive pedagogical accomplishments, a key aspect of interesting quests is not just emotion or surprise but rather meaning, something that Tosca acknowledges but does not expand upon in her statement that "the quest or mission format allows for a contextualization of the game's actions in a more or less meaningful story." This raises the questions of how to make quests more meaningful rather than less and how to analyze the ways that both designers and players create and enact meaning. Because spaces and objects in works of literature are often already treated by critics as having dense potential meaning, quests based on these narratives can inherit these meanings or complicate and challenge them. Designing a quest based on a work of literature is itself an act of interpretation by which the designer considers how a player will enact a meaning or range of possible meanings available in a text.

In *Twisty Little Passages,* Montfort offers an excellent example of how players may enact themes in games in his analysis of Andrew Plotkin's experimental interactive fiction *So Far.* Montfort argues that "the workings of the IF world and the themes of *So Far* must be enacted . . . for the interactor to make progress" (210). Montfort is discussing a text-based game in which the solutions of puzzles require the player to both uncover and act out a theme of relationships that are "so close to but so far from" perfection by moving various items (like the two posts of a gate or two radioactive bricks) into proximity without allowing them to touch. Montfort's example is representative of a larger tradition of games that conjoin meaning and action in gameplay rather than putting them in conflict, including both early role-playing games like *Ultima IV,* more recent ones like *The Elder Scrolls,* and experimental action-adventure games like *The Indigo Prophecy.* Rather than having to "break" the promise of meaning in order to maintain the interest of the quest, these games have replay value precisely because fulfillment of their challenges allows players to contemplate nuances of thematic implication through their active effort rather than through passive spectatorship. In such a game, the distance between Aarseth's "interpretative" and "configurative" functions diminishes, as does the difference between the "interpretative interactivity" that Zimmerman associates with literary narratives and the "explicit interactivity" that he attributes to games (Zimmerman 158, Aarseth *Cybertext* 64–65).

Meaningful games challenge Aarseth's criticism of narrative-based adventure games because of "the limited results they achieve (poor to non-existent characterization, extremely derivative action plots, and, wisely, no attempts at metaphysical themes)" (Aarseth "Quest Games" 367). On the contrary, many games contain rich and dynamic characterization, exciting yet meaningful gameplay, and a courageous engagement with metaphysical themes that is all the more compelling because the player is immersed in these ideas rather than a passive spectator of them. Appreciating these qualities allows both theoreticians and designers to learn from the artistic achievements of many games that feature quests, as well as from the history of quest narratives that enables these accomplishments.

A Spectrum of Quests

While there are quests in a wide variety of games, they fall along a spectrum in which narrative predominates at one end and action at the other. Games at the extreme ends of this spectrum are marginal cases, and a game that is too far toward one end may not contain quests at all but rather related forms of gameplay and narrative. For example, point-and-click adventure games with a heavy narrative component but little action are at the extreme narrative end of the spectrum. At the other end, massively multiplayer online games feature a profusion of quests but very little narrative, resulting in constant action that has little meaning.

Hence, MMOs fall on the "action" side of the spectrum of quests. In these extremely popular games, such as *Everquest* and *World of Warcraft*, millions of players can participate simultaneously in a vast, simulated world with many tasks. However, the emphasis on social interaction over the single-player experience causes the "main quest" to disappear, resulting in a proliferation of side-quests. These side-quests may contribute to an overarching set of themes, as Jeff Kaplan (a lead quest designer of *World of Warcraft*) suggests they do. However, the journey of a hero through a series of trials whose completion allow him to bring a meaningful item or insight back to his society is often absent. The "theme" of *World of Warcraft* is neverending war between racial factions, a bleak scenario that is not particularly conducive to meaningful gameplay.

Games at the center of these two extreme ends of the spectrum contain tasks that are most truly quests, conjoining activity and narrative into meaningful action. In the contemporary game market, single-player action-adventure games and role-playing games such as *The Elder Scrolls IV: Oblivion*, *Dreamfall*, and *Eternal Darkness* occupy this center. These games conjoin varied, energetically active gameplay with a powerful commitment to a long literary tradition of narratives about characters striving toward meaningful goals. However, there is nothing inherently fixed about these genres or these examples. An MMO could in theory conjoin gameplay and narrative to produce meaningful action, and some designers are striving toward this ideal. For example, *Dungeons and Dreamers* describes Richard Garriott's attempts to combine the virtues of single-player and multi-player games in *Tabula Rasa*, an MMO where individual characters can be at the center of a gripping storyline even while they interact with thousands of other subscribers (King and Borland 252).

The spectrum of quests constitutes a response to Aarseth's question, "Are there quests in all kinds of games?" In the most abstract sense of "goal-oriented activities," there can be quests in most kinds of games, but the tasks in certain genres of content and gameplay more closely fit the criteria of quests than others. Theoretically, there might be quests in arcade games from the 1980s, in combat games, in sports games, or in flight simulators. However, these are marginal examples, fitting some of the criteria of quests well but others only loosely. If one classifies games into genres based on their game-play, quests primarily appear with all their criteria intact in adventure games, action-adventure games, role-playing games, first person shooters, survival horror games, and massively multiplayer online games (MMOs).

If game genres are classified by content, such as the game's setting, back story, and visual appearance, then designers and players most often use the word "quest" to describe tasks in adventure games and role-playing games that take place in fantastic, medieval, or mythological settings. Designers of other content genres, such as action games set in urban environments, as is the *Grand Theft Auto* series, or martial arts action games like *Ninja Gaiden,* tend to use the word "mission" to refer to tasks that must be accomplished to make the game progress. The structure of these mission systems is similar to the quest systems of role-playing games like *Oblivion*, consisting of a main "plotline" or "story" comprised of various missions, along with a multitude of side missions. Designers and players often use "quests" rather than "missions" to describe the tasks in fantastic genres because the connotations of the word evoke knights in medieval romances rather than gangsters or ninjas. The word "quest" also implies that something more meaningful is at stake than stealing a car for the benefit of one's gang or assassinating a rival clan leader.

Like quest games themselves, the initiation that occurs in games runs a spectrum from more to less meaningful. In an MMO such as *World of Warcraft*, this initiation derives almost entirely from the achievements of one's character, registered in the power to destroy enemies as well as one's wealth and collection of valuable possessions. While Kaplan observes that the *World of Warcraft* designers do make quests in order to encourage exploration of a simulated world, players primarily gain a sense of personal achievement and a geopolitical familiarity with the fictional realm of Azeroth by playing the game for extended periods of time. Little is at stake in the ultimate failure or success of one's quests, which at best will gain a temporary victory for one's race in an ongoing war. In this sense, there is no "main quest" in *World of Warcraft,* but rather a proliferation of side-quests whose meaning is the strict-ly personal satisfaction of possessing a 60th-level character with an expensive suit of enchanted plate mail.

In contrast to *World of Warcraft,* the quest designers of *Oblivion* them-selves create a range of quests that occupy a variety of positions along a spec-trum of meaning and action. They display an awareness of these varying degrees of meaning in the structure and dialogue of the Mage's Guild quest line, a series of quests about the player's attempt to gain membership into an organization of scholarly wizards and to ascend through its ranks. The first seven quests give the player access to the arcane university by way of letters of recommendation, in imitation or parody of the contemporary academy. These tasks are fetch quests (recover a stolen staff, lost ring, or rare book), kill quests (destroy a rogue mage), and small dungeon crawls (find an exiled mage in a winding, zombie-infested network of caverns). Many feature interesting twists in narrative and gameplay, as when the search for a lost "ring of burden" at the bottom of a well requires a harrowing magical voyage underwater, which soon turns into a quest to investigate the evil actions of the insane quest-giver who sent the player on this doomed errand in the first place. On the whole, however, these early quests are relatively trivial, involving small-scale local conflicts within the guilds of particular cities.

However, when a player has completed these quests, they open up a new series of stages in this "quest line." The quest-giver of this line, an archmage named Raminus Polus, contrasts the earlier and the later quests in terms of the relatively greater meaning of the later ones versus the earlier ones. Referring to the petty motivations behind many of the early quests, he remarks, "You have no doubt seen much of the worst the guild has to offer" but adds "you are now ready for more meaningful tasks." The tasks are "more meaningful" in part because they allow opportunities for initiation in the sense of advancement through the guild, with a whole new sequence of leveled titles such as "associate," "apprentice" "journeyman," "evoker," and "conjurer." These levels repeat the pattern of initiation through overall levels and individual skills in *Oblivion,* which also allow the player to move from novice through apprentice and journeyman and eventually to master. However, Raminus Polus is contrasting the early quests with the late quests primarily because the latter ones reveal and alter a large-scale conflict within the guild, in which a group of evil magicians seek to revive the forbidden practice of necromancy. This overarching narrative emerges from the completion of the later quests, which are similar in gameplay (they remain fetch quests and kills quests) but more elaborate and engaging in terms of narrative. The NPCs within *Oblivion* and the designers of the game set up a scale of value in which exciting gameplay is a necessary but not a sufficient component of a meaningful and enjoyable quest.

Three Types of Meaning in Quests

Meaning is a highly complex term that has many facets in gaming, all of them connected by a sense of valuable significance that complements the pleasure of action for its own sake. The literary critical sense of "meaning" as a theme or idea conveyed symbolically through a work of literature is an important aspect of meaning in quest games but is only one type of meaning. If a player feels that a quest that she undertakes is a worthwhile expenditure of time and effort rather than an unrewarding chore, then this quest has meaning to the player.

There are at least three different ways in which quests can be meaningful, with several subcategories and ways in which these types of meaning can intersect and complement each other.

Meaning can refer to:

- the impact of the player's accomplishments on and within a simulated world, including
  — achieving greater power in this world and understanding of its lore, in gaming terminology as "leveling up" and in mythological terms as "initiation";
  — changing the shape of the landscape;
  — altering the political and moral balance of the game world;
  — changing the player-avatar's relationship with her companions or other NPCs;
- a narrative backstory that conveys emotional urgency by revealing why the player-avatar is performing an action and what effects this action will have;
- expressive, semantic, and thematic meaning: ideas symbolically encoded within the landscape, objects, and challenges of the quest and enacted through it.

Players' uncovering of thematic meaning through the completion of a quest can sometimes entail literally deciphering a secret message in a puzzle. More often, however, the world itself is the puzzle. The ways that different players go about completing quests "reconfigures" these meanings, allowing players to experience them in many ways.

This enactment of meaning is potential and metaphorical in quest narratives but actual in quest games. In narratives about quests, characters perform deeds that have meaning, often allegorical. For example, *The Quest for the Holy Grail* follows a pattern in which a knight's performance of a series of complex actions is followed by an explanation of the spiritual significance of each part of these actions by a wise figure, such as a monk. This explanation is usually complex yet blunt in its delivery, as when a monk says to Sir Galahad, "Sir, you asked me just now the meaning of the mysterious task you fulfilled, and I will gladly inform you" (63). In a postmodern narrative, these meanings might change according to the interpretation of the reader. If the plot is significantly ambiguous, a reader's interpretation may also affect the imagined "outcome" of these events in her mind. However, in both postmodern and premodern narratives, the characters' actions for the most part remain the same from reading to reading. Moreover, the reader does not have to exert effort to cause these events to occur because they will be narrated no matter what. The reader exerts cognitive and interpretative effort to determine what the actions performed by a character mean after they have occurred. In contrast, players of quest games must sometimes determine what their actions mean in order to perform them correctly. Their meaning is discovered or created by a player through action, so that the action itself is meaningful. It is not just the events that are "realized" or "actualized," in Juul's terms, but the meanings of these events as well.

For example, *Oblivion* is thematically "about" the struggle of good and evil and the necessity to act heroically to fend off destruction of self and society, although this theme must be actively pursued by the player in order for it to communicate. Thus, if the player chooses primarily to wander the world of Tamriel seeking buried treasure in dungeons, she would avoid exposure to this theme but would miss large portions of the actions available in the game. The main quest is emotionally and morally significant because it concerns the welfare of an entire simulated world, which the player "cares" about more strongly than a fictional world under attack because it is her actions that can save it. The main quest establishes its emotional significance in the opening stages of the game, in which the player must protect the emperor. The emperor, dramatically voiced by Patrick Stewart, issues a "call to adventure" by bravely facing a death prophesied in ominous dreams and rescuing the player character from jail so that he can save Tamriel. The side-quests elicit similar forms of emotional investment through character development and dramatic voice acting, leading the player to care about an unfortunate NPC who has lost a valuable item or close friend.

Meaning as Initiation

Quests are meaningful because they immerse players in dramas of initiation, defined as a gradual movement up through formalized "levels" of achievement into a progressively greater understanding of the rules and narrative in a simulated world. Initiation also entails insight into how this world comments imaginatively upon "real" events, circumstances, and ideas. Designers create an activity out of the quest structure by lengthening and repeating the phase of initiation described by Campbell, which originates in the trade guilds of the middle ages and the mystery religions of ancient Greece and Rome. The impetus behind quests is achievement, motivated by a drive to overcome difficulties and to better oneself, both in the virtual form of one's "avatar" and in the real-world skills developed through extended playing. What Frye glosses over as the "minor adventures" and "perilous journey" leading up to the hero's final battle becomes the center of quest in games, because these episodes are the greatest source for action (187). As Campbell writes, the hero "must survive a succession of trials. This a favorite phase of the myth-adventure. It has produced a world literature of miraculous tests and ordeals" (97). While the Campbellian elements of the initiation appear frequently in games, *Oblivion* reaches far back into the history and structure of initiation in order to produce compelling gameplay. There is a set of "quest lines" called "guild quests" related to the player character's membership and status within "guilds" devoted to particular professions in the game, such as a "mages' guild" of wizards, a "fighters' guild" of warriors and knights, as well as a shadowy "thieves' guild" of assassins and criminals. In massively multi-player online role-playing games (MMORPGs), these guilds facilitate community formation by offering support and a sense of belonging. At the same time, these organizations are based upon the trade guilds of the middle ages, which measured and validated a craftsman's increasing abilities. Hence, the "skill levels" associated with particular abilities like combat or alchemy derive directly from medieval guild vocabulary, including "novice," "apprentice," "journeyman," "expert," and "master." In a role-playing game, a character's abilities are measured by his "level," representing a summary evaluation of his experience within the game and his resulting abilities. Much of the motivation for extended play, which can take hours of mental exertion, comes from the desire to "level up" by gaining sufficient experience to ascend to the next level. The idea of achieving greater "levels" within an organization based upon skill and understanding comes from trade guilds, but also from the mystery religions and secret societies that preceded them and developed out of them, such as the Eleusinian mysteries or the Freemasons. For example, in the course of playing over many weeks or months, a player might attempt to move his character from a "first level" Spellsword to a "thirteenth level" Spellsword. This degree of formalized ascent through numbered gradations that bring new abilities and insights resembles the process of a "neophyte" of a mystical order becoming an "adept" or a new initiate into Masonry attempting to become a thirty-third degree Freemason."

Meaning as Narrative

While the primary type of meaning in quests is achievement in the form of initiation, a second form of meaning is derived from narrative, which motivates the player through a back story that gives urgency to a task, or rewards the player through an explanation of the events that occur as a result of the task's completion. A successfully completed quest may reveal what happened to lead up to it, such as "whodunit" in a murder mystery, or what will happen as a result of it, such as the fate of the empire after the demonic antagonist has been vanquished. While quests are not synonymous with narratives, the drive to discover what happened before or what will happen after the quest can be a powerful motivation to invest large amounts of time and effort in a game.

Thematic Meaning

A third form of meaning is thematic meaning, communicated when the player acts out a set of ideas that comment upon the simulated world of the game and the "real" world outside of it. This commentary can run the gamut from simple themes, such as a basic conflict between good and evil enacted in the game's battles, to sophisticated puzzles that conceal encoded meanings through the interrelationship of their parts. As in any other work of art, the themes enacted by players can fall into a wide variety of categories, including natural, psychological, political, and religious ideas. Designers can create quests with thematic meaning by drawing upon a tradition of symbolic correspondences that runs throughout quest narratives and through some of the most sophisticated quest games, which will be discussed in Chapter 1.

Notes

[1] Both game designers and literary critics acknowledge that quests often involve movement through space, and "journey" also etymologically descends from the Middle English *journee* ("day"), and the Latin *diurnata* ("a day's time, a day's work"). This implies that the journey is an extended enterprise that takes time and daily application.

[2] In acknowledgment of these innovations, Vogler himself suggested in the introduction to the second edition of his book that the hero's journey could furnish new materials for interactive narrative, which he understood in the mid 1990s as hypertext.

Designing Meaningful Action

Before you begin to design your quest, consider the big picture of the game's meaning. Why is this quest important to your players? What satisfactions will they gain beyond the usual ones of killing monsters and finding treasure? Will they gain a set of moral virtues, overthrow an oppressive political system (like the Rebels fighting the Empire in *Star Wars*), or uncover a code that unlocks the mysteries of the game's fictional cosmos?

In order to keep in mind this overarching picture of meaning and action, it can be helpful to understand the idea of symbolic "correspondences" that was crucial to the literary tradition of quest narratives that were popular in the middle ages and the Renaissance. These stories, such as the tales of King Arthur and the knights of the Round Table, were understood by their authors and readers as allegories. An allegory is a symbolic story or poem in which every element stands for an idea—often several ideas with multiple layers and components. When the Red Cross Knight battles the dragon in the first book of Edmund Spenser's epic allegory, *The Fairie Queen,* both author and reader see this dragon as

- a fantasy monster;
- a symbol of Satan;
- a personification of sin;
- an incarnation of England's political enemies, Rome and Spain.

Moreover, medieval allegory is built on a theory of correspondences in which symbols stand not only for other things but for other symbols as well, so that seasons of the year correspond to stages of human life, which in turn are associated with colors, parts of the body, precious stones, and animals. This tradition of interconnected allegorical correspondences is closely bound up with narratives about quests, as Piotr Sadowski argues in *The Knight on His Quest,* his book about the classic medieval poem *Sir Gawain and the Green Knight.* As Sadowski explains, the tendency of medieval authors to construct quest narratives built around densely interwoven symbols reflects "the universal medieval predilection to comprehend reality in terms of analogies, similarities, and correspondencies [sic]" (141). In other words, symbols are interconnected with each other in complicated ways that need to be mapped and displayed on tables in order to be fully visualized, although Sadowski argues that these correspondences were grasped quickly and intuitively by readers familiar with them.

In addition to standard allegorical devices, the poem revolves around a set of interlaced "correspondences" organized around five sets of five ideas, or "pentads," related to the "pentangle," or five-pointed star. As Sadowski explains,

> There seems to be no doubt that what interests the author, and what he is accordingly trying to convey to his readers, is not only the doctrinal meaning of the enumerated pentads, as well as their obvious relation to Sir Gawain, but also the relationships existing both within the pentads and among them. One perceives beneath the surface of the catalogued symbolic items an intricate system of interconnections and interdependencies, hinted at by the author in his repeated unambiguous statements about the "knotty" and interweaving nature of the pentangle. (128)

The author of *Sir Gawain* explains these connections when he describes the pentangle, but a full appreciation of them requires the active work of readers like Sadowski, who compiles them in several tables that resemble the programming of a game. For example, Figure 1.1 is Sadowski's table of the correspondences between five sets of five items (or "pentads") that the author of *Gawain* lists when pausing to interpret the pentangle on Gawain's shield. (The Middle English words for the five virtues of a knight are roughly equivalent in modern English to generosity, fellowship, purity, courtesy, and compassion.)

This table strongly resembles the virtue system that emerges in a "walkthrough" of *Ultima IV,* the gameplay of which is nonlinear and therefore must be represented as a table. Andrew Schultz's walkthrough (see Figure 1.2) offers a small concordance of these virtues.

	1st Cycle	2nd Cycle	3rd Cycle	4th Cycle	5th Cycle
Five Wits	sight	hearing	smelling	taste	touch
Five Wounds	right hand	left hand	heart	right foot	left foot
Five Virtues	fraunchyse	felaschyp	clannes	cortasye	pité
Five Fingers	thumb	index	third finger	ring finger	little finger
Five Joys	Annunciation	Nativity	Epiphany	Resurrection	Assumption

Figure 1.1. The five cycles of the five pentads contained in Sir Gawain's pentacle.

Virtue	Prin- ciple	Stone Color	Class	Town	Dun- geon	Mantra	Com- panion	Shrine
Honesty	T	Blue	Mage	Moon- glow	Deceit	AHM	Mariah	EC OJ
Com- passion	L	Yellow	Bard	Britain	Despise	MU	Iolo	FM IA
Valor	C	Red	Fighter	Jhelom	Destard	RA	Geoffrey	OF CE
Justice	TL	Green	Druid	Yew	Wrong	BEH	Jaana	AL EJ
Sacrifice	LC	Orange	Tinker	Minoc	Covet- ous	CAH	Julia	DC NJ
Honor	TC	Purple	Paladin	Trinsic	Shame	SUMM	Dupre	MP FB
Spiritu- ality	TLC	White	Ranger	Skara Brae	Hyth- loth	OM	Shamino	XX XX
Humil- ity	O	Black	Sheperd	Magi- nica	Abyss	LUM	Katrina	NI OH

Figure 1.2. Andrew Schultz's concordance of the *Ultima* virtues.

The Virtue System in Ultima IV

This resemblance is more than coincidental, since the designers of many successful quest games have built their games around simi- lar principles. Richard Garriott's *Ultima IV: Quest of the Avatar* (the fourth installment in his popular and long-running series of *Ultima* games) is a paradigm for an innovative, popular quest game that cre- ates meaningful action through a system of correspondences. Richard Garriott deliberately sets up an intricate system of correspondences between a set of moral virtues and the representational features of the game's simulated world, including its colors, villages, and directions of the compass.[1] As players battle monsters, seek out hidden shrines, and search for magical artifacts in each of the game's subquests, they are acting out the game's allegorical meanings (or failing to act them out), in such a way that gameplay gradually reveals these correspondences, and successful completion of the quests necessitates an understanding of them.

In *Dungeons and Dreamers*, King and Borland explain that Garriott "locked himself away with books of literature, poetry, philosophical con- cepts, and a white board, bound and determined to break life down into its fundamental principles," thereby taking a "programmer's approach to moral philosophy." Garriott himself explains that he set up this virtue system in response to fans and angry antivideogame activists who were "reading things into my games that were simply statistical anomalies in the programming. They thought I was putting messages into the game" (72–74). Garriott embraced this interpretive impulse in both fans and critics by deliberately programming ideas into *Ultima IV,* making the entire game an "Easter egg" (a video game term for secret messages inserted by designers) of hidden meaning instead of scattering these eggs here and there.[2]

For example, the number of virtues which a player's character has attained, as well as the number of runes and stones, were stored on a byte, which is comprised of eight bits. The virtue system, with its eight-part correspondences, derives in part from the Eightfold Path of Buddhism, but also from the eightfold structure of a basic programming unit. The order of the bits also reflects the correspondences of the virtue system, with the 0 position in two separate bytes standing for both the blue stone and the virtue of honesty that it represents. This is one instance of how Garriott made the arbitrary constraints of binary programming language into an expressive medium. Details of the programming structures underlying *Ultima IV* can be seen at the "technical page" of Joshua Steele's *Ultima IV* site, the "Moongates Ultima IV Annex," at http://www.moongates.com/u4/Tech.asp.

As King and Borland explain, "if people were reading this much into his games without him actually putting messages there, the games were clearly vehicles for provoking thought. Maybe he should use that power. He didn't want to be dogmatic about any particular message, but he was developing a more complex vision of the universe" (72). While *Ultima IV* does have an elaborate virtue system, Garriott's ideas of meaning and communication in games emphasize interactivity over didacticism, since he "wasn't interested in teaching any specific lesson; instead, his next game would be about making people think about the consequences of their actions" (73). Contemporary theories of allegory, such as those of Gordon Teskey as summarized by Wayne Erickson, have emphasized a game-like interactive experience of virtue that is shaped by players' decisions (Erickson 12). Indeed, Edmund Spenser's *The Faerie Queen,* a series of quest narratives about knights searching to attain various allegorical virtues, is a precursor to the *Ultima* games if not a direct inspiration of them.

Correspondences in Morrowind and Eternal Darkness

Games like *Ultima IV* and the narratives that inspired them suggest that quests can contain the most meaningful action if their simulated worlds are constructed around principles of correspondence and analogy. Quest designers have long known that they can make the player's experience more satisfying rather than frustratingly episodic if they give a specific number of related quests, often involving the collection of a set of related items to make a single one. The quests can have an even more satisfying sense of depth if these numbered parts correspond to ideas, spaces, objects, and other features of the game that address all of the senses, including hearing and vision. Examples include the eight pieces of the Triforce in the *Zelda* series; the twelve episodes and twelve runes in *Eternal Darkness*; the eight virtues, towns, artifacts, dungeons, colors, and mantras in *Ultima IV*; and the seven trials in *Morrowind.*

These analogies should be integrated not only into the structure of quests but into the gameplay, whether through the game's spaces, its magic system, or its interface. This idea of correspondence existed in the allegories of the middles ages and extends to nineteenth-century theories of art, such as the synaesthesia (one sense corresponding to another) advocated by Symbolists like Charles Baudelaire. A form of art that addresses all the senses through a combination of drama, painting, text, and music has been referred to as a "total art," and Marie-Laure Ryan observes that contemporary aspirations toward virtual reality (including its approximations in video games) continue this tradition. She writes of "the influence of such creators as Wagner and Artaud, for the popularity of a conception of total art that insists on the involvement of all the senses in the artistic experience. The closest to this ideal is the opera, with its blend of music, dance, drama, poetry, stage design, costumes, and light effects" (55). For example, Richard Wagner's operas (including his version of the Grail quest, entitled *Parzival*) were built on architectural correspondences among elements of a primordial, cosmic alphabet, sounds, and story elements. Games add the element of interactivity to this total art, so that the correspondences between aspects of the game can be integrated into actions that players perform rather than merely observing. The walkthroughs of *Ultima IV* and *Eternal Darkness* consist of charts of the games' interwoven correspondences, but these charts emerge from gameplay and are useful primarily because they help the player to progress and eventually win the game.

Another highly popular game built on a system of symbolic correspondences is the survival horror game *Eternal Darkness: Sanity's Requiem. Eternal Darkness* is structured around an invented language consisting of arcane runes, each with a different meaning and magical power that can be combined with others to create spells that enchant items, inflict magical damage, and reveal hidden portals. Three major runes of three colors (and one hidden color) correspond to three alignments associated with the game's three Ancients (demonic, Lovecraftian deities), which in turn correspond to the bodily, psychic, and magical attacks of their minions. One of the strengths of this game is the way that the game's symbolism is integrated with its gameplay, so that players uncover the mysteries of the runes of the Ancients through their use of the game's magic system, puzzle-solving, and combat.

At the same time that players learn about the feuds between the Ancients and their schemes to return to the world, they also learn the practical consequences of the power relations between the three runes (which can trump each other in magic and combat through a system that resembles rock–paper–scissors). Indeed, it gradually emerges that the Ancients themselves are playing a vast cosmic game whose stakes involve the preservation or destruction of human good in the face of overwhelming darkness and insanity. While Glassner has thoughtfully critiqued the opening sequences of *Eternal Darkness* because the player chooses the rune that will determine the alignment of his enemies without knowing the consequences of this decision, I would argue that it is precisely this sense of gradually disclosed meaning that makes *Eternal Darkness* so compelling and addictive. At any rate, this was the intention of its lead designer, Denis Dyack, who explains that the building of a world for the game is the first priority of his company (a principle that he continues to follow in the *Too Human* trilogy, a thematically rich game based on Norse mythology).

A third highly popular quest game that incorporates these correspondences in its gameplay is *The Elder Scrolls III: Morrowind,* in which the player's main quest is driven by the desire to interpret (and possibly fulfill) a mysterious prophecy revealed through dreams and ancient texts. The elements of this prophecy are organized in sevens, including seven dreams, seven visions, seven riddles, and seven trials that the player must overcome in order to gain seven objects that will allow him to become the incarnation of "the Nerevar," a mythical hero in charge of reuniting the people of Morrowind.

The active attempt to embody virtue also appears in *Morrowind,* where the main quest consists of the player's attempt to fulfill a prophecy of the reincarnation and return to power of a long-dead hero called "the Nerevar." When the player's status as this hero is tested by a tribal wise woman, she cryptically responds, "You are not the Nerevar, but you may become the Nerevar." She explains that to attain this status, the player must pass seven trials, themselves recorded only as riddles whose meaning must be determined and enacted through gameplay. Another term for the reincarnated form of this hero is "the Incarnate," implying that like the avatar of *Ultima IV,* he embodies the power necessary to defeat the enemies of the dark elven tribes known as the Dunmer.

Allegory and Avatars

Both symbolic correspondences and the relationship between avatar and self in the quest can be understood through the literary tradition of allegory, in which readers identify with protagonists seeking various virtues in order to cultivate these virtues within their own lives. Games intensify this relationship between imagined and everyday life through the player's control of an avatar that is both a digital image of a body and an extension of the player's everyday, embodied identity. Tasks that players undertake within a fictional world require the cultivation of real-world qualities, such as patience, planning, and effort.

In *Massively Multiplayer Online Role-Playing Games*, Kelly argues that while MMOs may initially appear to be a distraction from endeavors in "RL" (the mildly pejorative slang term that MMO players use to refer to "real life"), they can actually act as "distilled and purified practice versions of real life." They become "life simulators" in the same way that flight simulators educate pilots (85). Kelly briefly notes that this tradition derives from allegory when he writes that "MMORPGS also act as allegories for spiritual development. Think of them as interactive *Pilgrim's Progress* stories or *Jataka Tales* for the 21ˢᵗ century" (87). Indeed, he directly invokes the metaphor of a "training ground" used by the character Deetsan in the "Through a Nightmare, Darkly" quest of *Oblivion*, writing that "with all of these correlations between the stages of physical life, spiritual life, and game life, it appeared that what a lot of people were doing was using the game world as a practice space or a training ground for spiritual and emotional pursuits" (90). Kelly agrees that this process of training can occur most effectively when the player sees her avatar as an extension of her real-world self rather than an escape from or contradiction of it. He writes, "When they see that their virtual selves are not really separate from their real selves, when their virtual lives are really branch offices of their real lives, when their avatars are not objects to be manipulated but manifestations of their own thoughts and desires, some players even learn enough from their second lives inside the game world to improve their first lives in the real world" (91).

While Kelly's argument is insightful, quest in games can be more and less allegorical, and strategies for creating meaningful action can best be understood through the history of quests in games and literature. The "virtue system" of *Ultima IV: Quest of the Avatar* was overtly concerned with the allegorical acquisition of virtues through the control of a virtual self. When a player asks the NPC Lord British (a pseudonym for designer Richard Garriott and one of his in-game representatives) about the keyword "avatar," he responds, "The quest of the avatar is to know and become the embodiment of the Eight Virtues of Goodness." *Ultima* is playing with complex implications about what James Paul Gee calls "situated and embodied meaning," a "learning principle" of video games by which players understand concepts within the concrete context of gameplay rather than as abstractions (83–84).

Yet, *Ultima* is also using "avatar" in the sense of "the embodiment of a god," a feature of Hindu mythology and religious practice that fits with its requirement that the player "meditate" on "mantras" (the Hindu term for sacred syllables used to focus the mind on religious ideas) associated with each virtue. As Shay Addams explains in *The Official Book of Ultima*, Garriott learned about this mythological concept from a documentary on the Dead Sea Scrolls and applied the term in its religious sense before it took on its cybercultural usage (43–44). Hence, the player's quest to "embody" virtues is complicated, operating on many levels of metaphor and simulation. The player is embodied in a physical body that types at a keyboard, controlling a small animated "avatar," or digital representation of a body. The player then undertakes a quest to transform this digital body, or "avatar," into the embodiment of virtues, which Garriott intends to be applicable to the lives of physically embodied players.

Indeed, the introduction to *Ultima IV* dramatizes the player's entrance into the world of digital simulation, graphically and textually describing a back story in which the player is transported from the United States in the 1980s to the medieval realm of Britannia. Moreover, Garriott eschewed the "kill quests" that often define MMOs, in which players indiscriminately slay an arbitrary number of beasts in order to gain trophies to bring to a quest-giver. Instead, his concept of "the quest of the avatar," as explained by Lord British if the player inquires about the word "quest," entails an ethos or habitual ethical stance toward the world: "It is to live a life constantly and forever in the Quest to better thyself and the world in which we live." These quests are given at eight towns distributed over the land of Britannia, so that the game's symbol system encourages full exploration of the simulated world. Indeed, the practical design of quests might most productively begin with the design of the game's spaces, which will shape gameplay on every level because players will be exploring them constantly in the course of the game.

A Sample Exercise and Design Document: Sir Gawain's Quest

Before we discuss level design, however, it is wise to think about the ideas that will shape your quest. You won't know exactly how these ideas will play out until you are actually in the process of design, but a little planning early on can save a lot of work later and avoid a "pointless" or formless hack-and-slash

RPG (with which the market is largely glutted already). You might want to draw up a table of the journal updates, spaces, characters, and challenges that will make up your quest.

The process of planning out all these aspects of a game in written form is called writing a "design document," and *Fundamentals of Game Design* by Rollings and Adams gives many useful suggestions on how to build such a document for many different kinds of games (62–65). Building a design document for a quest game, especially one based on a literary quest narrative, requires a slightly different approach in that each component of gameplay must be simultaneously fun and meaningful. To illustrate what such a document might look like, imagine a sample quest design exercise in which designers have been asked to transform the medieval poem *Sir Gawain and the Green Knight* into a quest game. Below, I have listed some potential design challenges for such a game as well as a worksheet filled in with some suggested solutions for these challenges.

Sir Gawain and the Green Knight is one of the most popular quest narratives, entertaining and rich enough to appeal to both English professors and game designers. It is a short narrative poem from the middle ages describing the knight Gawain's quest to survive a beheading game proposed by a magical knight in green armor. The Green Knight asks Gawain to take one stroke at his head with an axe, provided that the Green Knight may return the blow one year later. Gawain beheads the Knight, who magically reattaches his own head and tells Gawain to meet him in a year to receive the return stroke. Gawain must voyage to the mysterious Green Chapel to honor his part of the game, and along the way he overcomes various temptations to behave dishonorably. In particular, he has to withstand the temptation to have an affair with the wife of his host, Sir Bertilac, by playing a game in which he must give the host anything he has "won" in exchange for anything the host killed while hunting. Gawain honorably gives the host two kisses but keeps a magic girdle given him by the host's wife in the hopes that it will protect him from death. When Gawain meets with the Green Knight, the knight pretends that he will cut off Gawain's head but gives him only a single nick in punishment for keeping the girdle. The Knight then reveals himself to be Sir Bertilac in disguise and encourages Sir Gawain (and generations of literary critics) to think about the meaning of imperfection, love for life, and honor.

Because of this poem's classic status, it could be used in any game design or literature course. At the same time, it is a deeply exciting and fun story, which itself includes various "games" that involve a range of human activity, from religious to erotic. Making this quest narrative into a quest game will take work, but game designers, educators, and students could all benefit from thinking about how to do this. As Sadowski argues in *The Knight on His Quest*, the poem is constructed around the temporal structure of the quest, defined as "a pattern, typical for the chivalric romance as well as for the heroic epic as its historical prototype, which shapes the story's action according to a general regulating narrative principle." He specifies that "the quest is to be understood as a sequence of events and adventures involving the main protagonist(s), leading toward some goal or solution. The sequential nature of the quest implies a linear, goal-oriented and purposeful movement in time from one important event or stage of action to another, usually framed within a fictitious life span of some exemplary individual" (51).

We will start small by focusing on only a small part of this quest, which adapts parts of the first two sections, or "Fitts," of the poem (included as Appendix B in this book). The exercise will also be broken up into the component parts of the quest according to our four-fold plan of skillsets:

1. level design;
2. NPC creation;
3. object creation;
4. scripting.

In this first exercise, we will build two locations: Camelot (where Gawain first receives his quest from the Green Knight) and the Green Chapel (where he voyages to fulfill his quest). Between these two locations, we will build a landscape of intervening obstacles, including cliffs, wild beasts, and monsters. To give Gawain his quest, we will create the Green Knight, as well as a few other Arthurian characters, such as King Arthur himself and the hunter Sir Bertilac. We will also build Gawain's inventory, which includes the shield with the pentangle and the green knight's axe, both highly symbolic quest items. As a scripting exercise, we will create various "magical" effects associated with Gawain's quest.

Throughout, we will seek to integrate the possible range of meanings in the poem with the gameplay of the quest, focusing on the intricate system of fivefold correspondences that will operate much like the "virtue system" in *Ultima IV*. As the poet explains, the five points on the pentangle, or five-pointed star, on Gawain's shield can be interpreted as signifying many important things in the poem that come in fives. These include the five senses, the five fingers on a hand, the five wounds of the crucifixion, the five mysteries of the Virgin Mary, and the five virtues of knighthood. Throughout our exercise, the question will be how to allow players to enact these various intricate correspondences as well as the themes of truth, temptation, and virtue at the same time that they have fun in their challenging quest. Later exercises in the book will allow designers more freedom, but this one will break down the component parts of the assignment in tutorial fashion so as to guide beginners in their work.

Sir Gawain Design Document

To begin planning your quest, you need to think about the following components.

1. Constructing the Spaces of the Quest through Level Design

What environments will the player explore? What geographical obstacles, such as mountain passes and rushing streams, will she surmount? Where will players need to travel in order to fulfill their task, and where will they return in order to complete it?

Key environments might include:

- a banquet-hall in Camelot;
- the forest between Camelot and the Sir Bertilac's Castle;
- Sir Bertilac's Castle (anteroom and banquet-hall);
- the forest between the Sir Bertilac's Castle and the Green Chapel;
- the Green Chapel.

2. Setting the Stages of the Quest through Journal Updates

Next, list the journal updates that the player will receive upon completing key actions in the quest. Taken together, these updates will form the "story" of the quest, but remember that they should not be only a narrative of the events that occur. Instead, you should be writing from the perspective of the player, using sentences with "I" that summarize what the player has done and what tasks he should accomplish next if he wishes to proceed in the quest. You may suggest alternate courses of action that different players might undertake, but be careful. A "choose your own adventure" narrative with too many branching paths can become difficult to program. Instead, let the rules of the game shape players' possible decisions based on how they take or discard objects, what strategies they use to fight enemies, and where they go spatially on their journey.

For example, the journal stages of the quest might read as follows.

- *Journal Update 1*: A Green Knight has challenged me to join in his beheading game. If I agree, I should take his green axe and cut off his head, but I will have to let him do the same to

> me in a year. If I do not agree, I will live but may be dishonored.

- *Journal Update 2*: I have cut off the Green Knight's head. I must now seek out the Green Chapel where I can honor my part of the bargain.
- *Journal Update 3*: I found a beautiful castle in the wilderness. My host, a hunter, has made a strange bargain with me. I am to spend three days with his wife while he hunts. He will give me all the game that he kills, but I must also give him whatever I "win."
- *Journal Update 4*: The Hunter's wife has given me a girdle, which she says is magic and will protect me from any harm. I am not sure whether I should give it to the Hunter or not.
- *Journal Update 5*: I have located the Green Chapel. I must now allow the Green Knight to cut off my head. If I keep the girdle, it might protect me. On the other hand, I will be forfeiting my honor as a knight by betraying my word and the emblem of "truth" on my shield.

3. Making the Objects through Quest Items

List several objects that figure prominently in the quest. These are more than just "props" to decorate an environment or the everyday weapons, armor, and scrolls that players will carry in their inventories. Rather, the "quest items" are the objects of the player's search and the famed artifacts that will allow her to complete it. If you need examples to help you think of these objects, imagine the "One Ring" that Frodo must bear to Mordor, the magic sword "Excalibur" that Arthur pulls from the stone, and the portions of the Triforce in the *Zelda* games.

For example, the player might locate and use the following items:

- one shield with a pentacle;
- one magical axe, made of a shining green material;
- one girdle, a love-token from the hunter's wife that may or may not have "magical" properties protecting him from harm.

Gawain might also symbolically gain the five virtues of a knight by retrieving the following plot items in a series of fetch quests:

- the Armor of Courtesy;
- the Shield of Beneficence;
- the Helm of Compassion;

- the Sword of Pure Mind;
- the Ring of Brotherly Love.

4. Designing the Challenges of the Quest through Scripting

Scripting is a form of "event-based" programming that specifies the rules governing possible events that may occur in the quest and the conditions that the player must strategically fulfill to bring them about. For example, will a door open only if a player has a key? Will a monster attack only if a player approaches within five feet of a cave entrance? Will an NPC respond to a player in one of two ways depending upon whether the player has accomplished a task first? Consider how you are going to measure these conditions. Can any of them be expressed mathematically?

Scripting is the most essential element of the quest because it is the glue that connects its elements and makes the player's experience more than a series of random interactions with a simulated world, but rather a consciously planned set of possible events that will occur only when players fulfill certain challenges. During the later design portions of this book, we will return to the various aspects of the Sir Gawain exercise and design document, discussing how various theories of the quest and game design skill sets might be used to solve them.

Role-Playing Construction Sets

Having considered the big picture of quest design in terms of history, theory, and the overall planning of a design document, designers must think about the technologies for implementing these ideas. The most useful tools for educational and independent designers to make their own quests are the construction sets and toolsets packaged with recent role-playing games or available for download. These include the Aurora Toolset, which accompanies the role-playing game *Neverwinter Nights,* the NWN2 Toolset that is included with *Neverwinter Nights 2,* and the Elder Scrolls Construction Set, which comes in two versions associated with *The Elder Scrolls III: Morrowind* and *The Elder Scrolls IV: Oblivion.* Each of these toolsets allows users to construct game environments, objects, characters, and challenges using prefabricated art assets.

Building game variants, often known as "mods" or "modules," is a matter of dragging and dropping these elements into various render windows and altering them using complex but manageable menus reminiscent of a web design tool like *Dreamweaver.* Such toolsets are ideal for learning to design quests, which are often built into the gameplay structure of the games that are being modified. The construction sets help temporarily circumvent the need for a large team of artists, musicians, actors, and programmers required to develop a game from scratch. Although commercial game designers will eventually need to develop their own art assets and programming in order to have the rights to sell their game, toolsets are an excellent way for educators and independent designers to learn to design quests and prototype them. Commercially successful games have occasionally emerged from "mods" of existing games and game engines, such as *Counterstrike,* a first-person shooter that is a mod of *Half-Life.* Also, many independent game designers currently purchase more generic game-building tools, such as Torque and Blender, to construct their games rather than building an engine entirely from the ground up. Hence, using game construction sets is worthwhile experience for aspiring designers in a variety of settings.

This book will discuss the Aurora Toolset in its main chapters and the NWN2 Toolset (also known as the Electron Toolset) in an appendix. The Aurora Toolset is both user-friendly and inexpensive, since the first installment of *Neverwinter Nights* that it was included with has been released since 2002 and can now be purchased for twenty dollars (or less in "bargain bins" at used video game stores). This toolset has been widely applied in educational contexts ranging from Henry Jenkins's "Education Arcade" at MIT to interactive storytelling workshops at the University of Alberta and multiplayer journalism simulations at the University of Minnesota. The Aurora Toolset has now been supplemented by a slightly more complex and graphically detailed second installment called the NWN2 Construction Set. Abandoning the "tile-based" approach, in which game environments are built by dragging small squares of landscape or "tiles," the NWN2 Construction set offers a richly customizable construction set in which every detail of gameplay, environment, and character appearance can be manipulated in nuanced ways. For the purposes of the exercises in this book, either version of the toolset will work well.

The first resources in learning these toolsets are the online tutorials available on various websites, produced both by official employees of the game companies associated with each toolset and by dedicated modders in the community of fans. These should be your first resource in constructing your own quests, although most of the tutorials available online do not proceed past the level of basic world construction, object placement, dialogue trees, and scripting. As the modder Skydiver observes in a quest tutorial (a happy exception to the general lack of tutorials on the specific subject of constructing quests), quest design "encompasses just about every aspect of modding in one package: item creation, possibly interior building or landscaping, NPC creation, dialogue, and scripting. Unfortunately, that means while you can find separate tutorials on each of those things, a good comprehensive quest-making tutorial is hard to find."

There are some tutorials available on constructing quests, but they tend to teach only how to design a generic fetch quest or kill quest. What is needed, then, is a comprehensive set of tutorials that explores each aspect of quest design with an eye toward how they all fit together within a scheme of meaningful action, as well as an awareness of the principles of production that extend across each of them. My tutorials and exercises are intended to fill this gap, but it makes sense to use them in conjunction with all of the collective wisdom of experienced modders available on the Internet. Here is a series of links to some of the best online resources.

For the Aurora Toolset, the best materials available online are the official tutorials in the "For Builders" section at the official Bioware *Neverwinter Nights* website at http://nwm.bioware.com/builders/toolsetintro.html. The "Toolset Intro" on this same website will take designers through the basics of building an area, while the "Module Construction Tutorial" offers a detailed walkthrough of the most central elements of module building, including world design, object placement, NPC creation and dialogue, and a little scripting. Accomplished modder Celowin has written a more in-depth set of eleven scripting tutorials, available at the *Neverwinter Nights* Vault and packaged with the excellent downloadable scripting resource, the *Neverwinter Nights* Lexicon at http://nwvault.ign.com/View.php?view=other.Detail&id=695.

The Spaces of the Quest

Goal-Oriented Spaces

After a designer has an overall sense of the meaningful action in her game as well as an overview of the toolsets for creating it, the first step in creating quests involves the building of spaces, since a landscape is required for players to act within. Both narratological theories of the spaces of the quest as well as ludological inquiries into game-space can help to construct the most effective levels and worlds of quests. Aarseth's emphasis on the movement of the "player-avatar" through space is a recurrent feature of many definitions of quests, both in game theory and literary theory.

Studying the spaces of the quest in games and narratives can lead to a set of design principles which involve the construction of an allegorical universe. The design of spaces in games is often referred to as "level design." However, most action-adventure games and single-player RPGs are no longer set exclusively in dungeons, as were some of the early role-playing dungeon crawls such as *Wizardry*. Consequently, the spaces of these quests can more accurately be referred to as "world design," in which the designer develops an open-ended geography through which the player can move. Designing the spaces of quests is a matter of planning increasingly more remote, difficult to access, exotic locations in which quest-givers more and more relevant to the quests can be found.

This terrain will include many enclosures, such as dungeons and castles, that can be entered and explored. Consequently, designers have to think both in macro terms (associated with the world map of a fantastic land) and in micro terms (associated with enclosures within this land). On the micro level of dungeon design, the spaces should give the player an overall sense of the direction of her ultimate quest target, while introducing challenges of disorientation that intervene. These can include dead-end passageways, multiple forking branches that wind around and return to the same location, secret passages, staircases, trap doors, and other labyrinthine features.

While quest games often occur within the dream-like spaces of the initiatory road of trials, movement through these disorienting spaces is more urgent and goal-driven than the "navigation" associated with hypertext or the "exploration" featured in early adventure games. The player experiences a drive toward a target in space, and every object or character that intervenes between him and this target is an obstacle that must be overcome. This does not mean that movement is only in one direction. The player may backtrack to find hidden buttons or keys to open doors, as well as exploring thoroughly to discover any hidden resources (like health packs) or secret spaces (like hidden levels or secret passages). Yet, despite these circuitous movements, the player of a quest game always experiences an acute desire for progression that manifests itself as an almost instinctive sense of where to go next. Stéphane Natkin reinforces this idea in *Video Games and Interactive Media,* in which he argues that "a level is made up of a collection of quests" (37). Natkin defines a quest as a succession of objectives, obstacles, and solutions that are distributed through a maze-like space in order to guide the unfolding of various narratives through gameplay (37–38).

Tiered and Leveled Spaces

This spatial instinct is elicited by careful planning on the part of designers, who create particular spaces that communicate an experience of progression. Hence, designers of quest games often construct leveled or tiered structures, such as spiraling towers and ziggurats. The player knows where he should go next even without a map, both because he is always looking for the space that he has not yet explored and because he knows that he should attempt to move upward to the next level whenever possible.

The Oblivion towers in *Oblivion* follow this architectural pattern masterfully, orienting the player towards his goal through an upward spiral of spatial movement and escalating difficulty. The player must venture into at least three of these towers to complete the main quest of *Oblivion* and may enter many more in order to acquire further experience and allies for a future battle. In each of these side-quests, the overall goal remains the same: close the gate to the plane of Oblivion by removing a "sigil stone" from the uppermost chamber of a large tower.

After closing a few of these gates, the player begins to master the architectural principles by which the towers are constructed, despite the variations that the designers build into each tower in order to increase their challenge. The player learns that there is a central well-shaft with a geyser of lava, with winding ramps twisting upward toward the top chamber, or "Sigilium Sanctis," and the sigil-stone. Each of these ramps has a series of doors that branch off into passageways and chambers that the player is forced to explore because many of the ramps end in dead ends, preventing an uninterrupted ascent through the main well-shaft. Instead, the player must find a way through side-chambers, back into higher levels of the main ramps, and then back into the side-chambers. These potentially confusing routes become clear once the player realizes that he should always attempt to take the path through the side-chambers that moves upward, taking the door at the highest point with the hope that it will lead to a passageway to the next ramp. Many of these passages follow naming conventions that the player can learn, so that a doorway to the "Hallways of Dark Salvation" indicates a midlevel passageway that will lead to a higher-level ramp. This diabolical architecture is more than just a gratuitously twisted aesthetic feature.

Movement through these spaces often has an allegorical component, since locations have symbolic names and structures in the same way that those in medieval and Renaissance allegory do. Each Oblivion tower and all of its passageways and chambers have names that fit with the theme of a particular plane, such as negative emotions, mutilation, or natural disasters. Upward-winding circular corridors called "the halls of shame" or "the shrine of anguish" cannot help but evoke the allegorical locations within Dante's medieval circles of hell, as well as other bleak symbolic places like "the slough of despond" in *Piers Plowman* or "the dark tower" that Childe Roland approaches. While the poet John Milton observes that "long is the way / And hard, that out of Hell leads up to light," the player experiences this struggle in upward-seeking battles that last for hours, living out the full meaning of Aarseth's term "ergodic" (requiring the exertion of work) (Milton 282).

This space mirrors the leveled progression of character development in the process of initiation central to the gameplay of role-playing games. When a player accumulates sufficient experience points within a role-playing game, her character moves to a new "level." Level in this context refers to a measurement of the character's achievements in a formalized system of rankings that allows the player to see at a glance the relative power and skill of a character. For example, a player might have a level ten mage with access to a specific set of magic spells and skills. To "level up" in role-playing terminology means to attain a new level, with accompanying increases in the strengths and skills assigned to a player's character.

At the same time, a level often refers to a demarcated spatial area with a particular set of challenges that must be overcome before a player can move to the next area. The leveled ascent up spiraling towers or ziggurats is the spatial equivalent of leveling up one's character, as acknowledged by the leveling up messages in *Oblivion,* which congratulate the player: "You have ascended to *x* level." Both are images of initiation through movement, either in the literal sense of spatial climbing or the metaphorical sense of character development and achievement.

Outward Movement

Quest Hubs

In addition to upward movement, a repeated pattern of venturing into a perilous, unknown place and returning appears throughout many quest games and is visible on the maps that are often used to travel quickly between locations. The *Oblivion* quest map is dotted with "hubs" of known locations, like cities, surrounded by scattered, unknown locations (like ruins, caves, and forts) that the player ventures into in quest of adventure. Upon completing an adventure, he returns to a known location to inform the quest-giver and receive a reward. Hence, he moves laterally outward and then inward, as when he travels from a city along a road or across the countryside to a ruined mine and then returns to the city. For example, the map in *Undying* shows one central hub (the family manor) and a network of five outlying locations (such as the Mausoleum, the Standing Stones, and the Pirate's Cove). The completion of each quest ends in the vanquishing of one of the five demonic siblings and the return to the manor to acquire the clues as to which location should next be visited.

The map of *The Elder Scrolls III: Morrowind* is also constructed to reflect the relationship of its side quests and main quests. As in many quest games, including *World of Warcraft,* this map consists of locations that can be referred to as quest "hubs"—places such as cities and forts, in which quest-givers distribute quests and to which the player must return to complete the quests. The player begins at a small, out of the way location (such as the outpost of Seya Deen in *Morrowind*), in which few activities are available, and the quests that can be undertaken are simple and easy in keeping with the player's low level. As the player progresses in the game, she gradually moves from this location to other "hubs," such as the town of Balmora, from which all of the quests given by Caius Coscades originate. These quests require the player to voyage to increasingly remote, inaccessible, and dangerous locations, which in turn contain their own set of more difficult quests. Eventually, these quests take the player into new regions of the world, such as the far northern regions of the Urshilaku camp, where the seven trials of the Incarnate begin.

This progression from quest hubs is a deliberate strategy on the part of designers to motivate players to explore the simulated world that they have created, as Jeff Kaplan explains in "Questing in *World of Warcraft.*" Kaplan enthusiastically confirms the interviewer's suggestion that "quests are being used as a mechanism to encourage the exploration of the world." He elaborates, "We think it's fun to travel all over, and we put in breadcrumb quests to encourage the players to do so." This classification of "breadcrumb quests" refers to tasks that lead the player into new areas like a trail of breadcrumbs.

However, the meaning of spaces within the context of narrative varies greatly from game to game. Because *World of Warcraft* lacks a "main quest," the organization of its vast geographical expanses is episodic and disconnected in the same way that its quests are. Kaplan explains that "the ongoing story of Warcraft is subtly woven into the quest system, and over time will coalesce more and more into a pattern that can be seen." This weaving is quite subtle indeed, since, as Kaplan argues, it largely consists of ongoing battles between various factions who occupy areas of the continent of Azeroth. The "pattern" emerging over these spaces can involve only an escalating war, which may reach cataclysmic proportions but which remains combat between factions. Spatially, *World of Warcraft* delivers precisely what its title implies: an infinite battlefield for a never-ending war.

In contrast, the spatial organization of the province of Vvanderfell in Morrowind reflects the interrelationship between main quests and side quests. As the game progresses, the player discovers that his ultimate task is to fulfill the prophecy of the Nerevarine, proving his status as a reincarnated leader destined to drive invaders out the land and establish the rule of a benevolent god. He must fulfill this prophecy by revisiting the ruins of Dagoth Ur, a stronghold of the god where the Nerevarine hero died. This central object of the main quest is also given spatial centrality, appearing directly in the middle of the Morrowind map. However, the challenge of this quest as the player's final task is conveyed spatially through forbidding, impassable mountains that surround Dagoth Ur on all sides, except for a single portal protected by a magical barrier called the Ghostfence. The designers convey that this challenge can only be surmounted by the most accomplished player in the endgame phase of *Morrowind*.

The strategy for world design needs to be focused on obstacles of terrain (mountains, ridges, pits of lava, lakes and oceans, forests) that intervene between the player and her target. The attempt to locate the Urshilaku camp in *The Elder Scrolls III: Morrowind* is a brilliant example of a spatial odyssey, created by obstacles that prevent the direct travel from Morag Tar to the Urshilaku camp (which is due north). Instead, a player must travel north to the foyada (volcanic ridge), follow it northwest across rocks with swirling red dust, struggling upward to find a path over the rocks and not to lose the trail. Then, one must swim around the headlands and hurry east through ancient ruins inhabited by deadly daedra (demons).

At the same time, the "seven trials" that the player must pass in order to reach this endgame are distributed spatially across the many villages that surround the center of Dagoth Ur concentrically. Movement across the world of Morrowind weaves back and forth between these hubs, branching off into outlying areas that involve side quests or exploring random ruins and dungeons, finally leading the player into the map's center. In order to create these initiatory spaces, designers must acquire skills of level and world design, and they can improve the construction of these spaces by keeping in

Theory

mind the traits most specific to both quest narratives and quest games. These spaces should be

- fantastic;
- dreamlike;
- allegorically arranged to convey ideas through their layout;
- organized to create a sense of progression through difficult ascent;
- labyrinthine.

Collectively, these spaces should also consist of "quest hubs" built for the purpose of distributing and coordinating players' tasks.

Dungeons and Labyrinths

Upward and outward movement is often alternated with the character's descent into perilous underground mazes known as dungeons because of their origins in *Dungeons and Dragons*. These mazes are inverted versions of the tiered ziggurats and winding towers through which players often ascend in quests, since progressively lower floors of these dungeons are known as levels. The further a player descends in these levels, the greater perils she faces and the greater rewards of experience and treasure she receives from successfully destroying monsters.

Progress in a dungeon is often also a form of initiation in that it moves a player closer to the labyrinth's secret, since the lowest and furthest chambers of the maze frequently contain a magical item that is the object of the player's quest. Movement through a dungeon yields an understanding of its architectural principles of construction, which often follow patterns in which locked gates earlier in the maze can be opened using keys, buttons, or pressure plates found at a later point. Players learn to anticipate the ways that passageways wind and branch into corridors and dead ends, as well as to interpret an automatically generated map to see what areas they have not yet explored.

The exploration of a dungeon corresponds closely to the phase of initiation known as "descent into the underworld," which both Frye and Campbell describe through the recurrent mythological image of the labyrinth. Venturing into a dangerous underground space is a recurrent motif associated with the passage through trials because it signifies confrontation with the monstrous forces of darkness, whether conceived as a natural fear of the dark, the manifestation of unconscious contents, or a metaphysical battle with evil. Campbell argued that the figures associated with these labyrinths would reappear with even more terrifying force in societies that had lost touch with their mythologies. He writes that "if anyone—in whatever society—undertakes for himself the perilous journey into the darkness by descending, either intentionally or unintentionally, into the crooked lanes of his own spiritual labyrinth, he soon finds himself in a landscape of symbolical figures" (101). Frye associates the same "symbolical figures" with the mythological motif of descent into the belly of the whale, of which he writes that "the image of the dark winding labyrinth for the monster's belly is a natural one, and one that frequently appears in heroic quests, notably that of Theseus" (190).

Whereas Theseus ventures into the labyrinth only once, RPG designers maximize the potential for activity in this motif by creating many quests that involve descending into multilayered dungeons distributed throughout a vast world, or "dungeon crawls," as they are known in gaming culture. In the main quest of *Oblivion*, players must descend into a vast, winding labyrinth to find the armor of Tiber Septim. The side quests of this game include many other dungeon crawls as well as ruins scattered over Cyrodil.

While many scholars of postmodern literature interpret the labyrinth as an image of the indeterminate interpretative paths that different readers may take through works of literature, doing so strips this image of the historical context that makes the labyrinth itself signify so richly. As an environment in which players confront the challenges of darkness and overcome them through exploration and combat, the labyrinth reenters quest games as a contemporary location for initiation. The caves covered with painting murals at Lascaux are sometimes cited as primitive precursors to virtual reality and gaming because they are thought to have been used as spaces in which tribe members were initiated into the myths depicted there by being immersed in them.

Branching structures are crucial for the construction of such labyrinths, but much of the controversy surrounding branching in gaming and interactive storytelling originates in a confusion about spatial and temporal branching. When Glassner and Crawford decry branching structures in interactive storytelling, they are referring to junctures at which a narrative could fork in two or more possible directions because different plot events occur in time (Crawford 124–25, Glassner 239–59). They criticize this strategy because it either limits the interactivity of the story severely or results in unfeasibly large story files with large amounts of wasted content. If the story branches once at each plot point, it will soon grow exponentially into a large number of branches, most of which a player will not experience unless she takes the trouble to play back through the game multiple times. Programming each of these branches soon either becomes restrictive or involves an unrealistic amount of labor; therefore, Glassner and Crawford reject branching structures in favor of procedural storytelling, based on algorithmic rules that set parameters for player action without restricting it to predefined paths.

When game designers such as Natkin praise branching mazes as a model for level design in adventure games, they are referring to spatial branching (37–40). Because scripting of various events, such as encounters with monsters, can be associated with particular locations, a player's triggering of a given event may depend upon his taking of a particular fork in a maze. However, the other events are available to be triggered whenever a player enters these areas, rather than being automatically closed off. Access can be restricted to particular events through spatial barriers and objects, such as requiring a key to open a given door to a new set of passages. Distributing quest objects and targets through the branches of a labyrinthine structure is an effective strategy for balancing the freedom of interactivity with the purpose of a quest.

Allegorical Spaces

In order to increase the sense of the quest's purpose, the spaces should themselves convey encoded meaning through their layout. This scheme of meaningful landscapes "remediates" allegory, to use Bolter and Grusin's terms for the reworking of one medium in terms of another. Bolter and Grusin observe that in digital art "naïve allegory is common, as we see, for example, in the computer game *Myst* with its allegory of the end of the book" (136). By "naïve allegory," they refer to art with an "obvious message," presumably to be contrasted with heavily ironized, ambivalent allegory, such as that theorized by some postmodern literary critics. They regard the "losing" endings of the computer game *Myst,* in which the player is entrapped within imprisoning books instead of being able to move freely through the space of computer graphics, as an allegorical critique of the book. At the same time, Bolter and Grusin argue that the book is remediated by the game's interface and plot.[1]

However, the tradition of creating meaningful spaces originates in literary allegories that are far from naïve and that encourage a degree of engagement that prefigures digital games. As Wayne Erickson argues in *Mapping the Faerie Queen: Quest Structures and the World of the Poem,* the starting and ending points of the knights' quests in Spenser's poems themselves convey meaning. These quests begin in historical sixth-century Britain and then proceed into Faeryland, thereby conjoining the historical and political concerns of epic poetry with the private, fantastic themes of chivalric romance (87–117). Moreover, Erickson points out that Gordon Teskey's recent theories of Spenserian allegory emphasize a "game of 'interpretative play,'" in which readers learn not just by example but "by becoming engaged, through the play of interpretation, in the theory of virtue" (12).

While Erickson and Teskey are not discussing new media, the combination of Erickson's focus on the imaginative spaces of the poem and Teskey's interest in its elicitation of readers' active involvement suggests that Spenser was already striving for the synthesis of "immersion and interactivity" that Marie-Laure Ryan upholds as the ideal of digital art. Aarseth's evocative phrase for video game representations of space, "allegories of space," turns out to have another dimension besides the one that he focuses on. Aarseth argues that the spaces of digital games can be "allegories" of space only because they consist of digital implementations of automated rules necessary to create a game rather than of actual physical or social laws. He writes, "In other words, the topology of even the most 'open' computer generated landscapes makes them quite different from real space, and controlled in ways that are not inherent in the original physical objects they are meant to represent. This makes them allegorical: they are figurative comments on the ultimate impossibility of representing real space" (169). This is true, yet the spaces of quests can be "figurative comments" on a wide variety of other actions and ideas, especially the goals of the player and her relationship to a larger simulated world.

Dream Spaces

Joseph Campbell argues that the entrance into a spatial realm separate from the ordinary world is the first stage of the hero's adventure proper. He writes, "Once having traversed the threshold, the hero moves in a dream landscape of curiously fluid, ambiguous forms" in which he undergoes the trials that constitute the initiation phase of his journey (97). Campbell ascribes several features to the space of the adventure that set it apart from ordinary space and that are literalized in the simulated space of quest games. He suggests that the space of the quest is a dream landscape because it takes place at least partially in the imagination. The movement of fluid forms is metaphorical in the case of a quest narrative, which is often characterized by descriptions of dreamlike, shifting images. Similar movement is intensified in the case of a digital simulated space, which can actually change and be explored in ways that are partially metaphorical in written texts.

Aarseth insists on this difference between a written text as a metaphorical space that can be imagined by a reader versus a digital cybertext whose simulated space can be physically explored through the exertion of effort (3–4). However, a digitally simulated space is technically not an "actual" space either because it is a moving configuration of pixels on a screen that requires the player's imagination to be explored. Hence, quest games intensify a potential for imaginative exploration that was already present in narratives;

Theory

the spaces of quest games and quest narratives differ not fundamentally but in the degree to which they are simulated and imagined. Henry Jenkins aptly makes this connection between simulated and imagined spaces of quests and quest games when he argues that "games fit within a much older tradition of spatial stories, which have often taken the form of hero's odysseys, quest myths, or travel narratives" (122). Working from the perspective of narratology, Jenkins tends to underemphasize the active overcoming of challenge that is crucial to Aarseth's definition of the quest. However, Jenkins also observes a strong relationship between quest games and their origins in epic and myth that Aarseth neglects.

The player's movement through space in the form of an avatar allows him to enact meaning, so that the actions he undertakes in simulated space have significance in terms of progressing further in the game as well as thematic implications. In *TechGnosis,* Erik Davis argues that game players move their avatars through a space that is not only dreamlike and changing but also dense with allegorical meaning. Davis writes:

> In some ways, *Adventure* (and the countless adventure games it spawned) sticks the user into a first-person allegory. Like Dante or the knights-errant in *The Faerie Queene,* whose environs Coleridge described as 'mental space,' you wander through a rigorously structured but dreamlike landscape patched together from phantasms. These images usually possess more than a surface meaning, since they conceal clues and abstract relationships that, if figured out, will send you further into gamespace. (253)

Davis's analysis reaches deep into the history of gaming and literature to *Adventure,* the first text-based adventure game, and to Renaissance allegory and Romanticist analysis of its imaginative effects, both of which are in turn derived from medieval romance. Davis's use of the term allegory raises difficult theoretical issues because some critics view an allegory as having a single, rigid moral idea that it attempts to teach its readers, while other, deconstructionist critics have tried to show that allegory is inherently self-contradictory and unstable.

Davis also associates the dreamlike landscapes of games with allegory by way of Angus Fletcher's observations that allegories often take place in bizarre, fantastical spaces. Campbell's description of a "dream landscape" plays out over and over again in a variety of different quest games, in which the surroundings through which the avatar moves are compared to a dream either overtly or indirectly. Hence, the significant landscapes of dreams are places where the player can be separated from the "ordinary world" and initiated into a meaningful world that operates according to different rules. Dreams disobey the logic of everyday life, suspending its rules in favor of a bizarre and surreal associative stream of consciousness (whether theorized in Freudian, Jungian, or cognitive terms). In a sense, games are already dreams and dreams foreshadow games, so that to put a dreamworld within a game is to make a "dream within a dream," a metagame twice removed from mundane reality.

These dreams within games create initiatory spaces that allow players to be immersed in a fantastic, supernatural environment while at the same time thinking about what it means to play a game. Hence, many quest games contain spaces within the game that are demarcated from the rest of the game's "real world" as a dreamspace or dreamworld, suggesting the horror writer Poe's phrase "a dream within a dream." These spaces include

- "the Winter" and "dreamnet" in the game *Dreamfall;*
- "Oneiros" in Clive Barker's *Undying* (an allusion to the word "oneiric" or "dreamlike," derived from the ancient Greek word for dreams);
- Henantier's "dreamworld" in the "Through a Nightmare, Darkly" sidequest of *Oblivion.*[1]

In the chapter of *Dreamfall* entitled "A Dream within a Dream," Zoe discovers her own powers as a "dreamer" who can dream while awake, maintaining a dual awareness of dreaming and reality that duplicates the player's double identity as player and avatar. The dream worlds in games are places where designers reflect on the principles and benefits of their own game design. These reflections occur in the form of dreams because dreams were the closest approximation of digital games before this technology appeared. In dreams, one moves through a simulated space that addresses all of the senses, including sight, sound, and touch. A dreamer both is and is not himself when he dreams, since his sleeping mind and immobile body make the dream possible, but he may take an entirely different imaginary form within the dream (as when one dreams of oneself as aged, wounded, in an animal form, or as a ghost).

Spaces and Avatars

Action and movement through space are possible in quest games because of the involvement of the player as active participant rather than as spectator who only identifies emotionally with a character. Aarseth's phrase "player-avatar" suggests the complex hybrid identity that the player takes on as she identifies with a virtual representation of herself on screen. The player's relationship to an avatar involves a dual consciousness of an embodied, everyday, "real" identity that is playing the game and an avatar that the player directs within the game. [2] Despite these differences in perspective, the relationship of a player to an avatar builds upon the metaphorical "identification" of sympathy and admiration that the reader of a narrative feels for the hero.

The player of a game experiences this metaphorical identification as literal in the sense that, for the duration of the game, the player *is* both player and avatar. This double identity descends from Western quest myths' simultaneous thematic concern with the discovery of self and the knowing of an Other. Quest myths have always encouraged identification with a hero and suggested ways that the readers or audience might imitate the hero's behavior in their own lives, including his assimilation of opposites that the society regards as dangerous or threatening.

The player of a quest controls an avatar who passes trials to acquire greater levels of skill and accomplishment, but the close relationship between player and avatar means that the achievements of the avatar are accompanied by real development on the part of the player. The designers of *Oblivion* include self-reflexive commentary on the initiatory benefits of games for players in the side-quest "Through a Nightmare, Darkly." In this quest, the player must rescue a magician named Henantier, who became trapped in a nightmare after he constructed an amulet that allowed him to enter his own dreams. The NPC Deetsan, Henantier's friend and the head of the Mages' guild, explains, "Henantier constructed a magical device he called the Dreamworld amulet. With this device, one can enter his own mind and experience dreams. When you enter your dreams with the amulet, you're in full command of a dream-like replica of yourself." In cybercultural terms, this "dream-like replica" is an avatar. Deetsan in *Oblivion,* like many characters in *Dreamfall,* is using the metaphor of dreams to reflect on the mechanics and psychological function of games.

The events in this "Dreamworld" are crucial to understanding the role of this side quest, which consists of games within the game. Like Campbell's trials, these games are explicitly referred to as tests: the "test of patience," the "test of courage," the "test of perception," and "the test of resolve." While the tests undertaken by an avatar might seem to have little relationship to the development of the player, Deetsan explains that "All your thoughts, your dreams and your talents travel there with you. Think of it as exploring a new land, but a land within your own mind." She more explicitly sets forth the purpose of these trials when she says, "Henantier created the Dreamworld to see if he could use his dreams as a training ground to help better himself." She thus suggests that Henantier can benefit from playing a game in which he overcomes trials through an avatar, and this assertion also applies to the player's own self-improvements.

The "test of patience" does require a great deal of patience from the player, who must decipher the cryptic symbols on a scroll to find a path across a grid of pressure plates, where a single over-hasty misstep leads to the avatar's death and a required repetition of the task. The "tests of perception" and "resolve" also require observation of minute traps in a dark landscape as well as the persistence to engage in extended combat with difficult enemies. The "courage" test may draw less upon real-world courage than the others, although the realistic simulation of diving into underwater caves without knowing the way back up to air does induce at least a small amount of fear that has to be overcome. These games are indeed the training ground that Henantier envisioned, and they test not just memorized facts or a set of cognitive skills but strengths of character akin to allegorical virtues.[3]

Level Design

Role-playing construction sets are extremely useful in designing the spaces of quests, since they allow a beginner to create detailed, fantasy-themed environments in a relatively short amount of time. They are better for the purpose of quest design than a level editor like the Unreal Engine, which is designed for creating first-person shooter environments consisting of abstract, minimalistic architecture. Role-playing construction sets are also best for producing the fantastic and neomedieval environments common in quest narratives, though some modding is possible in order to introduce visual styles that suggest other genres, such as science fiction or "realistic" history. The RPG construction sets are also useful because they are not just "level editors" but also toolsets that integrate spatial environments with functions for creating NPCs, conversation trees, and scripting.

Which toolset a designer uses to construct her environments depends upon her preferred working style, degree of expertise, and desired appearance and spatial perspective on the simulated world. The Aurora Toolset, Bioware's first version of their construction set packaged with *Neverwinter Nights,* is highly modular, with a variety of preexisting tilesets that make world building a matter of well-planned dragging and dropping. The *Neverwinter Nights 2 Toolset* expands on this basic principle, allowing for more subtle environmental effects and detailed textures but keeping the basic ideas the same. The *Morrowind* and *Oblivion* versions of the Elder Scrolls Construction Set offer more finely nuanced control of environments at the price of a steeper learning curve, since the camera controls of this world are so complex as to require a great deal of skill to manipulate smoothly. The Elder Scrolls Construction set is also less "modular" than both versions of the *Neverwinter Nights Toolset,* which are designed for creating stand-alone "modules" rather than expanding an existing world. Building worlds within TESCS means placing locations in nooks and crannies (or bare swaths of wilderness or recovered underwater land) within the already teeming simulated world of Tamriel.

No matter what construction set designer's use, there are several considerations that should be kept in mind when designing the spaces of the quest:

- embedded meaning;
- a balance between challenging obstacles and exploration and a sense of progression;
- the organization of spaces according to "quest hubs."

The first principle suggests that world design should be organized meaningfully, with a consideration of the patterns that will emerge from the placement of villages, dungeons, and geographical features such as mountains and lakes. It can be helpful to think of the world both as an environment that the player will explore from his perspective (whether first- or third-person), as well as an overarching pattern that will be visible only from an aerial or "bird's-eye" view. Postmodern American author Thomas Pynchon, famous for his game-like novels, describes the aerial view of a suburban landscape as resembling a "circuitboard" in its "hieroglyphic sense of concealed meaning," implying that there is some secret encoded in the land itself that is visible only when its overall pattern is grasped (24). Similarly, Garriott designed the world of *Ultima IV* so that each village in Britannia would correspond to one virtue in Ultima's "Virtue System," while each dungeon would represent the opposed vice.

In practical terms, designers can also derive a model from world-famous maze designer Adrian Fisher, who has constructed multiple "symbolic" mazes, such as the one at Leeds Castle, which gradually reveal an intricate image to people who stand on a viewing platform found as they explore the maze. One of the mazes most relevant to quest design, especially to the sample quest of *Sir Gawain and Green Knight,* is based on *The Dream of Poliphilo,* an Italian allegorical poem from the Renaissance that features a "water labyrinth" representing the five senses. Fisher designed a maze in the shape of a five-pointed star much like the one on Gawain's shield, with an animal emblematic of each sense at each of the points. Designers doing the first exercise of this book might consider designing at least one of the areas on Sir Gawain's quest in the shape of such a star. When I did this sample exercise myself, I made five rooms in King Arthur's castle at Camelot, each distributed roughly at the points of a pentangle. In four of these rooms, I put "terrain" and "placeable objects" from the Aurora Toolset associated with each of the four elements of the ancients (air, water, fire, and earth); the fifth room is associated with the fifth element (spirit) at the top of the star. I put a fountain in the water room, a gust of wind in the air room, a burning statue in the fire room, and a mound of dirt with rocks in the earth room. Each of these rooms contained a treasure chest with one piece of Gawain's armor, corresponding to one of his knightly virtues.

In building these symbolic patterns into the world of the quest, it is crucial to keep in mind that they must not be applied mechanically, but rather integrated into the aspects of good level design that will encourage fun gameplay. The pattern of "objective," "obstacle," and "solution" described by Emmanuel Guardiola as characterizing the quest should be distributed strategically across the levels of the game in order to balance difficulty with reward (36). Instead of regarding the tilesets and placeables of a construction set as mere stage-sets of beautiful scenery that will be in the background of the game, a designer should place geographic elements in such a way that they force players to interact with them as obstacles that must be overcome to progress. To the extent that it is possible within the rules of gameplay, players should have to ford streams, wind their way up treacherous mountains, leap across yawning chasms, and hang from narrow precipices.

Tutorial #1: Designing Areas

1. Boot up the Aurora Toolset.

2. Click the "Create New Module" button.

3. Name the module something appropriate and descriptive of the quests that you want to make. "Sir Gawain's Quest" might be appropriate for the first exercise.

4. You must create one area for your quest to have a functioning module. The Aurora Toolset offers several tilesets based on common environmental themes, such as "City Interior" and "Forest." Choose carefully, since the modular character of this toolset will leave you with access to only one tileset per area, limiting your options for the "tiles" (prefabricated pieces of terrain) that you can use. You can always create more areas and experiment with different tilesets, but plan ahead

Practice

so that you do not find yourself trying to put a cavern in the "Rural Winter" landscape where caverns are not available.

5. Select the size of your area. I find that "Medium" works well for experimentation, since "Large" is too overwhelming and "Small" too restrictive. The first step in learning any toolset is developing the ability to manipulate the "camera" in the game, a term borrowed from film to suggest the perspective from which the designer will view the environment. In the Aurora Toolset, the commands used to move the camera are relatively simple, provided you have a mouse with two buttons and a wheel.

    - To pan left, right, and forward, hit "ctrl" and drag with the left mouse button.
    - To zoom in and out, roll the mouse wheel forward or backward.
    - To rotate or tilt the environment, click and hold the mouse button; then move the mouse left, right, or forward. This allows you to turn the grid along all three axes (the *x*-, *y*-, and *z*-axes).

There are also buttons underneath the viewing screen that allow you to pan and turn the grid, but using the mouse is more efficient and allows more finely nuanced control. To have a strong sense of how players will experience your quests, you should play the actual game *Neverwinter Nights* (or whichever game a given construction set is based on). This particular game allows players to adjust the camera in some of the same ways that you can as designer, but they will most effectively be able to view your environment from a "bird's-eye" position slightly above their avatar's shoulder and at an angle. This is the convenient way to view and move through *Neverwinter Nights,* although players can effectively zoom in to observe details on objects. Design accordingly; you do not want to assume that players will see every detail of every object or that they will be directly in front of objects (although this would be the case in first-person role-playing games such as the *Elder Scrolls* series).

6. Observe the various palettes available in the toolset, which you can identify by mousing over them briefly. In particular, focus on the palettes at the right side of the screen, especially the uppermost left icon ("Terrain"), the second icon from the left on the bottom ("Doors"), and the table icon fifth from the left side of the screen ("Placeables"). These are the three buttons that you need to design environments,

Practice

starting with "Terrain." Press the "+" buttons on the three lists below to expand the types of tile that you can place to construct your environment. By clicking any of these items, you can select a single tile (or group of related tiles under "Groups") to place on your grid. Try clicking on one of these tiles, which will cause a semitransparent or "ghosted" version of this tile to be attached to your cursor.

7. Move your cursor over the grid in the center of the screen to experiment with various positions for your tiles. When the rectangles surrounding the tile turn green, you have found an acceptable position for the tile or tile group. While the tile is still ghosted, you can right-click to cause it to rotate, 45 degrees at a time. Once a tile has been placed, it cannot be rotated, but it can be deleted and then replaced. Placing tiles takes some getting used to, since tiles often do not fit together quite as expected or desired. You may find, especially when creating interiors, that you have to place and erase tiles several times in order to find a combination of rooms and corridors that will connect up. Remember to shift your camera controls to make sure that players will have an unbroken path through the areas; any obstacles to movement should be deliberate on your part rather than a design flaw resulting from not connecting two rooms.

8. Place several tiles in order to create the first environment in your quest. Remember that everything you place should have a purpose. Avoid clutter for its own sake. When transforming a literary narrative into a quest, you can often allow the choice of tilesets to be shaped by the details of the author's description, but you should also exercise your own creativity and be flexible in order to create your own living, interactive environment rather than an exact copy of the literary work. For the "Sir Gawain's Quest" module, I used

- the "Interior Castle" tileset for Camelot and Hautdesert;

- the "Forest" tileset for the Forest of Trials (an area that expands upon the quick summary of Gawain's adventures fighting monsters in North Wales);

- the "Rural Winter" tileset for the Green Chapel.

A literal adherence to the book might have required "frozen wastes" for the Green Chapel area (or the nonexistent "frozen forests" option), but this tileset is limited to ice pits and variants on an "Evil Castle." The Green Chapel, though described by Gawain at one point as similar to hell, is supposed to be integrated into nature, covered in moss and nestled in the caverns to fit with the character of the Green Knight as an immortal, evergreen nature spirit (as well as a possible embodiment of the resurrected Christ and/or a disguised Satan). For this purpose, the "rural winter" tileset allowed me to use the "Raise/Lower" tool to elevate parts of the landscape into cliffs, creating an ominous, frozen valley of death through which Gawain can voyage as if descending into the underworld. Four instances of the "Turf House" tile group facing in opposite directions, combined with carefully placed graves, shrines, and snowdrifts, create the ambiguous blend of natural and underworld imagery that allows players to experience the multiple possible meanings of the Green Chapel as they approach it. The wintry valleys also provide an obstacle-ridden, maze-like environment that forces the player to find this Chapel through navigational trials rather than walking easily up on it.

The key improvement of the *Neverwinter Nights 2 Toolset* in terms of level design is a vastly detailed terrain editor that allows designers to use brushes to raise, lower, and smooth out terrain. This editor allows for extremely nuanced control of the appearance of an area, which could be used to guide the player along certain pathways using environmental cues or to place obstacles in his way that add challenge to gameplay. However, some of these features imply a degree of micromanagement that could become counterproductive; in other words, if you are too focused on setting the blade size of the grass in a particular area, you might forget the overall mood that a setting is supposed to evoke.

Level Design Exercise #1

Use the Aurora Toolset to design an environment based on the description of the mysterious castle of Hautdesert from *Sir Gawain and the Green Knight.* Keep in mind these guidelines. In this space, the player will be tempted by supernatural forces, so its outward appearance should be inviting yet perhaps a bit sinister. The castle is the dwelling of the Green Knight in disguise, so you might want to prominently display the color green with all of its symbolic associations. At the same time, this area should have an atmosphere of mystery and magic, conveyed through its elevation from the rest of the land and its shimmering white architecture. Sadowski offers useful guidelines for creating a meaningful environment when he writes:

> [T]he structure is depicted as rising high above the valleys and marshes and is situated—as castles usually are—on a hill ("abof a launde, on a lawe [mound]," 765, also 768, 788). Its walls shone and shimmered from afar (772), as did the chalk-white chimneys (789–90), and the whole structure, for all its architectonic splendor, looked like paperwork ("pared [cut] our of papure hit semed," 802), enhancing the effect of visionary and dreamy ethereality. The elevated position and consequently the status of the castle are emphasized later in the poem by its name "Hautdesert" (2445), a 'High Place' or 'Hermitage'. (153)

Sadowski's analysis of the location of Hautdesert can be implemented with the improved landscaping/terrain editing features of the NWN2 Toolset, especially the ability to shape masses of land on which to place a castle rather than the restriction to modular tiles and limited capabilities to raise and lower land. Building the Green Chapel, a mossy, cavernous mound with a simultaneously verdant and infernal atmosphere, is possible with NWN2 in a way that it is not with the original Aurora Toolset. Try to make this environment as interactive as possible, so that there are many objects that can be examined, opened, and picked up.

Level Design Exercise #2

Design one of what Wayne Erickson (quoting C. S. Lewis) calls the "allegorical cores" from Book One of *The Faerie Queen,* where meaning is concentrated. As the introduction to this work in the *Norton Anthology* suggests, "Houses, castles, and gardens are often places of education and challenge or of especially dense allegorical significance, as if they possess special, half-hidden keys to the meaning of the books in which they appear" (360). For example, try creating the House of Pride from Book I, Canto IV, perhaps with a golden exterior surrounded by crumbling sand to suggest the outward appeal and precarious dangers of arrogance. Remember that it is not your goal to follow every detail of the text exactly, but rather to create a space for players to interact with the ideas associated with a location.

Level Design Exercise #3

Construct three quest "hubs" from which a quest-giver will assign tasks to the player and to which the player will return when each task is completed. Make each hub progressively further away from the player's initial starting location, and use geographical indicators to suggest that the quests in each hub will be more significant and difficult than the last. For example, the first hub might be a small village, while the second might be a larger encampment, and the third might be a vast city.

Practice

Level Design Exercise #4

Construct a short quest based on Edmund Spenser's *The Faerie Queen,* Book I, Canto XI, in which the player as the Redcrosse Knight battles the Dragon. Book I is a classic quest narrative, as the introduction to this piece in the *Norton Anthology* suggests: "Book 1 is almost entirely self-contained; it has been called a miniature epic in itself, centering on the adventures of one principal hero, Redcrosse, who at length achieves the quest he undertakes at Una's behest: killing the dragon who has imprisoned her parents and thereby winning her as bride" (361). This quest is the Redcrosse Knight's attempt to gain the virtue of Holiness and overcome a beast representing his personal, political, and spiritual enemy.

The first exercise in this project is to construct the space of the quest and to place the objects and creatures in it. The following items are suggested but not required:

- one brazen tower in which Una's parents are imprisoned;
- one large red and black dragon;
- one Well of Life that can restore the player's health as he battles the dragon;
- one Tree of Life (with healing apples) that springs up at a certain point in the battle, such as when the player has been wounded and his hit points drop below 5.

The Well of Life could be represented as an actual well or a spring with a stream of crystalline water emerging from it, preferably with restorative powers, so that the player can run to it and use it as a power-up. You can accomplish this function by painting a trigger around the pool and scripting a heal function that will be activated whenever the player enters the pool. Chapter 4 of this book, which deals exclusively with scripting, can help to design this portion of the game. Both the Tree of Life and Well of Life need to be designed carefully to produce engaging gameplay. In the narrative of *The Faerie Queen,* Redcrosse Knight discovers these healing locations or they appear to him in his moment of greatest distress, one on each of the three days that he is battling the dragon. They emblematize Christian salvation, which in Spenser's thought can redeem righteous souls by the grace of God when they least expect it.

Notes

[1] Other examples of dream worlds within games include the "nightmare mode" in the Edgar Allan Poe game *The Darkest Eye* and the "Shadow Out of Time" sequences in *Call of Cthulhu.*

[2] James Paul Gee argues that the negotiation of multiple identities required by the relationship between the player and his viritual representation is one of the primary "learning principles" inherent in games.

[3] The concept of games as a "training ground," referenced three times by Deetsan, may also allude to one of the earliest historically influential computer role-playing games entitled *Wizardry: Proving Grounds of the Mad Overlord*.

The Characters of the Quest

While it is tempting to jump directly from the spaces of the environment to the interactions that will be scripted there, several intermediate steps between level design and scripting need to be filled in. The first of these steps is the creation of NPCs, or "non-player characters." This acronym refers to any character in the game except for the player, ranging from the kings and princesses who give quests to the multitude of "extras" who add to a sense of realism by having mundane conversations with the player. Designers must have environments in which to place NPCs before they can be painted, and it makes the most sense to have NPCs before assigning the objects that they will give and receive. Only when the spaces, NPCs, and objects are in place is it possible to attach scripts to any of them that will regulate gameplay, although this flow of scripts should be kept in mind from the beginning of the quest design when one is setting up journal stages.

Propp's Dramatis Personae

In terms of theoretical background, the critic of quest narratives most useful in constructing these characters is Vladimir Propp, though Joseph Campbell and Carl Jung also offer helpful suggestions for character models. Andrew Glassner cites Campbell and Vogler in his analysis of the characters in the Zelda games, and Jeannie Novak describes the archetypes of "hero," "shadow," "mentor," "allies," "guardian," "trickster," "herald," "protagonist" as inspirations for character design (Novak 148–52). However, *Fable* is one example of a game that suffered from relying too heavily upon archetypal structures of the hero's journey for its NPCs and avatar. Thus, the hero character whose identity the player assumes is automatically named "Hero," and the hero's mentor is named "Mentor." Jack of Blades, the villain in this game, might as well be named "Villain," since his dialogue and appearance are a blatant composite of Darth Vader and other megalomanical, somewhat cartoonish villains from a variety of sources.

Despite *Fable*'s moments of rich simulation and exciting gameplay (such as the boss battle with Jack of Blades), the role of its NPCs seems a bit contrived and imitative, as when the "Mentor" mechanically gives the player "quest cards" with standard "heroic" tasks. He also delivers voiced-over advice that sounds like Obi-Wan Kenobi's instructions "to use the Force" but without any of the drama of this moment in *Star Wars Episode IV*. The use of archetypes as models for characters can give a sense of mythic grandeur to games, but it is not enough by itself to create well-designed NPCs. How then can a designer benefit from the archetypes and characters of literary narratives and literary criticism without falling into a pale imitation of these works that is also weak in gameplay?

Propp's dramatis personae may actually be more useful than either Campbell's or Vogler's character models in that he posits a certain number of "functions" that could be "distributed" among character types. In Propp's system, the characters are defined by what they do, not necessarily by their belonging to a set of psychological archetypes in the collective unconscious. Propp suggests that a set of "dramatis personae" recur in all folk tales and are defined by the "functions" that they perform in the tale, such as giving the hero an item. While Propp's theory of narrative (part of a broader set of methods for analyzing the structures of art called "Russian formalism") predates the invention of computer programming languages, he did strive for a scientific precision in his vocabulary that is derived from the same mathematics that influenced these languages.

Despite ludologists' hostility toward Russian formalist narratology, Propp's "functional" approach fits remarkably well onto the scripting languages of game construction sets, in which NPCs are not "characters" in the literary sense but rather objects that call functions. For the most part, games do not describe characters at great length, although cinematic cut-scenes may help to establish some depth of background or personality. Rather, NPCs exist almost solely to perform functions in relation to the player, assisting in the quest or providing challenges to completing it.

Because of this emphasis on gameplay, every list of archetypes or functions needs to become a set of actions that a character can perform, help the player to undertake, or obstruct the player from performing. Ultimately, these actions should be programmable in precise terms. In other words, designers should consider each NPCs gameplay function, in both the Proppian sense and the programming sense. Propp's dramatis personae include

- "villain";
- "donor";
- "helper";
- "princess";
- "her father";
- "dispatcher";
- "hero";
- "false hero" (84–86).

The most essential NPCs in role-playing and adventure games are quest-givers, who correspond roughly to Propp's idea of a dispatcher. These characters offer tasks to players and sometimes give information as to how to embark on these tasks (such as a target location on a map or the name of another NPC to talk to). Quest-givers also offer a reward when the quest is completed, after which they may propose a secondary quest, or the next part of the quest. Donors and helpers carry over almost directly from Propp, except that their donations and assistance bear directly upon gameplay. There are also characters other than quest-givers who offer items and information that will help the player, such as the location of a precious item or of a needed location, which often involves sending the player to another NPC. A donor will perform essentially the same actions of giving valuables in both a narrative and a game, though in a game the items must provide a strategic advantage in combat, commerce, or navigation.

Villains also transfer directly from Propp, though the need for repetitive action in a game's core mechanic suggests that there should be many minor villains as well as the central antagonist. Villains of any type stand between the player and his goal, prompting him to play strategically in order to overcome them. These characters need not be human and may include dragons, evil wizards, monsters of all sorts, and vagabonds.

Thus, converting Propp's list into terms of gameplay, a "villain" can

- attack a player physically;
- steal items from a player's inventory;
- set traps for a player;
- cast damaging spells on the player;
- block the player's movement into a space that she needs to enter to complete a quest.

Encounters and Dialogue

The unit of interaction with these NPCs is the "encounter," which refers in role-playing terms to any exchange that a PC and an NPC have, including talking, fighting, persuading, giving, or receiving. One form of the encounter is the conversation, which can take place through dialogue trees (forking branches of options for dialogue that players can speak along with appropriate responses from NPCs) or through lists of available "topics" for conversations. Because the focus of a game is play rather than passive reading, conversations should be kept short and focused on action, but they can still carry complex instructions for meaningful gameplay. For example, in *Ultima IV*, there is a very narrow range of conversational options available based on the constraints of programming in the mid 1980s, so that players can ask only one-word commands such as "name," "job," and "health." Yet Garriott managed to develop a richly detailed network of quests without any complex journal system, because characters knew pieces of gossip that would send players all over Britannia in search of items and other NPCs, who often directed players to yet more NPCs for further conversations.

Quests are dialogue and journal driven in their basic structure. Hence, the two "simple quest" tutorials in the NWN Lexicon are essentially tutorials in the dialogue editor and the journal editor. The tendency of these tutorials to focus on dialogue and journal entries at the expense of other elements of quest design can be frustrating at first in that the many aspects of the quest (its spaces, objects, actors, and challenges) are not as well-integrated as in the "quest window" of *The Elder Scrolls Construction Set*. A "plot wizard" of the Aurora Toolset does serve some of these functions, yet it can constrain the scripting of quests through its structure.

Despite the apparent limitations of dialogue-driven quests, Daniel Erickson has argued that well-written interactive dialogue is itself a form of game design because it can allow players to make interesting choices. Erickson emphasizes the interactive potential of dialogue in his GDC 2007 presentation "A Craftsman's Guide to Interactive Dialogue." Erickson argues that all in-game dialogue should be in the service of interactive fiction and hence should allow players to shape this dialogue in ways that they could not in a novel or short story.

Erickson offers three main guidelines and several smaller points for writing game dialogue, many of which can be applied specifically to quest design. Since quests are devices for maintaining momentum within a game, the maxim of "keeping players in the moment" is especially important. Erickson's suggestion to "pace the amount of dialogue delivered at once" means that NPCs should speak only about two sentences at a time, and PC responses should be much shorter than those of NPCs. At the same, time in the case of quest dialogue, PCs should have more than just the opportunity to say "yes" or "no" to the quest (or, worse, only to say "yes"). Erickson's other principles of "reinforcing the player's personal fiction" and "making choices matter" suggest that if quests are delivered in the form of branching dialogue, players ought to be allowed choices not only of taking or refusing the quest, but of taking and refusing the quest for different reasons. The dialogue in NWN2, though not written by Bioware or Erickson's team, does a masterful job of allowing players to express varying degrees of nobility or wickedness in their motivations and a variety of attitudes toward law and order. These responses may mean the difference between being accepted into the town Watchmen or Moire's gang of thieves, or between receiving 500 gold versus shifting one's alignment in the direction of lawful good for saving orphans without recompense.

When designers convert a narrative into a quest game, they often need to find ways to adapt complex character interaction, with nuanced dialogue and elaborate back stories, into a few conversational options that will quickly result in action. In some cases, characters who appear only briefly or do little in terms of action within a literary text may need to appear directly on stage, as it were. For example, the evil magician Clinschor rarely appears directly in the Grail stories, where he is instead mentioned indirectly as the inventor of the Marvelous Castle and its magical traps. In a quest game, however, players need to talk directly to Clinschor and perhaps fight him, since this NPC creates an opportunity for fun, spell-casting gameplay. In order to plan the role of NPCs in gameplay, designers should ask what information a given character will have about locations, items, and events that will figure into various quests. This decision is not complex when there is only one quest involved, but assigning one quest per NPC will be rare in most role-playing games of any complexity. Consequently, writing dialogue may be a matter of planning out a series of conversations that NPCs will have for each possible quest that they might offer, as well as seemingly random bits of gossip that may actually offer clues to given quests.

NPC Creation and Dialogue Trees

Vladimir Propp provides an excellent guide for character creation through his concept of recurrent functions in quest narratives performed by a rigorously categorized set of character types. Erickson suggests ways to enrich and complicate these functions through interactive dialogue trees that offer players a rich array of choices in refusing or accepting quests. To put these theories into practice, designers can begin by creating NPCs using the creature wizard in the Aurora Toolset.

NPC Creation Tutorial #1: Building Characters Using the Creature Wizard

1. Pull the "Wizards" menu to "Creature Wizard."
2. Select "Race." Click "Next."
3. Select class and level. Although you may not have thought of your NPCs as belonging to one of the predefined character types from *Dungeons and Dragons*, you should consider what actions they might need to perform in the course of the quest. Will they cause a magical event to occur by conferring special

powers on the player? If so, they might need to be a high-level mage or cleric. Will they need to stand up to a fight with the player in order for the gameplay to be challenging? If so, they might need to be of a high level or to have particularly high attributes of strength and dexterity.

4.   Select the "Appearance" tab. Here, you can modify individual body parts of some humanoid creatures by mixing and matching various heads and limbs from the drop-down menus.

5.   Click on the "Inventory" button below the NPC preview window to bring up an expandable list of items that can be equipped as well as a visual representation of the various slots into which these items can be placed, such as the "Armor" slot and the "Cloak" slot.

Scripting Tutorial #2: Constructing Fetch Quests Using the Dialogue Wizard

1.   Right-click on an NPC and select "Properties" from the drop-down menu.

2.   At the bottom of the NPC properties window, click the "edit" button next to "conversation."

3.   As Bioware's programmer David Gaider explains, quest dialogue nodes need to be constructed with the node that will appear last at the top of the screen. In selecting a dialogue node, the NWN engine searches the conditions attached to each of these nodes to see if each one fulfills the conditions required to run it. In programming terms, this means that the conditional statement "returns true."

In the early stages of the quest, the conditions attached to the final statement, as when the NPC rewards the PC for completing a task, will return false until the player progresses further. Therefore, the engine will cycle down through the rest of the nodes until it hits the first one that registers true. This programming technique is called dialogue "fall-through" because the engine will "fall through" each node that returns false until it reaches one that returns true. If you need to change the order of your dialogue nodes, all you have to do is select the node by left-clicking and then dragging it to your desired location. Release the node in the space between the actual dialogue nodes, since if you drop it directly onto the node, it will not "stick."

4.   In a basic fetch quest, only three nodes are needed, in the following order:

- Thank you for retrieving my lost item.
- Will you go on a quest to retrieve my lost item?
- Hello, I need your help.

For each of these items, the player must be able to respond by choosing from two branches, either by accepting the quest or refusing it.

- For the lowest node, players should be able to listen to or ignore the NPCs request for help.
- For the second to lowest node, players should have the opportunity to accept or refuse the quest.

5. Make each of the NPC nodes by right-clicking the word "Root" and pulling the menu down to "Add." This will add a node to the root by opening a window for you to enter text that the NPC will speak. To make sure that each node is spoken by the NPC, reselect the "root" each time before you press "Add." As Daniel Erickson emphasizes, this dialogue should be "paced," with no more than two sentences at a time.

6. To add possible PC responses, right-click on an NPC node (such as "Will you help me?") and select "Add." Each time that you reselect the NPC node, you will add another possible PC response, creating branches of dialogue. By adding NPC responses for each of these PC choices, you can cause the NPC's comments and requests to change according to the player's actions.

Remember that these nodes are only the skeletal structure of quest dialogue. Fetch quest dialogue (and fetch quests in general) is often parodied because designers approach it in a clichéd and simplistic way. However, fetch quest dialogue does not have to be dull. The quest template is like any other form, whether the structure of a sonnet or symphony, whose sophistication depends upon the user. Because you will have to repeat the basic structure of the fetch quest many times in your module, you should try to construct variations on this dialogue that offer different options for taking and refusing and to phrase the NPCs invitation in a way appropriate to her circumstances.

7. Once you have your skeletal dialogue structure, you need to give the toolset a way to test whether the player has actually completed the quest. You do this by setting and testing local variables that track the progress of the quest. For the first few

Practice

times, you can do this with the "Script Wizard" that works in conjunction with the toolset, but eventually you will want to master the process of setting variables so that you can build your own specific scripts.

The numbers used to track quest progress are called "integers," and they are usually given a name starting with an "i." You should make your variable name unique and easily identifiable, since in complex modules you may have many variables that you need to identify. For example, in the Sir Gawain quest, you might name your variable "iGawainQuest." Following the example of Merriman's "Simple Quest" tutorial, you could assign a variable of "100" to the moment when the player accepts the quest and "200" to the stage when he completes it.

- To set a variable using a wizard, select the node that you want to appear only when the conditions have been fulfilled. Then, select the "text appears when" tab in the lower right-hand corner of the screen. On the window that says "what conditions would you like to test for?" check the "Local Variable" box and click "Next."
- In the "what local variables have to be set" window, put the name of your integer (such as iGawainQuest) into the window, and enter the value that you are testing for in the "Constant Int" window.
- Now click the "Add" button, which will cause a programming expression to appear in the "Local expressions" box. Be sure to remember this step, since otherwise your integer will not be tested for.
- Click "next" and enter a name for your script. I usually use the initial of my name, a string identifying my quest, and a number to suggest what stage of the quest the script is attached for. For example, the first script for testing a variable might be "jlh_gawain_001."
- Repeat the above steps to test for the quest's completion by attaching a script to the final line of dialogue that the NPC says when the PC has completed the quest, such as "Thanks, but I don't have any tasks left for you right now."

8. The last and crucial step of scripting a quest is to test whether the player has fulfilled it, which can be done with a fetch quest

by monitoring whether the PC actually has the required item in his inventory. You can do this by attaching a conditional script to the node in which the NPC congratulates and rewards the player for completing the quest. In the "what conditions would you like to check for" window, check the box that says "Inventory Item"; then fill in the tag of the item that the player is looking for, such as "the shield of truth." Then, click the "Add" button, next, and give the script a unique name.

9. To reward the player, select the node in which the NPC congratulates him and click on the "Actions Taken" tab. You can check multiple rewards, including experience, gold, and items, filling in the parameters of each as you go.

Practice

The Objects of the Quest

One of the most central functions of NPCs in quest games is giving and taking valuable objects, as well as directing the player toward them. The search to locate or destroy valuable objects plays a central role in multiple quest narratives, ranging from the Christian salvation emblematized in the Holy Grail sought by the Arthurian Knights to the One Ring that Frodo bears to Mount Doom.

Appropriately, role-playing games abound in objects, which can be organized into "tiers" according to their relative functional and thematic importance.

- At the lowest tiers are minor and largely useless objects that give a sense of realism to a simulated world, such as yarn, calipers, and carrots. In the *Elder Scrolls Construction Set,* these objects are classified as "clutter," implying that they are placed into an area as a decorative afterthought and have little impact on the quests that take place in these spaces.
- A second, higher tier includes functional objects that help players to perform more effectively in the game, including weapons, armor, and potions. These objects are often the rewards of quests or are gathered as booty while raiding dungeons in the course of quests.
- However, there is a third level of items that are often designated as "quest items" or "plot items," either within the in-game inventory or the construction set. One explanation for this special designation of quest item is that these objects play an essential role in the back stories behind a quest. Another is that these items often possess great magical power within the rules of the game. Yet these two attributes would at best produce only a mediocre quest item: a +10 Longsword with a complicated story about how it was lost in an elven palace centuries ago.

Symbolic Quest Items

In contrast to such generic objects, quest items emblematize meaning in the way that they are integrated with gameplay. In *Ultima IV,* the *Codex of Ultimate Wisdom* can only be gained through a mastery of all of the correspondences in the game's virtue system, displayed in a complex rune within the book (see Figure 4.1). This object encodes all of the game's symbolic cor-

Figure 4.1. Symbol from the Codex of Ultimate Wisdom. (See also the back cover.)

respondences, representing geometrically and through color how the three principles (Truth, Love, and Courage) combine to produce the eight virtues. For example, blue (the color of truth) directly produces the virtue of honesty (a blue line) and combines with love (yellow) to generate justice (green). Rather than functioning as a static emblem whose meaning is didactically forced onto the reader, the symbol in the codex appears after players have retrieved eight colored stones from the bottom of eight dungeons and thereby interactively experienced the correspondences that the symbol encodes. Players discover and produce the meaning of this emblem through their own achievements in quests as well as their own shortcomings in violating or losing these virtues in gameplay.

Similarly, the Tome of Eternal Darkness contains all of the runes in *Eternal Darkness* (see Figure 4.2). The Tome holds the keys to the game's cosmology, but it also forms the game's interface, containing the magic system for combining runes into spells, inventory, journal, and maps. The Tome of Eternal Darkness is an object that characters in the game acquire in cutscenes, marking them as those chosen to fight the demonic Ancients and filling them in on the meaning of their battle. It is also an object that allows players to interact with the game.

Both the *Codex* and the *Tome* are excellent quest items, but not all such objects must be books. All of the standard objects that fill this role—such as gems, pieces of armor, staffs, cloaks—can carry meaning in similar ways.

The quest items in a game should possess several if not all of the following qualities:

- symbolism;
- function within gameplay;

Figure 4.2. Rune Chart from the Tome of Eternal Darkness, compiled by Simalcrum.

- value in the game economy;
- a distinctive appearance from other objects in the game world.

Symbolism means that the item should suggest an idea or emotion that is connected in some way to the lore of the game world or the mythologies that it draws upon, such as the ancient Greek legends that inform the action RPG *Titan Quest.* When Sir Gawain and Parzival go off in quest of the Holy Grail, they seek it not just for its powers, even though these often include the ability to conjure up infinite amounts of delicious food or to heal a wounded king. Instead, they seek the Grail because it embodies sacrifice, holiness, and salvation. Indeed, this item is worthy of being sought out because of its rich lore, ranging from the religious reading in *The Quest for the Holy Grail* that represents it as the cup which caught Christ's blood at the crucifixion, to Wolfram von Eschenbach's account of it as a vessel where the "neutral" angels hid during the war in heaven.

While not all games need to have such an involved back story surrounding their items, the richest quest items that will keep players immersed in a game for hours at a time are those that do have some symbolic associations.

Figure 4.3. Symbolic objects in the *Ultima Online* interface.

These items should be sparse, iconic, and mysterious, like the ones found in fairy tales and romances. For example, much of the action in *The Elder Scrolls III: Morrowind* is motivated by the player's search for the star and crescent that will prove him to be the reincarnated hero called the Nerevar. All of the prophecies that the player collects as scrolls, books, and conversations concern this "mark of the Nerevar," and it is the desktop icon that emblematizes the entire game of *Morrowind* visually for players. Hence, the mystery of this mark and the player's eventual discovery that he is actually seeking a ring in the shape of a star and a crescent helps to drive the quest.

Similarly, Garriott also developed iconic objects that correlate with each of the virtues (see Figure 4.3) displayed in the character creation sequence of *Ultima V* and the interface of *Ultima Online.*

Each answer to the questions about ethics in the character generation process is associated with a virtue and a small two-dimensional icon, including a sword for valor, a chalice for honor, a heart for compassion, scales for justice, an open hand for honesty, an ankh for spirituality, a tear for sacrifice, and a shepherd's crook for humility.

The Tattoos in *Planescape: Torment*

The role of symbolic objects in gameplay appears even more pervasively in the tattoo system of *Planescape: Torment,* a method of documenting quests and translating these achieved narratives into gameplay advantages. In *Planescape: Torment,* a player's quests can become inscribed as symbolic glyphs that both tell the story of his chosen accomplishments and directly impact

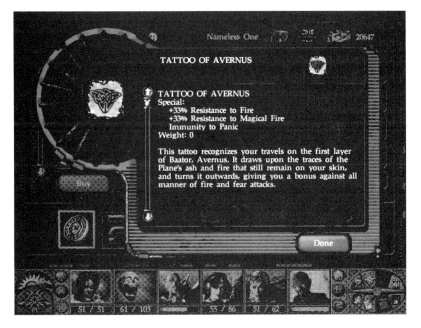

Figure 4.4. The Tattoo of Avernus in *Planescape: Torment.*

gameplay. Justly and persuasively redeeming a fallen angel grants the player access to the "Tattoo of the Redeemer," with bonuses to charisma and intelligence. These tattoos are especially rich features in that they respond to the player's choices in nuanced ways, reflecting his particular decision in resolving a quest with multiple options, such as the "Tattoo of Sebastion's Fall," which becomes accessible only if the player decides to betray a quest-giver. The tattoos record the most minor side quest and the most monumental task alike. Match-making between two lonely young people earns a "Tattoo of Joining" that boosts the player's charisma, while descending into hell brings him the "Tattoo of Avernus," bestowing resistance to fire and immunity to panic (see Figure 4.4).

Each tattoo has its own glyph designed especially for the game, resulting in a system of quest symbols specific to *Planescape: Torment,* configured on the player character's body in response to the player's actions. There can be no better image of the reconfiguring of meanings within a quest system.

The tattoos that emblematize each side quest in *Planescape* culminate in the "Symbol of Torment," (see Figure 4.5).

This complex sigil, one of many signs inscribed on the Nameless One's back, emblematizes the history and cosmology underlying the player charac-

Figure 4.5. The Symbol of Torment.

ter's forgotten memories. Its meanings emerge as players uncover elements of this narrative in gameplay, acquiring a "Blade of the Immortal" in this shape and learning a devastatingly powerful spell called "Rune of Torment" that summons the design. As the Nameless One converses with an otherworldly tattoo artist, the four points of the design are revealed to correlate with four party members who have adventured with the player character in the past and may have joined him again. Lead artist Chris Campanella divulges that "the Planescape universe is so steeped in myths and symbology that very shortly after starting on the project, we all started creating shapes that evoked the combination of threat and otherworldliness that was this realm." Hence, the two halves of the blade, one rusted and the other pure, emblematize the Nameless One's struggle with his own power-mad mortality, embodied in the Transcendent One and enacted in the game's final boss fight. These objects both function within gameplay and document the underlying meanings of the narrative background of their games, constituting what Campanella calls "visual backstory."

Propp and the Absent Object

Quest items like the Rune of Torment drive players to uncover the symbolic resonances of a narrative through gameplay, making these items susceptible to study from the standpoint of both ludology and narratology. In *Morphology of the Folktale,* Vladimir Propp argues that the search for an absent object to fulfill a lack or desire is often the driving force in folktales that feature quests (34–35). Indeed, various forms of object transfer operate as recurrent functions in the folktales that he describes, such as a key function in which a "donor" gives the hero an item, often in the form of a "magical agent" (43–46).

These functions can inspire various forms of gameplay involving the seeking and finding of objects. Propp summarizes their combinations in one of his most complex diagrams, indicating the many possibilities for these events to occur in conjunction with other motifs. They include

- "transference";
- "indication";
- "preparation";
- "sale";
- "find";
- "appearance";
- "swallowing";
- "seizure";
- "offer of service" (47).

In other words, a donor might give the item directly to the hero, prepare it for him, or sell it to him.

Similarly, Joseph Campbell (and his popularizer, Christopher Vogler) both refer to the hero's "seizing" of an object, sometimes described symbolically as a magic sword or an "elixir" (245). In the many myths and stories that these two critics examine, the object takes myriad forms other than these two symbols, but Campbell and Vogler use the sword and the elixir to suggest the idea of an item that is either a powerful tool, like a sword, or a potion of great restorative or protective power, like an elixir. As in Propp, a wise old man or mentor also often gives the hero a magical "talisman" that will help him on his journey. This talisman is perhaps best represented in popular form when Obi-Wan Kenobi gives Luke Skywalker his father's lightsaber (Campbell 69–77).

Theory

Hitchcock and the McGuffin

In addition to the theories of quest objects advanced by Propp and Campbell, the idea of an object as the driving force of a narrative also appears in more recent cinematic contexts. In Francois Truffaut's *Hitchcock*, the director himself explains that he used the term "McGuffin" to refer to an object in a film that is unimportant in itself but that motivates the plot (138). For example, a stolen weapon might function as the McGuffin in a James Bond movie, even though little of the actual film is dedicated to explaining the significance of this item. Another famous McGuffin is the golden suitcase with uncertain but valuable contents in Quentin Tarantino's *Pulp Fiction*. While Hitchcock's concept of the McGuffin downplays the significance of the object, more experimental and abstract cinema sometimes places the focus on objects themselves, which acquire symbolism that may exceed the interest of characters or plot. Such objects include the many strange and mysterious objects (such as blue keys, boxes, rings, and roses) that recur in the films of David Lynch. These films have a game-like atmosphere reminiscent of adventure games like *Myst* and *King's Quest*, where the emphasis on object collection foregrounds these treasures and artifacts over the unconsciously or deliberately thin characters.

   Despite these similarities between game items and Proppian, Campbellian, and cinematic uses of objects, narratological approaches to the role of objects in games must be supplemented by a ludological analysis of their role in gameplay. Objects in games are interesting primarily from the viewpoint of what the player can do with them. Hence, Propp's catalog of events that can take place involving object transfer in folktales is most useful to designers as a reminder of the many different ways that these items could be used in gameplay. For example, player characters might engage in all of the following object transferences, corresponding to Propp's functions:

- buy items from a merchant;
- acquire money to buy possessions by selling other treasures;
- fetch artifacts whose existence has been indicated by another NPC;
- trade items;
- discover treasures hidden in dungeons;
- win loot from defeated monsters or enemies.

   Each of these activities can result in the acquisition of the object, but the event of taking the object is often less important than the strategic maneuverings that lead up to its acquisition, which constitute interactive gameplay. For example, a large part of the action in *World of Warcraft* and *Neverwinter Nights 2* involves bartering. In gameplay terms, trading consists of dragging items back and forth in "merchant" windows to buy and sell them and calculating the exchanges that will enable the player to buy the supplies that will allow his party to survive, conquer enemies, and complete quests. Unlike a reader's spectatorship of a hero who acquires treasure, the strategic effort required to attain an object in games give the player a sense of pride in possessing this item that results from its use value. The player becomes proud of and attached to the treasures he has amassed in the course of slaying enemies precisely because they allow him to destroy further enemies and overcome future obstacles.

Object-Oriented Programming and the Lore of Quest Items

The use of objects as tools in gameplay mirrors the role of "objects" in programming, as in the phrase "object-oriented programming." An "object" in programming terms refers to any collection of variables and functions that can be called, in contrast to procedural programming, which runs sequentially through a series of rule-based actions. An object, in programming terms, may or may not have a counterpart in the simulated world of the game. For example, a window displayed on the screen might be an object, composed of variables and constants that define its visible appearance and function. A treasure chest in a game might also be an object in the programming sense if it consists of functions that check what it contains and define how it should behave when opened. On the other hand, an "object" displayed on the screen in a game that the player cannot interact with, such as a dresser or a table, might not be defined as an "object" in the programming sense. Such objects would only be static backdrops, akin to the sets or scenery in a drama rather than its props.

Yet the utilitarian role of objects in gameplay and programming does not undermine their symbolic functions as vessels of meaning or their narrative background as indicators of a larger back story. Edward Wesp argued in his 2005 presentation at the Modern Language Association Convention that the drive to acquire objects in *Everquest* challenges literary understandings of games because players do not seek to interpret these objects. He explains that players do not think about the treasures that they acquire as critiques of consumerism in the same way that readers of *The Great Gatsby* might interpret Gatsby's possessions. While Wesp may be right about some gamers' attitudes, he ignores the reality that designers often do create objects with a

Theory

narrative back story in the form of "lore," which enhances the object's interest in gameplay and permits replayings as this lore is more completely uncovered. As Kelly explains, the lore of a game consists of all the fictional information about its imaginary setting (69–71). Despite Aarseth's claim that MMOs like *Everquest* epitomize "post-narrative" discourse, players of MMOs often describe what Kelly calls the "lure of the lore" as the experience of shaping an ongoing novel by participating in its action (70–71).

Lore can consist of the fictional world's mythology, its history, its science or pseudoscience, and its politics. Items are often wrapped up in the lore of the game, as reflected in the "item description" tabs in games like *Neverwinter Nights 2.* Many items in these games have paragraph-long descriptions detailing the appearance and function of these items and telling the stories of their invention. In *Morrowind,* the early fetch quest from Caius Coscades to recover a Dwemer puzzle-box leads to the player to investigate a strange dwarven civilization in which every stray cog, gear, and precious metal cup suggests a society whose mechanical abilities as craftsmen were its strength and its downfall. Dwemer artifacts are also carefully balanced in the game's economic gameplay and the rules for transporting inventory items, since they are both extremely valuable and very heavy. They can be sold for a great profit, but only if the problem of transporting them is solved through the use of transportation or "lightness" spells. This balance of lore and gameplay challenge is characteristic of *Morrowind,* leading to its excellent reviews as a deep, rich role-playing game.

Ludological and narratological approaches can come together in quest items, especially those that are split into multiple parts that must be recovered in successive side quests or stages of the main quest. Sometimes, these items form a whole when reassembled, while at other times they constitute a "set," such as all the pieces of a magic staff or all the jewels of a certain number. Reassembling the parts of an artifact is a standard, recurring device in role-playing and adventure games, including the pieces of the Knight of Diamond's armor in *Wizardry II,* the eight portions of the Triforce of Wisdom in *The Legend of Zelda,* and the shards in *Neverwinter Nights 2.* As the parts of the disassembled item are put back together, so often is the narrative that underlies them.[1]

In the case of detective narratives, these narrative fragments are sometimes placed physically within the text as "clues," which consist of minute and often mundane objects that will tell the story of a murder when scrutinized and reassembled like the pieces of a puzzle.[2] Jenkins refers to stories that are told using clues in the form of objects in the game world as "embedded narratives," though he gives examples of elements of game spaces that players observe rather than of objects that they collect and use (126–27). Collected quest items can often be wielded in the game to gain a substantial strategic advantage, since the fragments of a staff or suit of armor can be activated individually or reassembled to form a magic artifact of great power, which necessitates ludological analysis of their gameplay. The principle of reassembling a quest item that stands physically for the narrative and meaning of a game is known as the "rod of many parts," a principle of quest design that can help designers to create exemplary artifacts.

The Rod of Many Parts

Ken Rolston, long-time inventor of pen-and-paper RPGs and lead quest designer of *Morrowind* and *Oblivion*, has declared that "the greatest story is the rod of eight parts." Hal Barwood, who worked as a lead designer for LucasArts and in his own company, often quotes Rolston's maxim as a guide for constructing storylines in games by associating a complete story with a whole object and then breaking this object into parts. In Barwood's words, this process involves "corporealizing and then atomizing" the story, that is, giving it a physical form and then splitting this form into pieces. This principle of quest design comes from many games that charge players with seeking out the parts of a magical rod or artifact that has been broken. In his lectures, Barwood refers to this principle as the "rod of eight parts." (The disagreement as to whether the rod has seven or eight parts has to do with varying sources for the first appearance of this structural principle. The exact number of parts is less important than the principle itself.) Barwood traces his understanding of this principle to conversations with Rolston at a game design workshop that they both attend.

Barwood's model is an excellent structural description of a design principle in many successful games, but it is important to note that this idea also has a historical lineage. The rod of many parts is heavily grounded in the history of RPGs, originating in a 1982 pen-and-paper module for *Dungeons and Dragons* numbered "R7" and entitled *"Dwarven" Quest for the Rod of Seven Parts*. In this scenario, adventurers seek out the seven fragments of a magical staff called the Rod of Law. Each of these sections has its own magical properties that combine when the staff is reassembled to provide the strength to vanquish the Queen of Chaos. Each part of the Rod of Seven is named after one word of a Latin sentence, with each section reading respectively *"Ruat," "Coelum," "Fiat," "Justitia," "Ecce," "Lex,"* and *"Rex."* This phrase translates to "Though Chaos Reign, Let Justice Be Done. Behold! Law Is King" (boxed set, insert).

This completed sentence demonstrates how players can assemble not just a magical artifact but also an idea, an invocation of law in the face of

Theory

chaos and an expression of hope that one virtue might rule over another. Moreover, each word in this sentence is a part of gameplay, a magic "command word" that can cast a spell. Players gradually become embroiled in the large-scale conflict between law and chaos without fully understanding the significance of the items that they are acquiring. Hence, the meaning of the quest is emergent, acquired through the complex manipulations required to find all parts of the staff. As the scenario book explains, "The quest for the *Rod of Seven Parts* begins when the player characters embark on a search for the first piece or when they fortuitously acquire it. It might be quite some time before the PCs comprehend exactly what they've started." The complex rules by which each part's magical powers function, either alone or in combination, and influence players' behavior to become more lawful require that players engage actively with each portion of the rod and with the greater principle of law in order to progress in the game.

The "rod of seven parts" principle carries forward from this 1982 module through the early CRPGs. *The Bard's Tale II: The Destiny Knight* (1986) featured this principle, requiring players to locate and acquire the seven parts of the "Destiny Wand" in order to slay the evil mage Lagoth Zanta. A similar activity carries forward through the location of the eight pieces of the Triforce of Wisdom in *The Legend of Zelda* (1986) and its many sequels. A similar principle operates in the recovery of the "spiritual medallions" that mark "quest status" in *The Legend of Zelda: The Ocarina of Time,* Hal Barwood's primary example. Indeed, the very series of games that Ken Rolston would later join, *The Elder Scrolls,* featured this motif in its first installment, *Arena* (1994), in which the player's quest is to help the emperor escape by finding eight sections of the Staff of Chaos. Rolston's insistence that the "greatest story is the rod of eight parts" (instead of seven parts) may result from the association of the earliest pen-and-paper appearance of this idea with its first occurrence in the *Elder Scrolls* franchise that he would later head.

The centrality of the "rod of parts" quest in early CRPGs and its continued popularity suggests its usefulness as a strategy for designers. In essence, designers should consider ways to motivate their quests by the acquisition of an object of great power, then break this artifact into pieces and place them strategically throughout their game world in ways that will prompt players to explore and overcome challenges.

Conclusion

Quest items mediate between the perspectives of narrative and gameplay, meaning and action, because they often are set apart from other items precisely by what *cannot* be done with them in the rules of the game. Checking the "Quest Item" or "Plot Item" checkbox in the *Aurora Toolset* or *The Elder Scrolls Construction Set* causes an item to become indestructible because it cannot be discarded from the player's inventory, since to do so would be to stop the progression of the game's story. Paradoxically, objects become quest items as a result of being partially removed from gameplay and pulled into the narrative underlying the game. At the same time, quest items allow players to perform actions that they could not otherwise accomplish, such as opening an interdimensional portal or casting a spell to destroy the ultimate boss. Thus, a quest item operates in an in-between space of games, both bracketed outside of the action because it cannot be sold or given away by the player but also extremely powerful within crucial moments of gameplay.

With items like this in mind, the question arises as to how designers can create such objects. Designers with educational or literary aims should start by consulting the books whose themes they are adapting, which often provide detailed descriptions of especially significant items. Designers can also scour dictionaries of symbols, tarot cards, heraldic coats of arms, and the books of psychologist Carl Jung, with their illustrations from mythological and alchemical texts. Secret alphabets, including runes, ancient, and foreign languages can also evoke a sense of mystery and a drive to decode these secret symbols. The use of such alphabets in J. R. R. Tolkien's books, the *Ultima* games, *Eternal Darkness,* the upcoming *Too Human,* and countless other adventure games and RPGs should testify to the efficacy of these symbols. These elements resonate with significance and give the game a sense of mystery and fun—the same sense of encoded significance that made the *Da Vinci Code* franchise so wildly popular.

Designing Quest Items

The easiest way to make quest items is to modify a blueprint for an existing item in the game system, adding enchantments and tweaking its appearance until it fits your design goals. The following tutorials and exercises will teach you how to do this, along with more advanced object creation skills such as creating custom objects in *Gmax* (a free version of *3ds Max,* a professional modeling tool).

Object Creation Tutorial #1: Building Quest Items with the Item Wizard

While designers can modify the blueprint of an existing item, it is also possible to create items using the Item Wizard in the Aurora Toolset.

1. Pull the "Wizards" menu down to "Item Wizard."
2. Select Item Type. For example, I might want to create a key to open the chests with Gawain's armor in them.
3. Select the palette that the item will appear under. This is a convenient way to locate items as you build, since they will be stored like the colors of paint on an artist's palette on the right side of the screen, where they can be accessed and placed in the render window at any time. Carefully choose a palette to place your items in so that you can find them later. It is often easiest to put the items you create in the "Special" section of the "Custom" palette, using an organizational scheme that distinguishes between the numbered sections, such as "Custom 1." Perhaps all of the items from the first area go in "Custom 1," and all those in the second area go in "Custom 2."
4. Click "Finish," and check the box that says "Launch Item Properties."
5. Give your item a unique tag, ideally in all capitals, since this makes some scripts work better (as noted by Celowin). Keep track of this tag, since it will be used to refer to the item when you are scripting object-related functions, such as transferring the object from an NPC to a PC or causing it to disappear.

Practice

Object Creation Exercise #1

Design the magical girdle that the lady in Hautdesert gives to Sir Gawain. Keep in mind that there is significant scholarly debate over whether this girdle is actually magical at all, as well as arguments about what it suggests regarding Sir Gawain's imperfection. With these debates in mind, what magical properties should the girdle have?

- Does it protect Gawain against bladed weapons, such as the Green Knight's axe?
- Does it allow Gawain to regenerate health once per day, in keeping with the associations of the color green with evergreen plants and the natural "resurrection" of vegetation each spring?
- On the other hand, is it simply an enticing artifact with no magical benefits, or perhaps even with powerful hidden detriments (such as moving Gawain's alignment toward evil, weakening his wisdom statistic, or making him more susceptible to harm rather than less)?

Object Creation Exercise #2

Create two of the following items, with appropriate visual appearances and magical properties.

- Frodo's ring
- Excalibur
- The Redcrosse Knight's Shield
- The Holy Grail (for the truly ambitious designer only)

Object Creation Exercise #3

Drawing inspiration from the tales of the search for the Holy Grail, design and attach appropriate scripts to the Bed of Marvels in the evil sorcerer Clinschor's Castle, which hurls rocks and crossbow bolts at whoever sleeps on it. This exercise requires some scripting abilities, which will be discussed in Chapter 5. For example, in the Aurora Toolset, the magical effects associated with the bed could be a userdefined event triggered by "OnActivate" or "OnDisturbed," since there is no standard animation for sleeping on beds.

Importing Custom Items

When educators and beginning designers start to consider the possibilities of adapting a videogame toolset to specific texts or educational applications, they often ask whether it is possible to bring a painting or image from outside the game into the toolset. This is possible through the creation and importing of custom content, such as models produced in three-dimensional modeling programs like 3ds Max and Maya. Because these programs require a great deal of expertise and work to effectively produce results, it is wise to check existing content produced by communities of modders before attempting to make your own. For example, one hakpak produced by the modder "Loge" and available in the *Neverwinter Nights Vault* features a variety of shields with heraldic devices. A similar hakpak of "holy symbols," produced by the modder Lisa, also contains many mystical symbols, such as an ankh, several crosses, and a pentangle. Many such items have been collected in a large Community Expansion Pack for the Aurora Toolset, which can be downloaded and installed to bring a wealth of user-made items into *Neverwinter Nights* modules. Modders can follow these examples and then create unique items through the use of Photoshop manipulation and three-dimensional animation software.

Object Tutorial #2: Installing Hakpaks

1.　In the Aurora Toolset, a hakpak is a bundle of related files that the toolset can recognize as constituting one object. To use a hakpak in the game, find the folder named "Hak," located in the *NWN* folder. Drag the hakpak into this folder.

2.　Load your module. From the edit menu, select "module properties" and click the "custom content" tab.

3.　From the dropdown menu, select the names of the hakpaks that you would like to be accessible from this module.

4.　Click the "Add" button.

5.　Use the "Item" wizard to create a new item, launch its properties, and then select the new "Appearance" number that will use the hakpak you have installed. For example, by installing the "Lisa's Holy Symbols" hakpak, I can incorporate a staff with a golden pentangle on the top that will suggest the one on Sir Gawain's shield. Other "symbols" in this hak include a staff with an ankh (the "looped cross" that is the ancient Egyptian symbol of eternal life) that would work well in an Egypt-themed game or one inspired by the *Ultima* series.

Modeling Custom Items

Creating such objects often involves building them rather than using prefabricated artifacts within a game itself, and custom content requires three-dimensional modeling skills. This is the use of a software application to sculpt images, such as new weapons and creatures, in three dimensions. When working with role-playing construction sets, the software applications most useful for this are Gmax (the free version of the professional modeling program 3ds Max) and Blender (an open-source program that is rapidly becoming popular in independent game development).

For the purposes of this book, Gmax is the most useful program because it is highly compatible with the first version of the Aurora Toolset. This compatibility allows models to be exported from the Aurora Toolset, modified in Gmax or used to produce guides for new items, and imported back into the Aurora Toolset. Gmax is no longer officially supported by Autodesk, the company that makes 3ds Max, but it can still be downloaded for free from http://www.turbosquid.com/gmax. Several individuals and independent development teams have made utilities and scripts that enable importing, exporting, and modifying materials between the Aurora Toolset and Gmax.

NWMax is a general purpose utility that grafts onto Gmax itself, operating as a large attached program or "plug-in" (http://nwmax.dladventures.com/). Blender Tools is a more recent and popular open-source modeling tool, but its compatibility with the Aurora Toolset is limited by the lack of reliable exporter scripts, except for a somewhat incomplete utility called Neverblender. (However, Blender is the best utility for custom content in *The Elder Scrolls* Construction Set.)

Three-dimensional modeling is an extremely complex subject to which many books are already devoted, but designers can acquire basic modeling skills to useful ends if they remember the principle of meaningful action as the basis of their design. These designs do not have to be the most polished or professional models. Rather, they need to be

- symbolic;
- useful in gameplay;
- revealing of the game's underlying narrative.

With these guidelines in mind, the best place to begin learning Gmax is the "Making a Sword" tutorial available online from http://www.cs.ualberta.ca/~games/299/lab/MakingASword4.pdf, an exercise in modeling and skinning a sword and importing it into the Aurora Toolset. The most comprehensive resource on importing custom content into the Aurora Toolset is the *Custom Content Guide,* by Eligio Sacateca, at http://nwvault.ign.com/View.php?view=Other.Detail&id=99. A modder must have considerable expertise in basic modeling skills before she can import objects into the toolset, so it also makes sense to work through some of the tutorials that accompany Gmax before working extensively with the *Custom Content Guide.*

An object in the sense used by three-dimensional modelers is composed of dots, or vertices, in space linked by lines to form geometrical shapes called polygons. These polygons usually consist of at least three dots but may contain up to four or five in the current generation of toolsets. Each polygon is a face of a three-dimensional solid, and modelers build objects by connecting faces to form a mesh, or network, of polygons over which they stretch a "skin" of two-dimensional images called a texture. To build such an object, modelers pull and push some faces out of the surface to form cylinders, bumps, and other raised spots. This process is called "extrusion." Modelers also slice faces to divide them into contoured surfaces for modeling, and they bevel these surfaces to round them or create a slope. Using only these techniques, one could create a crude three-dimensional image, perhaps using a two-dimensional picture as a guide and then extruding its various lines to form faces.

Practice

As you do these exercises, imagine a simple geometrical image that might become the object of the player's quest, such as a cross, rune, ankh, or pentangle. Perhaps one of these abstract geometrical shapes is embossed on an artifact such as a rod, shield, or amulet. While it is technically possible to place such items under the "miscellaneous items" category in the Aurora Toolset, where they will appear as a generic gray bag with only a two-dimensional "portrait" to indicate their identity, they can become more integrated into gameplay if they are modeled three-dimensionally whenever possible.

Object Creation Exercise #4

Design a symbolic object based on an artifact in a literary text or one of your own choosing. Try to incorporate an abstract geometric icon suggestive of an idea into this object, such as a sigil, glyph, or emblem similar to the tattoos in *Planescape: Torment* or the runes in *Eternal Darkness*. To do this, make a three-dimensional object and retexture it by wrapping a two-dimensional image around it in order to customize its outward appearance. Possibilities include:

- Design the Redcrosse Knight's shield, incorporating the red cross and white background whose multiple possible meanings have been analyzed by Frye.

- Design Sir Gawain's shield with a golden pentangle, showing the interlacing of the five lines.

- Design a set of rune plates with an alphabet or array of symbols of your choosing, such as Norse runes, alchemical or astrological signs, Sanskrit mantras, or your own custom symbols. These plates, consisting of a plane attached to a model, can be used in puzzles designed in Chapter 5.

Step 1: Export the Models to Gmax

1. Download "Neverwinter Explorer," a program used to view all the files that represent objects in the Aurora Toolset. http://nwvault.ign.com/View.php?view=Other.Detail&id=248

2. Navigate to "NWN Main Data," then "data\models_01.bif," then "models."

3. Select "ashto_041.mdl." This is the model file (abbreviated with the filename "mdl") for a tower shield. "Sh" stands for shield, "to" stands for tower, "04" is the model number, and "3" is the color of the model. Pull the "resources" menu on the

top toolbar down to "export," select the folder that you want to export the file to, and press "save."

4. Start up "NWMax." In the "NWMax" plug-in box at the left hand side of the screen, expand the "Mdl Loading" rollout and browse to the folder where you exported the mdl file. Click "import" and wait for the model to compile. When it is visible, press the "select by name" button and select the model "g_AShTo_04." This is the part of the model that represents the front plate of the shield, where you will be applying a texture with a symbol crucial to your quest.

Step 2: Retexture the Object with a Bitmap

1. Use a free trial version of Photoshop or a free image editor like GIMP to construct a simple two-dimensional image, or bitmap, that you would like to apply to the 3D model. This texture should be 128 pixels by 128 pixels in size and saved in "tga" (TARGA) format, as shown in Figure 4.6.

2. Select your 3D model in Gmax. In this case, make sure that you have selected "g_AShTo_04" (the front plate of the shield).

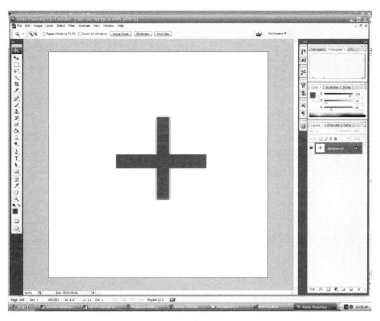

Figure 4.6. A red cross texture.

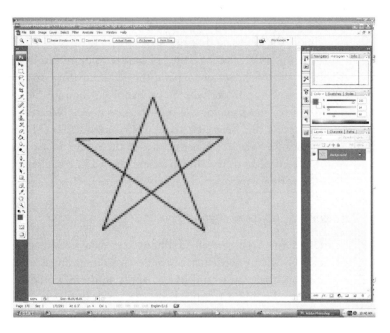

Figure 4.7. Pentacle texture.

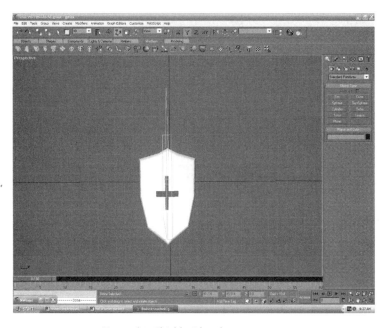

Figure 4.8. Shield with red cross texture.

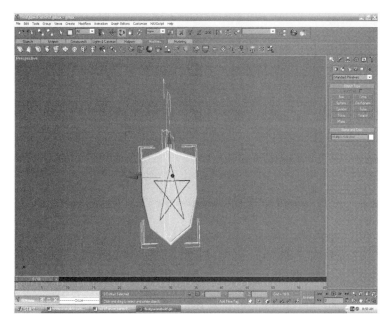

Figure 4.9. Shield with pentacle texture.

3. Click the "Gmax Material Navigator" at the right top corner of the screen.

4. Click the "New" button. Select "standard" from the "New Material" window that pops up.

5. Click in the gray square next to the "diffuse" box under "Blinn Basic Parameters."

6. Select the black square labeled "Bitmap."

7. Click "OK" and browse to the bitmap that you want to apply.

8. Select the "show map in viewport" button (a blue and white cube).

9. Select your object, such as a plane, in the "Perspective" viewport. Click "Apply."

Step 3: Export and Package the Textured Files

In order to view these models within the toolset, you will need to export them and package them as a "hakpak." In order for your shield to be imported into the toolset without error messages, you will need three files in this hakpak.

Figure 4.10. A backpack image of the redcross shield.

First, you need the model with your texture applied to it, saved with a model number and color number higher than any of the existing models in the toolset. If the highest model number for a tower shield is "04," your shield number should be "05." I saved the pentacle shield as "ashto_051" (a tower shield with model number five and color number one). Next, you must include the texture file itself, saved with a file name ending in "_tex" and with the extension "tga." I named my pentacle texture file "gawainshield_tex. tga." Finally, be sure to also include a "backpack image" that will represent the shield in the player's inventory and in the process of building the custom shield within the toolset. This file must start with "i," as in "iashto_051.tga." It should be a frontal outline of the shield shape, 64 pixels wide and 128 pixels tall (see Figure 4.10). These files must have exactly the correct names in order to be recognized by the toolset.

When you have all three of these files assembled, you need to package them as a hakpak.

Step 4: Making a Hakpak

1. Open the "NeverwinterNights" directory from your hard drive and then the folder "nwn."
2. Open the utilities folder named "Utils" and start up the NWN Hak Pak File Editor, named "Nwhak."
3. Give your hakpak a title and description in the appropriate fields; then drag all three of the files associated with the shield (mdl file, texture file, and backpack image) directly into the "Resource" window at the bottom of the editor.
4. Save your hakpak with a recognizable name, such as "sirgawainshield.hak."

5. Open the Aurora Toolset and add the hakpak. Go to "edit," "module properties," and select the "custom content" tab. Next, go to the "add" button, pull the list of hakpaks down to the one with your shield in it, such as "sirgawainshield.hak," and press "add." Press "Ok," and then press "Yes" at the prompt that warns of the dangers of adding hakpaks, and wait for the module to "build," as it checks for any errors or conflicts with your work.

6. Under "Wizards" at the top of the toolbar, select "item" wizard and select "Tower Shield" from the list as "Item Type." Give the item a name, such as "Sir Gawain's Shield," in the next window.

7. Select "Special" and "Custom 1" as the palette for this item.

8. From the blueprints toolbar, select "Paint Items"; then right-click your shield and select "Edit." Select the "Appearance" tab and browse through the backpack images that appear. Your new backpack image should show up as the last of these images, with the name you gave it in the hakpak, such as "iashto_051." Click this image, and a preview of your textured three-dimensional shield model should appear.

9. Paint this item anywhere in your module, where it can now be equipped by any character within the game.

Notes

[1] In narratological terms, this resembles the way that the Russian formalists suggested that the fabula (or complete sequence of events in a story in chronological order) must often be reassembled out of the syuzhet (fragmented, partially non-chronological tale with devices such as flashbacks and foreshadowing).

[2] This metaphor for detective stories as a fragmented narrative whose pieces must be re-assembled like the parts of a puzzle appears in early critical essays, such as R. Austin Freeman's "The Art of the Detective Story," and is summed up by Heta Pyrhönen in her analysis of the formal structure of detective stories in *Murder from an Academic Angle* (Freeman 14, Pyrhönen 27). Henry Jenkins uses the detective story as the "classic example" of the reassembly of the complete "fabula" out of the fragmented "syuzhet" (126).

Practice

The Challenges of the Quest and Quest Systems

The Challenges of the Quest

In order to move through the initiatory spaces of the quests, players must overcome trials, and quests can be classified in part by the challenges that they provide and the initiations that result from overcoming these obstacles. A typology of quests would also include features such as the player's objective, the actions that she must undertake, and the quest's location. To construct a "grammar" of these quests like that proposed by Aarseth, one would also need to examine the ways in which plot-lines inspired by literary genres give rise to quests or develop out of them. Although quests are not synonymous with narratives, story-lines offer an important motivation for undertaking quests as well as a reward for completing them.

Taking into account features of both action and narrative, online communities of players have developed semiformal classifications for quests, which have been further formalized in official "strategy guides."[1] R. V. Kelly 2 offers a similar classification scheme of quest types in MMORPGs (30–34). These schemes can be strengthened through close analysis of quests in games like *Oblivion*. In *Oblivion*, there are "fetch quests," "delivery quests," "dungeon crawls," "escort quests," and "kill quests." These categories can be further divided into subcategories, combined with each other, and melded with narrative back stories to produce a wide variety of possible quests.

Fetch Quests

In a fetch quest, a character must find a valuable, often magical object and return it to an NPC for a reward. While the term fetch quest is often used critically by gamers because this device sometimes seems clichéd, the original "quest for the holy grail" is itself a fetch quest.[2] Despite the familiarity of the form, the interest of such a quest depends upon the value and meaning of the object sought as well as on the challenges that must be surmounted to reach it. In *Oblivion*, the four middle quests in the main quest-line involve finding Azura's star, the armor of Tiber Septim, a great Welkynd stone, and a great Sigil stone and bringing them back to the Martin Septim. Fetch quests in *Oblivion* range from mundane but sometimes charming "collection quests," such as looking for twelve scales from a rare breed of Slaughterfish, to cosmic, such as the search for a Great Sigil Stone. The slain emperor's heir uses this stone to close one gate to the hellish plane of Oblivion and open a doorway to the "paradise," where the final battle between good and evil takes place. A frequent variant on the fetch quest could be referred to as the "delivery quest" (less formally known as the "fedex quest"), in which a player must carry an item from one character to another.

Combat and Kill Quests

"Kill quests" or "assassination quests" require the player to slay monsters or hostile NPCs, either as an end in itself that remedies an injustice or as a means to an end, since the gaining of an item in a fetch quest often requires the defeat of many enemies. Kill quests involve extensive combat with monsters, resulting in the intense violence that many opponents of video games criticize. However, this violence is no more intense, detailed, or gratuitous than that practiced by Odysseus as he engages in his "kill quest" to slay the Cyclops or the suitors. Examples of combat in chivalric romance could go on endlessly, since large parts of the action in these narratives involve ritualized jousting and swordplay between knights, not to mention the slaying of roving beasts and dragons. Digital games put the responsibility for this violence on the player, who must acquire the dexterity and persistence necessary to destroy his enemies as well as making choices about when and where to act violently.

As with all quests, the purpose and meaning of the violence determines the consequences of the player's actions. It is equally possible in *Oblivion* to murder random citizens or to destroy a demonic lord, but one action will put the player's avatar in jail while the other will result in a quest reward. Combat constitutes one of the key trials by which the meaningful conflicts of quest narratives are manifested, as well as one of the most fruitful opportunities for narrative to be converted into action.

Quest games require players to acquire active skills at virtual combat rather than making them spectators to another character's violence. Players develop the ability to perform various types of attack, including both light, quick blows and heavy "power attacks." Depending upon the degree of action in the game, combat might also entail complex "combo moves" involving the rapid pressing of buttons in specific combinations to execute a variety of subtly different blows and blocks. Players also master an arsenal of weapons and defenses, whether medieval implements, such as swords and armor, or more modern weapons such as revolvers and flame-throwers. In games like *Oblivion* and *Undying,* players may also gain skills in magical combat, including offensive and defensive spells, as well as healing mechanisms like the "health packs" common in first-person shooters and the healing potions of RPGs. In the most active and least meaningful form, combat challenges may entail assignments to slay a particular number of monsters and to bring back trophies, like pelts and horns, to a quest-giver.

However, combat can more meaningfully occur as a means to an end, such as gaining access to a spatial area of a dungeon or level that is blocked by a fearsome creature. These monsters are the equivalent of the "threshold guardians" that Joseph Campbell describes as obstacles to passage into any unfamiliar, dangerous, and supernatural region in which the hero's initiation occurs (77). In games, these monsters frequently appear guarding buried treasure in dungeons, like the undead Blade warriors who must be fought at the end of each level of Tiber Septim's shrine in *Oblivion.* Indeed, Erik Davis describes the "bosses" guarding the end of each level as "faint echoes of the threshold-dwellers and Keepers of the Gates that shamans and Gnostics had to conquer in their mystic peregrinations of the other worlds" (244).[3]

Combat challenges are often quite difficult, requiring an expenditure of time, energy, and mental activity far rivaling what is needed to follow along with the action in even the most dynamic and complex combat scene in a quest narrative. In addition to the quick reflexes often dismissively cited by critics of video games as their only benefit, virtual combat is a test of resolve, mental focus, and strategy. The more that this violence is contextualized by the back story of a quest, the more meaning it can potentially accrue, so that the player of a game is mashing buttons and pushing joysticks in the name of large-scale personal, societal, and cosmic stakes. Frye saw this conflict as the heart of the quest, constituting the phase of "conflict" or "agon" by which the heroic protagonist would overcome his monstrous, demonized antagonist. Thus, Frye declares that "the central form of the quest-romance is the dragon-killing theme exemplified in the stories of St. George and Perseus" (189).

Frye sees this violence as a vehicle for an epic conflict between good and evil that gestures back to the apocalyptic mythologies from which it sprang. At the same time, he argues that the conflict in quest-romances tends to be abstract and "dialectical," relying on a stark contrast between positive and negative forces that he explicitly compares to the workings of a game. Frye writes:

> The characterization of romance follows its general dialectic structure, which means that subtlety and complexity are not much favored. Characters tend to be either for or against the quest. If they assist it they are idealized as simply gallant or pure; if they obstruct it they are caricatured as simply villainous or cowardly. Hence every character in romance tends to have his moral opposite confronting him, like black and white pieces in a chess game. (195)

This epic struggle between good and evil is actually more a feature of Frye's and of Campbell's source materials than of Campbell himself, whose Nietzschean rhetoric and attraction to Eastern mysticism leads him to represent the hero's trials as a subsuming of all opposites, including moral ones. Yet Frye could easily be describing the world of *Fable*, in which the moral decisions advertised as the one of the key selling points of the game tend to fall into black and white choices to protect the innocent or victimize them, resulting in the player either opposing the villainous Jack of Blades or becoming increasingly like him in his search for vengeance. Frye's analysis of combat in quests suggests that "kill quests," which could function as potential fodder for the accusation that video games are gratuitously violent, are in fact at the heart of epic and romance that lend inspiration to quest-games.

Another type of quest is the "escort quest," in which the player must guide an NPC from one location to another while protecting this character from enemies. In *Oblivion* one such quest involves bringing the slain emperor's heir, Martin Septim, from the besieged town of Kvatch to a refuge in Weynon Prior. A final quest type, known as the "dungeon crawl," is classified by the location that the player-avatar moves through, since a "dungeon" refers to an underground labyrinth filled with monsters guarding treasure. The player must explore the passageways of this maze in order to find an item of value, an exit into another area, or a monster that must be dispatched.

Dungeon crawls are often conjoined with kill quests and fetch quests, as when the player must slay five undead soldiers evenly distributed in five areas throughout the dungeon in order to recover the armor of Tiber Septim. Combat literalizes Campbell's "threshold guardians," making them not just fearsome mythological characters but obstacles to the completion of a plot who must be overcome by the exertion of effort that Aarseth calls "ergodic" (*Cybertext* 1). A reader of a quest narrative may be frightened by a dragon but will never have to slay him, and hence will confront whatever narrative or allegorical evil he represents only on the conceptual level. A player of a quest game is forced to engage with a simulated representation of this enemy that fights back, delaying or potentially preventing altogether the completion of the quest.

Quest Systems

The challenges of quest games are woven together into a network of rules, tasks, and storylines called a "quest system," which is managed technologically by event-based programming, or "scripting." The most effective designers of quest systems will be those who understand both the relationships of many plot strands in quest narratives and the construction of rule-based challenges through scripting. While the quest functions as a structure in Frye's and Campbell's formalist and archetypal criticism, it operates as an activity in digital games. The most sophisticated quest games complicate and enrich the quest concept in a number of ways. Designers of role-playing games have introduced elements of multiplicity by creating not just a single quest, but a "quest system," often consisting of a "main quest" that must be performed in order to progress satisfactorily in the game and "side quests" that can be optionally completed in various order to receive rewards.

In practice, this often means that designers extend the portion of Campbell's second "initiation" phase, called "the road of trials" (97–109). In mythology, heroes must often battle monsters, seek out magical treasures, solve mysterious riddles, and complete other difficult tasks in order to prove their worth and complete their overall goals. Since games require action in order to maintain the involved interest of the player, this portion of the hero's journey furnishes the most material for game designers. Campbell argues that the "monomyth" is flexible, since "the changes rung on the simple scale of the monomyth defy description" (246). He also explains that these changes can include particular focus on some elements of the journey, omission of others, or various other combinatorial forms of multiplying and joining these components (246). Whereas Campbell is writing about the variations among myths, games include many of these changes within a single work, making possible a wide variety of morphological variations that unfold as the player plays.

The Elder Scrolls IV: Oblivion is one example of the simultaneous unity and multiplicity possible in a sophisticated quest system. *Oblivion* takes full advantage of the increased graphical capabilities and memory capacity associated with high-end PCs and new consoles, such as the Xbox 360 and the Playstation 3. In many ways it is the culmination of computer role-playing games produced throughout the 1980s and 1990s, including the first three *Elder Scrolls* games. Because of the power of the Xbox 360, the designers of *Oblivion* were able to produce a game of unparalleled complexity and richness, taking place in a vast simulated world in which every spatial and temporal detail has been crafted to allow for months of exploration. While three-dimensional graphics and artificial intelligence have been advancing in games rapidly since the early 1990s, *Oblivion* raises the bar on these achievements by producing a landscape in which every blade of grass, ripple on the water, and rare plant can be observed and interacted with. Yet all of these features are secondary to the primary engine that drives the game and makes it worth emulating as a model of well-constructed, creative design: its quest system.

Theory

The "quest system" in *Oblivion* refers to the organization of all the interrelated, goal-oriented activities comprising the objectives of the game. The quests in *Oblivion* consist of a "main quest" to restore the rightful heir to the throne and close the gates to the plane of Oblivion and many side quests, which are short, episodic adventures that allow the player to perform tasks for minor nonplayer characters, exploring the world of Tamriel and receiving rewards that aid in the main quest. The main quest of *Oblivion* is in many ways a hero's journey that begins when the player character is called to adventure by his fated meeting with the emperor. The cinematic trailer to *Oblivion* concisely proclaims its use of the hero's journey, to the accompaniment of operatic chanting, symphonic music, and shots of the game's sweeping landscapes and battles. In fiery letters, the subtitles appear: "In the shadow of evil / From the ashes of an empire / A hero will rise. / The fate of the world / rests in the hands of one." These brief sentences prophesy the narrative that will emerge from the main quest if it is successfully enacted and completed by the player. This narrative is then followed by a statement of the quest in the imperative form: "Find him [i.e., the new heir to the assassinated emperor] and close shut the jaws of Oblivion," cementing a close relationship between the narrative of the hero's journey and the gameplay that emerges from it.

Thus, in *Oblivion* the player character is called to adventure by the Emperor, who charges him with the task of bringing an amulet to Jauffre, the captain of the loyal legion of imperial bodyguards. Jauffre acts as the player's mentor or helper in the form of a "wise old man," giving him useful items and advice and charging him to break the siege of Kvatch by venturing into the supernatural world of the first Oblivion gate. After closing this gate, the player begins the "road of trials" phase of initiation, starting with the "Path of Dawn" and proceeding through a series of descents into the underworld of Bleak Flats Caves, Tiber Septim's shrine, and the Miscarand ruins. When he has gained the rewards from each of these trials in the form of magical items needed to open a portal to Mankar Camoran's Paradise, the player faces his final ordeal in combat with the evil sorcerer. He then returns to the ordinary province of Cyrodil, where he must bring the ultimate boon of the amulet of kings to Martin. Finally, he witnesses the resurrection of evil in the apocalyptic, mythological confrontation of the demon Mehrunes Dagon with the avatar of the benevolent god Akatosh.

Main Quests and Side Quests

Like *Oblivion,* many action-adventure games and single-player role-playing games feature a profusion of side quests and a "main quest" that revolves around a hero's quest and an apocalyptic battle between good and evil. For example, as Noah Wardrip-Fruin points out, the writers of the recent RPG *Fable* explain that their ambition was to create a game "driven by the 'classic' hero's journey elements."[4] Hence, the completed main quest of *Fable* (and its expanded version, *Fable: The Lost Chapters*) follows the pattern of the hero's journey even more closely, although the game's more playful visual aesthetic lacks the tragic grandeur of *Oblivion* and makes the contents of this journey so abstract that they resemble the fable suggested by the title.

The player assumes the identity of a character with the blunt name of "Hero"—an everyman whose appearance and moral standing change radically according to the choices of the player. The "hero's guild" in *Fable* uses the word "hero" to refer to any extraordinarily powerful and skilled person who gains fame by accomplishing fantastic deeds, whether these actions are virtuous or infamous. This definition of a hero is on one level a departure from Campbell's theory, in which moral virtue is a prerequisite to the hero's humble self-sacrifice. However, Campbell also argues that virtue is not the hero's ultimate aim, since he must eventually embody all the unified opposites of good and evil (44). Hence, *Fable*'s invitation for the player to become a benevolent or a wicked hero is partially inconsistent with Campbell's pattern and partially supportive of it.

However, in the overall form of the completed quest, all of the stages of the hero's journey are clearly visible. As Noah Wardrip-Fruin explains in "Writing Fable, Part One," the writers of *Fable* originally wrote it as a short story that they consciously constructed according to the Campbellian schema, after which they broke this story into individual quests and animated scenes. "Hero" is orphaned by bandits who ransack his home village, murdering his father and kidnapping his mother and sister. A mentor named Maze befriends him and brings him to the Hero's Guild, where the wise old Guild Master trains and equips him. After a few preliminary adventures, he sets out to find the prophetic advice of a blind seeress in a bandit camp, battling the vagabonds along an abandoned "road of trials" and vanquishing Twinblade, the leader of the thieves.

Hero then overcomes further trials by rescuing a kidnapped archeologist, destroying a white werewolf or "Balverine," and gaining fame in the gladiatorial arena. He descends into the underworld of a haunted graveyard and its subterranean dungeon in order to rescue his mother, only to find himself imprisoned in the "belly of the whale" when trapped by his nemesis, Jack of Blades. After a harrowing escape with his mother, he follows Jack of Blades to an isolated mountain region, combating him in a long chase scene that culminates in a final battle in which Hero destroys his enemy. *Fable: The Lost Chapters* extends this main quest through a series of episodes surround-

Theory

ing the return of Jack of Blades in the form of a dragon, fulfilling both the resurrection phase of the hero's journey (in which the evil tyrant reappears for a final battle with the hero) and the dragon-slaying motif central to Frye's definition of quest-romance.

Despite the influence of quest narratives on quest games, the pattern of the hero's journey only partially describes the quest systems of *Fable* and *Oblivion*. In *Oblivion*, myriad side quests branch away from and intersect with the main quest, and there are also many random activities that the player may undertake while exploring the world of Tamriel. At the same time, the side quests in *Oblivion* constitute an encyclopedic compendium of possible quest types that, taken together, resemble a vast, episodic story-cycle like *1,001 Arabian Nights*. While these quests are not solely narratives, their designers show clear literary influences, since several side quests have plot-lines and punning, allusive titles influenced by various narrative genres. These side quests include detective investigations of a stolen painting ("Canvassing the Castle"), Gothic tales of vampires ("A Brotherhood Betrayed" and "Azura"), and tales of political and economic intrigue ("Unfriendly Competition"), as well as many stories drawing on motifs from folktales and mythology. The side quests include all of the tasks offered by the NPCs who inhabit the cities of Cyrodil, as well as the "quest lines" of the Daedric quests, the Mage's Guild, the Fighter's Guild, the Arena, and the Dark Brotherhood. These quest lines involve the player in perpetual activity, so that the game does not become a static, linear narrative. At the same time, the main quest keeps this action from becoming random and meaningless, offering purposeful structure to a welter of possible activities.

The Quest Menu in Oblivion

Purposive action is built into the quest system of *Oblivion*, whose central component is a quest menu. In *Oblivion*, this menu appears within the "maps" screen, which includes both a "world map" displaying all locations in the game and a "local map" with the player's closest surroundings, such as the city or building that he is currently exploring. The placement of the quest menu within the maps screen confirms Aarseth's idea that the avatar's movement through space is a key component of quests, but this movement is only one part of quests. Players move through the world of Tamriel in order to complete particular objectives, which are listed under "active quests," "current quests," and "completed quests."

These categories are represented iconically at the bottom of the interface as a chalice for active quests, a hand grasping a chalice for current quests, and three chalices stacked triangularly for completed quests. The use of cups to represent quests is a visual allusion to the quest for the Holy Grail, suggesting a strong and commonly-held association between this quest narrative and quests in games.[6] Moving over each of these icons brings up a screen with text entries describing objectives in the quest, and new entries are added as the player progresses through a quest or as he undertakes new quests. The text on these screens is a guide through the quests as well as a record of them. While players perform quests within the game's main interface, moving an avatar through a three-dimensional graphical space, players refer to the two-dimensional, text-based map and quest menu in order to determine what their next move should be.

"Current" quests are all the quests available to a player at a given time because he has chosen to accept them as a part of his goals. The player has the option to accept a given quest or refuse it, usually with the opportunity of accepting it at a later date by returning to the quest-giver after accomplishing other tasks. Because the world of *Oblivion* is teeming with NPCs with tasks to give, players usually have several quests pending at once, which could result in confusion about their current course of action. Hence, players can also move to another screen where they can choose at any given moment to make one quest the "active quest"—the task that a player has chosen to focus on. The active quest is a way of prioritizing a particular task, but this does not mean that players can forget all other tasks while working on the prioritized task.

Oblivion requires a form of multitasking in which the player remains aware of multiple goals even in the midst of a stressful challenge. A player may be working on many quests at once, storing them in his mind, since the exploration involved in pursuing one quest often turns up clues for another one. For example, a player might be searching underwater for a lost "ring of burden," precariously using a "buoyancy" spell to avoid drowning, and discover a "Nirnwood" root. If one of the player's current quests, though not active at this point, was to find ten of these rare plants for an alchemist, he would need to quickly remember this goal and acquire the Nirnwood root while underwater. The player considers all of the available activities on his agenda and chooses to actively focus on one of them. Upon completion of this activity, it then moves to the list of "completed quests," where the final entry in the list summarizes the quest.

Players could choose their current and active quests on the basis of what is most important to them in terms of the overall storyline, the development of their character, or curiosity about an innovative feature of gameplay or plot-thread. However, the main quest gains increasing urgency as the game progresses, often escalating to an apocalyptic scale that eventually overshadows other goals. On the other hand, a player finds that it is often necessary to complete various side quests before she is powerful and skilled enough (both in her avatar or her real-world identity) to complete the quest. Delaying the main quest for too long can increase its difficulty, since the power of enemies increases proportionally with the player's level in order to maintain challenge.

It is also possible to explore the province of Cyrodil for its own sake, battling wandering bandits and monsters as well as venturing into mysterious locations, such as ruins and dungeons. This gameplay imitates the "knights errant" of Arthurian romance and Spenserian epic, who wander the forests of their kingdoms awaiting whatever unexpected adventure might arise. The designers of *Oblivion* make it clear from the introductory paragraphs of the game manual that they intend players to be able to adopt varying degrees of structure in their gameplay, from strictly linear accomplishment of the main quest to picaresque wandering and everything in between (2). However, wandering almost inevitably pulls the player into quests even if he does not formally accept them, since dungeons contain monsters to be slain and treasures to be recovered that fall into a quest-line elsewhere.

While the text in the quest menu is primarily a record of the quest and not the quest itself, players can nonetheless determine much about the grammar of quests, especially their tense and mood, through this text. Each quest consists of multiple entries, usually four or five in number, describing what has happened or what the player has done to lead up to the quest, then suggesting a next course of action. These entries tend to take place in the first person past perfect and the imperative, following a pattern of "x has happened. I should or must go to y place and perform z action." For example, the quest entitled "Deliver the Amulet," reads "I've arrived at Weynon Priory. Now I must take the Amulet of Kings to Jauffre."

The first person point of view implies that the player, directing the avatar, is performing the action and making notes about it addressed to himself. The past perfect tense suggests action in the past that is still occurring, while the imperative mood suggests the requirement or obligation to a task that must be completed in the future. Even the final entries of "completed" quests tend to end in the future imperative, because the fulfillment of one quest must give rise to others in order to keep the game moving. This unusual combination of person, mood, and tense rarely appears in narrative except in the diaries of ambitious people focused on their short-term and long-term goals. Hence, the text in the quest menu may take the form of diary entries, and the record of quests in many role-playing games (such as *Neverwinter Nights*) is recorded in a journal.

An analysis of the quest text suggests that the process of questing is not merely the movement from performative to constative (i.e., action to story) that Tronstad suggests. Rather, the actions that players perform in quests are constantly becoming narratives of past events that give rise to future actions, which in turn become narratives. Moreover, players shift their focus to particular threads in a network of interconnected goals and paths, moving back and forth between tasks of greater and lesser urgency that in turn facilitate the accomplishment of other quests.

This temporal dimension of quests is further complicated by the goal-directed movement through space. Goal-oriented activity provides direction and orientation in both the metaphorical and the spatial sense, because the selection of a particular quest as active causes quest targets to appear on both the local and world map. These targets are arrows, colored red or green according to the degree of urgency and the nature of the target, that direct the player to the location of her next objective. The local maps show only territory that the player has already explored, so that within a maze she often sees several familiar corridors, a quest target arrow off in the distance, and a vast blank space of unexplored territory. This spatial representation also reflects the gap of the unknown that is necessary to maintain interest in the quest, as the player constantly keeps a long-term goal in mind and seeks to discover the intermediary steps necessary to reach this goal.

This uncertainty is similar to a reader's desire to know what happens next in a narrative but more immersive and intense. A reader may relax in the assurance that the questing character will progress (or fail) in his journey regardless of the reader's actions, whose only challenge is to follow the thread of the narrative or interpret its meaning. In the case of a quest game, the events of the story will not occur and the goal will not be accomplished unless the player exerts effort, often involving intense cognition and sometimes physical tension and stress.[7]

At the same time, completing a quest also results in a more intense sensation of satisfaction resulting from an accomplishment achieved by skill. In many cases, the reward for this accomplishment is the production of narrative, as players look back over the events that they have brought about or the mysteries that they have uncovered. Nevertheless, this narrative is only half of the equation, and the other half is not simply "interactivity" in the form of random changes that the player can create in the story. Rather, the player's pursuit of a definite goal with emotional, thematic, and personal meaning is key to the experience of questing.

Scripting Quest Systems

Once a designer has mastered the craft of scripting individual quests and of transforming literary narratives into quests, the next step is to consider creating networks of interrelated quests that take advantage of the quest systems built into game construction sets like *Oblivion*. The story of the quest for the Holy Grail is focused around a single fetch-quest for an invaluable artifact, but it involves hundreds of interwoven subplots that form a "story-cycle." There are also many versions of this cycle, such as Wolfram von Eschenbach's *Parzival,* the anonymous *The Quest of the Holy Grail* that is part of a larger cycle of tales about Lancelot, and the unfinished Grail romance of Chrétien de Troyes. This cycle grows even more complex if one includes its contemporary adaptations, such as Richard Wagner's opera *Parzival* or Dan Brown's popular novel *The Da Vinci Code.*

In these cycles, many strands of narrative weave in and out of each other, in a device that narratologists call "interlacing." As William Kibler argues in his preface to Chrétien de Troyes' *Arthurian Romances,* "The knights-errant who indefatigably make their way through a forest—that ancient symbol of uncertain fate—are apt to abandon at any time one quest for the sake of another, only to be sidetracked again a moment later; and when such things happen they behave as though their apparent vagaries were part of an accepted mode of living, requiring no apology or explanation" (69). This description of interlacing is also remarkably similar to the underlying programming principles of the quest system in *Oblivion,* of which Tom Dawson writes, "One of the greatest features of the game is the fact that it does not progress you automatically to the next stage in a quest. You can now rush off to the Kings Arms to find out about the house or, you can go off and save the world, or kill a few innocent civilians. It's your call." Dawson's point is that a quest "bump" in the *Oblivion* system only updates the player's journal with a suggested plan of action but does not require her to complete the quest. She can instead take up another quest and complete it to any degree, or begin several other quests simultaneously, shuttling back and forth between them like threads in a tapestry.

For example, one quest line might involve the challenges and events surrounding Parzival's quest for the grail in Wolfram von Eschenbach's *Parzival.* Parzival challenges the Red Knight and takes his armor, steals a ring and a kiss from a nearby maiden, encounters Anfortas (the Fisher King), witnesses the ritual of the grail but fails to ask the crucial question about the Fisher King's suffering, wanders for many years in the forest, does penance with a hermit, and eventually witnesses the grail and asks the question. Interlaced with this plot is the subplot of Sir Gawain's adventures, including the narrative equivalent of a side quest, in which the hideously ugly creature Cundrie challenges any knight to the adventure of the Castle of Marvels. While spending the night in this castle, such a knight must overcome a lion

Theory

as well as a magical bed that throws crossbow bolts and rocks. *The Quest of the Holy Grail* introduces even more subplots that might also function as side quests, following each of the knights through their adventures that culminate in Lancelot's acquisition of the Grail.

The key to transforming these narrative strands into a quest system is to recognize that players may experience them in a variety of orders, perhaps delaying the main Grail quest of Parzival in favor of the Castle of Marvels. Moreover, different players might respond differently to various challenges, perhaps asking the question about the Fisher King immediately or failing to overcome the challenge of Bed of Marvels because of its difficulty. To keep the big picture of this quest system in mind, the designer should ask herself: what meanings are at stake in these events, and how can they best be enacted through gameplay?

The answers to these questions will vary from designer to designer, just as interpretations of the texts vary from reader to reader. For example, Parzival's dilemma might involve conflicts between his instinctive compassion and his distrust of it in favor of a predefined code of honor that requires him to not ask impertinent questions of his elders. Similarly, in *Sir Gawain and the Green Knight,* the Beheading Game has at stake Gawain's struggles to maintain his honor in the face of his own temptations and reputation as a seducer, while not betraying his loyalty to Sir Bertilac or his courtesy to Sir Bertilac's wife. As Sadowski explains, Sir Gawain must chart a middle strategy of temperance between the various knightly virtues to which he is committed (172, 176). This strategic maneuvering resembles the ways that a player of the *Ultima* games must try to gain points in compassion (by not killing "non-evil" creatures) while keeping points in the conflicting virtues of justice and valor (by never backing down from a fight).

In order to allow players to enact some of these themes, the key in working out a quest system in response to a literary text is to plan the strands of various quest lines so that players will bring about some of the events of the text, though not necessarily in the same order or with the same outcomes. Designers may need to fill in many of the gaps in the text that are not sufficiently explicit, and they should think of the various activities that a player will need to perform to fulfill an event. In other words, what items might the player need to "fetch," what locations might he need to discover, and what enemies might he need to combat? Filling in these gaps is not a violation of a literary text, but a way of opening it up. However, the gaps that the designer must fill in are not just absent details of setting or character, but details of action expressed through gameplay, such as what Gawain did in the year of wandering that the poet summarily glosses over.

For example, in *Parzival,* the leading character finds Anfortas, the Fisher-king, and is directed by him to the castle of Munsalvaesche, where he sees the ritual of the grail and is given a sword. For this set of events to be a quest, the player should have to work to bring them about through gameplay, which should expand upon the themes implicitly at play within the text. For example, the player might need to fetch an item for Anfortas to prove his valor before being admitted to Munsalvaesche. Given that Anfortas is king of the Waste Land, an empty desert, the player should have to travel across vast expanses of space akin to the areas near the Red Mountain in *Morrowind.* There, he might fight various zombies and demonic creatures who have fallen under the spell of the Waste Land. Perhaps he must slay several of these for Anfortas, or bring Anfortas a vial of healing ointment (or a fishing pole) that will temporarily ease his pain.

If a designer wanted to work the overriding mythic symbolism of the Grail quest into the story, perhaps the player might recover a "golden bough" from a grove of trees guarded by a druid (as part of an ancient fertility ritual that some scholars believe to be at the root of the Waste Land story). Locating the grail castle itself should be a struggle, involving careful strategic management of weapons and healing potions to pass through the treacherous level of the Waste Land. Only after the player has successfully overcome these challenges will he receive the sword that Anfortas gives Parzival immediately in the narrative of *Parzival.* The player will have experienced firsthand the trials of a land that has lost its fertility and spirituality, and the sword that he gains will function less as a prop and more as a tool in gameplay that he has gained through achievement.

Scripting Reader Response

The theoretical goal of this extension through scripting is to render a metaphorical, interpretative interactivity as configurative and strategic. The designer must locate junctures of a story that have implicit interpretative interactivity and then set up challenges that allow players to play strategically in order to reach goals that are motivated by their own values. The challenge of such programming is that design decisions must be extremely precise to function within a game, while interpretative interactivity is inherently imprecise, "fuzzy," and uncertain. As Rollings and Adams explain in *Fundamentals of Game Design,* the difference between a "game idea" and a "design decision" is the difference between "dragons should protect their eggs" and an exact set of parameters for how close dragons will stay to their nests and under what circumstances (62). Hence, the challenge of a designer seeking to make interpretative interactivity into strategic interactivity is to render a conceptual ambiguity as a precise cluster of variables.

In terms of completing the final level design exercise from Chapter 1 based on Book I of *The Faerie Queen,* the ambiguity regarding the saving powers of holiness needs to become concrete in the player's strategic use of armor, the healing pool, and the apples from the tree of life. One source of ambiguity of the allegory comes from the difficulties of the armor of faith, which both protects Redcrosse Knight from the fires of the dragon and imprisons him in pain as the dragon's breath heats the armor. This armor is allegorically derived from a metaphor about girding oneself with Christian virtues in the biblical book of Ephesians. Spenser implies that virtue is both an asset and a liability, trapping the knight in the difficulties of a battle with evil even while it protects him with the last-minute salvation of the cooling well of life.

In terms of gameplay, these problems would need to be scripted as properties of the armor, spring, and apples. Donning the armor might grant the player a +10 AC bonus against creatures of evil alignment but inflict +5 damage per second of exposure to fiery dragon's breath. The player's attitude toward the protective powers of holiness then becomes a strategic decision whether to wear the armor. Similarly, the apples and spring are power-ups that heal the player by 5 hit points per apple and 20 hit points for each time he enters the spring of life. However, the spring only functions when the player is near death because he has less than 10 hit points left, and the power-ups only work if the player has both donned the armor of holiness and refused evil magical items offered by the wicked magician. The player would then find himself immersed in a set of strategic conflicts with both gameplay consequences and moral implications about the benefits and detriments of holiness.

There are many moments in quest narratives that are quite ambiguous, in which readers do change the text through their imaginative activity. We tend to associate these moments with postmodern texts, such as Pynchon's *The Crying of Lot 49* or Vladimir Nabokov's *Pale Fire,* which openly advertise their game-like qualities through multiple possible endings and paths through the text. However, older quest narratives can be just as interactive in a figurative sense, as when Gawain is faced with the opportunity to take a magical girdle (or belt) that may protect him from the axe blow that he must receive, but at the price of his honor. There is great scholarly debate over whether this girdle is actually magical or not, resulting in many possible interpretations of Gawain's taking of the girdle and even more speculations as to the physical and moral consequences that might have ensued had he not taken it. The

Theory

interpretative ambiguity of this plot event has to do with whether accepting this girdle, a love-token from the lady, is

- an act of cowardly betrayal of Sir Gawain's duty to his host;
- an understandable human fault reflecting Gawain's desire to protect himself from death;
- a positive, life-affirming act of love and nature that
  — Gawain misunderstands as a fault
  — but that the Green Knight sees as a token of allegiance with natural cycles of death and redemption.

Gawain views accepting the girdle rather than giving it to his host as an act of cowardice, an interpretation that is backed up by the single nick that the Green Knight gives him on the neck to symbolize this minor imperfection. In this reading, the girdle is not magical but only claimed to be so by Sir Bertilac's wife as a ruse to tempt Gawain. However, another reading could be supported by much of the text: the girdle is magical, and Gawain receives only a nick on his neck because the Green Knight cannot inflict any further harm. In this case, the acceptance of the girdle might actually be a wise and perhaps even salvational act symbolizing Gawain's love for life. Another possible interpretation of Gawain's choice is that he wants to honor and show allegiance to the lady who offered this token to him in the ritual of courtly love. In this reading, the tendency of King Arthur's court to laugh off or even celebrate Gawain's imperfection by wearing similar garters as a badge of honor might actually be a spiritually or socially correct response rather than a sign of moral laxity.

These alternate interpretations and their accompanying plot ramifications cannot be experienced by readers within the lines of the text of *Gawain*, but such interpretative possibilities can be read between the lines, filling in the gaps of the story imaginatively (in accordance with reader response theories of reading, such as those advocated by Wolfgang Iser). However, scripting these alternate events within a game can make them actual, in accordance with the rules of the game engine rather than in the rigid and difficult to program "choose your own adventure" format of branching paths.

This is the ultimate goal of quest design: to make actual the metaphorical interactivity of a quest narrative without sacrificing readers' abilities to pursue goals that are intimately tied in with their own values as evoked by the imagined world of the text. The purpose of scripting in quests is to establish a specific form of interactivity in which players must overcome challenges in order to cause a narrative to unfold. Failure to overcome these challenges will result either in a lack of progress in the quest or in a negative outcome, such as bodily injury or death. The two forms of challenge, combat and cognition, described in the previous theoretical section, can be brought about through a combination of individualized scripts and various wizards and palettes associated with placeables, NPCs, triggers, and encounters.

Scripting

Scripting and Quest Systems

The success of quest design will depend largely on the tools available for scripting and their integration with other design tools. In other words, productive quest design is greatly facilitated by a quest system, which prevents designers and students from having to implement the mechanics of a quest from scratch. It is theoretically possible to program one's own game engine from the bottom up, using low-level programming languages that compile directly into machine language, such as C++. However, this approach is extremely time-consuming, especially from the viewpoint of a humanities educator or a student with only a semester to complete a project.

Instead, many designers already use "scripting" languages associated with a particular game engine. As designers know, scripting does not refer primarily to lines of dialogue, as in the script of a movie or play (although scripting can control the dialogue of NPCs). Rather, scripting is a "high-level" programming language, far removed from the 0s and 1s of machine language. Because the game engine acts as a translator between scripting and machine language, scripting languages are much closer to everyday human writing in syntax and vocabulary.

The principles of scripting and their relationship to quest design remain the same across game engines. Scripting requires designers to think of a quest not as a single whole or as a story that is told by one narrator to a passive listener. Rather, designers must consider the ways that a quest can be accomplished and brought into being through the interactions of a player with landscapes, objects, and other NPCs. Scripting requires designers to think of events in terms of the conditions under which they might occur and their effects on other components of the game. "Conditions," taking the form of if–then statements specifying that an event will occur only under certain circumstances, are at the core of quest design. Similarly, programming statements that create "results" by setting certain variables and new conditions in response to player actions also give quests the combination of goal-based logic and interactivity that makes them unique.

Practice

Scripts are small programs that can be attached to anything, including objects, NPCs, nodes of conversation, and triggers. When the player performs a certain action or enters a particular area, or when a certain amount of time elapses, the script will run, causing an event to occur. Some scripts manage quest systems by updating a player's journal with new entries whenever she takes a certain branch in a dialogue tree, while modifying a variable that keeps track of the player's progress in a quest. Other scripts give a player certain items, open a door or portal, or set off a trap.

Scripting is the thread that binds together all the components of the quest, bringing together its spaces, objects, NPCs, and challenges into one goal-oriented activity. Designers can make their quests much more interactive by mastering the basics of scripting, such as

- functions;
- events;
- variables.

Scripting can be used to manage the challenges of the quest and the flow of its overall forms, including fetch quests and kill quests.

At the same time, designers can also attach scripts to the component parts of the quest to allow players to interact meaningfully with them. Scripts can be used effectively in conjunction with the spaces, NPCs, and objects of quests in the following ways:

- *Spaces*:
  — Attaching scripts to strategically placed triggers will create areas that respond when players enter them. These trigger scripts can start visual effects such as beams of light as well as gameplay effects such as healing or poisoned traps.
  — Attaching scripts to triggers can also create portals that open up in response to player actions and transport them to other areas. If the spaces of the quest are already symbolic, these portals can be used to create a conceptual "multiverse" like that in *Planescape: Torment*.
- *Characters*: Setting variables in conjunction with dialogue nodes and other actions can keep track of player characters' ethical viewpoints, or alignments, as well as their affiliation with other NPCs, or factions. NPCs, spaces, and objects respond differently to players' actions based on their alignment or faction.

Practice

- *Objects*: Attaching scripts to symbolic objects can create puzzles that allow players to enact or uncover hidden meanings in their environments.

Functions

The scripting languages used in both of the *Neverwinter Nights* toolsets are relatively easy to get started with, and skills in one are transferable to the other, since both are loosely based on the programming language called "C." As such, they have certain features in common. They are almost like a family of languages that share similar elements derived from their parent language, just as French, Italian, and Spanish have many similar words and grammatical structures derived from Latin.

The first thing to learn in these scripting languages is their basic syntax.

When you begin a script, you often start with the following lines:

```
void ()
{
}
```

"Void" is the designation for a type of "function," which refers to a set of programming lines that tell the program to do something, whether in the simulated world of the game or behind its scenes, such as performing a calculation. The blank parentheses indicate that this function does not require any numerical input to operate, while the designation "void" shows that this function causes an action to occur rather than calculating and returning a value. For example, here is a script from my sample Gawain module in which the Green Knight puts his axe in front of Gawain after Gawain accepts the offer of the Beheading Game.

```
void main()
{
   //Green Knight puts axe down in front of Gawain
   object oItem=GetObjectByTag ("GREENKNIGHTAXE");
   ActionPutDownItem(oItem);
   // Set local variable to show that Gawain has accepted the
   // Knight's challenge.
   SetLocalInt(GetPCSpeaker(), "nTalkedToKnight", 1);
}
```

The line "ActionPutDownItem(oItem)" is a function that causes the Green Knight to drop his axe, after the player chooses the strand in the dialogue tree in which Gawain accepts the game. In fact, the easiest way to learn to script is by attaching scripts like this to dialogue nodes using the "script wizard."

Practice

Scripting Tutorial #1: Attaching Scripts to Dialogue Nodes

1. To attach a script to a dialogue node, first select the node.
2. Select one of the three tabs at the right-hand corner of the screen.
   a. "Text Appears When" allows you to set conditions for when a particular node will appear, so that an NPC will say a line of dialogue only if a PC has a certain set of traits or carries a particular item, or if a variable has been set to equal something. This tab is ideal for testing whether a certain quest condition has been fulfilled.
   b. "Actions Taken" causes something to occur when a line of dialogue has been spoken, such as giving the PC a reward, taking an item from a player, setting a variable, or causing the NPC to trade with or attack the player.
   c. "Other Actions" causes another set of miscellaneous actions to occur when a line of dialogue is spoken. The most crucial of these options for quest design is the "Journal" pull-down menu, which updates the player's journal with both a topic and an entry, such as "Green Knight's Quest" and "2."
3. Follow the menus of check boxes and "next" buttons to specify which conditions must be fulfilled or which actions will occur in response to a particular node. If the script involves getting or setting a variable, specify its name and value.

For example, I have attached a script to a node in King Arthur's dialogue tree that causes the Green Knight to walk from the Camelot entrance gate to a point directly behind the player as soon as the king says, "I think I hear the footsteps of a giant Green Knight, who is walking up behind you." The effect of this script is to cue an action in the manner of a play or movie when the screenplay says "the Green Knight enters from stage right."

In addition to these cinematically scripted events that cause NPCs to perform actions in conjunction with dialogue, scripting can be used to generate interactivity. By attaching different scripts to dialogue nodes at alternate branches of the player's responses in a dialogue tree, a rudimentary interactivity can be created by which players will have a range of possible responses that correlate with various actions. Alternately, some dialogue nodes might consist not of spoken lines but of actions themselves, such as "[slit throat of NPC]." Such an approach resembles branching storytelling media, such as hypertext and the choose-your-own adventure books that allow readers to turn to different pages in order to alter the protagonist's course of action.

Practice

Scripts carefully attached to branching dialogue can help shape the progress of quests through journal updates and variables that change according to players' choices. However, if followed exclusively, this method of scripting causes gameplay to become dull because it resembles browsing a webpage by clicking on links rather than role-playing. Temporal branching structures limit the player's actions to a few choices selected through words rather through than simulated performance. In order to take full advantage of the "procedural," or rule-based, interactivity enabled by scripting, programmers need to use scripts to produce events in gameplay in addition to dialogue nodes.

Scripting Quests

To script the skeletal programming framework of quest, you should outline its stages along with the journal updates that will signal players of their progress in their quest as well as alerting them to the next step. You should also plan the conditions that make each stage kick into action (such as the player's entrance into a certain area or possession of a certain item) and the results of the stage (such as the addition or removal of an item from the player's inventory). Tom Dawson, in his "Anatomy of a Quest" tutorial, best explains this programming technique when he summarizes the underlying pattern of quest scripting as

- "Trigger a Stage, and do some changes to the settings to reflect the new status.
- Go into a hiatus, while we wait for the player to trigger the next action sequence.
- When triggered, do the actions, then when it's done, trigger the next stage."

In the case of the five-part fetch quest that begins the sample *Sir Gawain* exercise, the conditionals are the possession of a quest item, while the results are the receiving of a key that allows the player to unlock the chest that contains the next quest item. For example, the first stage of the quest has the following conditional under the "text appears when," which regulates when an NPC will speak a certain line of dialogue.

```
int StartingConditional()
{
  // Make sure the PC speaker has these items in his inventory
  if(!HasItem(GetPCSpeaker(), "SHIELDOFBENEFICENCE"))
    return FALSE;
```

Practice

```
    return TRUE;
}
```

This conditional checks to make sure that the PC has the Shield of Beneficence in his inventory before King Arthur congratulates him on finding it and suggests that he should seek the next item. A second script, in the "actions taken" tab, determines the results of this action.

```
void main()
{
  // Give the speaker the items
  CreateItemOnObject("firekey", GetPCSpeaker(), 1);

}
```

More generally, the conditionals should be local variables that keep track of progress in the quest, ideally set at fairly wide intervals (such as 5 or 10 rather than 1) so that intermediate steps can be inserted. The results should be the setting of new local variables that bring the quest to a new stage. As each variable is changed, the journal should also be updated to indicate the player's progress in the quest. Hence, the most important scripting functions to learn initially in designing quests are the ones that check and set local variables. In the Aurora Toolset, these variables must be named, checked, and set manually. However, David Gaider (a lead writer on *Neverwinter Nights*) also explains a procedure for setting them up in relation to dialogue. In the Aurora Toolset, the function for setting a local variable with the value of an integer is `SetLocalInt`. It must be followed by an object to which the variable is attached, as well as a variable name in quotation marks, and an integer value. For example, you might attach the following lines of script to a dialogue node:

```
        SetLocalInt (GetPCSpeaker(), "QUESTSTAGE", 1);
```

As Gaider explains, when the designer wants the computer to check whether a quest has been completed, she should write a script that sets up a new variable which returns true if "QUESTSTAGE" equals a certain value. Returning true means running a certain function rather than going on with the other scripts that were occurring before the computer encountered this one. Returning false means skipping this function and continuing with the processes that were already in motion.

Using Gaider's model but filling it in with our own variable names, we get

```
int StartingConditional()
{
```

```
int nAcceptedquest =
  GetLocalInt (GetPCSpeaker(), "QUESTSTAGE") == 1;
return nAcceptedquest;
}
```

The best resources currently available on constructing quest dialogue as a means of structuring this aspect of the game are David Gaider's tutorial on setting local variables and Iskander Merriman's "Simple Quest" tutorials available with the *Neverwinter Lexicon,* under the "Lyceum" and "Toolset" categories.

Scripting Kill Quests

While Merriman emphasizes that quests can be constructed without the use of scripts by focusing solely on the use of wizards, you can have much more flexible and meaningful quests by building your own scripts. A good way to learn to do this is by observing the scripts that the script wizard creates in order to find the functions relevant to quest design. For example, in a kill quest, a designer can place a script in the "OnDeath" handle of an enemy to update the player's journal, register the progress of the quest, and shift the player's alignment or faction in response to this violent act. This scripting prevents the awkward solution of making the player bring back the head of the monster as proof that he has slain it—a solution advocated by Merriman for beginners because it prevents one from having to script. A scripter can attain more versatility and directness by attaching scripts directly to the enemy that must be destroyed in the kill quest.

Scripting Tutorial #2: Scripting a Kill Quest

1.   First, select the creature that is the target of the kill quest.
2.   Right-click and select "Properties."
3.   On the window that opens, select the "scripts" tab.
4.   The slots on this window with pull-down menus are called "handles," which are boxes that allow you to attach custom scripts to an item, creature, area, or other object in a module. Locate the "OnDeath" handle, which regulates the events that occur when a creature dies.
5.   Next to the "OnDeath" handle, click the "edit" button to bring up a window where you can add custom scripts.
6.   To update the player's journal when an NPC has been killed, add the following script, replacing the journal category and stage with your own parameters:

```
void main ()
{
  object oPC = GetLastKiller();
  AddJournalQuestEntry ("journal_killquest", 175, oPC);
}
```

- In the script editing window, click the "save as" button and give your custom script its own name, such as "jlh_death-journalupdate." Always remember to give each script that you alter its own unique name so that you do not change the "OnDeath" script for all creatures in the module.

Remember that you must use the journal tag (e.g., "journal_dreamquest") for the quest, not the journal category name (e.g., "Dream Quest").

- To set a local variable that registers that the NPC has been killed, add the following code in this window:

  ```
  SetLocalInt(GetModule(), "iPhobosKilled", 1)
  ```

- Then, in the "text appears when" attached to the dialogue node that congratulates the player for killing the target, put the following;

```
int StartingConditional()
{
  // Inspect local variables
  if(!(GetLocalInt(GetModule(), "iPhobosKilled") == 1))
    return FALSE;
  return TRUE;
}
```

A similar approach can be used to have the engine update a journal as soon as an object is acquired in a fetch quest, rather than waiting for the player to return to the NPC who congratulates or rewards him. This approach can make the quest seem more articulated and easily absorbable in small segments, in which players are made aware of their progress after achieving each subgoal instead of slogging through a long dungeon crawl before being reminded that they have advanced. Journal updates like this can be especially important if the player has many pending quests in his journal and may have forgotten which magic swords and golden chalices he is looking for.

- To attach a script to an item that will update the player's journal when she acquires the item, place the following script in the OnAcquireItem event handle of "Module Properties" in Edit window:

Practice

```
void main ()
{
    // Get the object which was acquired
    object itemAcquired = GetModuleItemAcquired();

    if(itemAcquired != OBJECT_INVALID) {
        // Get the tag of the acquired item
        // If it is "my_item_tag" we got the right item
        if ( GetTag(itemAcquired) == "DreamShard") {
            // Get the object (player) who now possess the
            // item
            object oPC = GetItemPossessor(itemAcquired);
            // Add an appropriate journal entry to his
            // journal
            AddJournalQuestEntry ("journal_dreamquest", 150,
              oPC);
    }
```

Scripts Attached to Spaces

Scripting Triggers

The key to keeping gameplay interesting in quests is to correlate scripted events with the player's successful, unsuccessful, and partially successful completion of tasks. This can be accomplished by attaching scripts to placeable objects, NPCs, areas, and triggers, so that the quest progresses or fails to progress if the player opens a chest, attacks an NPC, enters an area, or steps into a specific trap. In scripting, "events" are instructions to the computer to perform an action in response to a set of conditions, including a user's interactions. Events often take the form of the word "On" followed by an action that could occur in relation to an object, area, or trigger. Examples include "OnOpen," which causes an event to occur when an object such as a chest is opened, and "OnDeath," which brings about an animation or other response when a creature dies.

A set of scripts centered around the function "GetEnteringObject" uses "triggers" to cause a journal update or other event when the player enters an area, which can be a useful effect if exploration is a key aspect of the quest. In this type of scripting, you attach a script to the "OnEnter" handle of a trigger or area. For example, a previous exercise asked you to script the Healing Pool of Faith that Redcrosse Knight falls into while fighting with the Dragon. You can do this by first putting down the tile group of water and then drawing a trigger around it using the trigger wizard. Draw four connected points, with a double-click on the last point to complete the trigger. Then, select this trigger and insert a script into its "OnEnter" handle. For example, to script the Healing Pool of Faith that Redcrosse Knight falls into, insert the following code:

```
void main()
{
  object oPCHeal = GetEnteringObject();
  ApplyEffectToObject(DURATION_TYPE_INSTANT, EffectHeal(7),
   oPCHeal);
  AddJournalQuestEntry ("journal_faeriequeen", 100, oPCHeal);
}
```

Scripting Portals

In addition to triggers that create an effect when a player enters them, it is possible to set up a trigger that transports a player instantly to a specified location in the current area or into a completely new area. Such a trigger functions as a portal, and a model of innovative portal use can be found in *Planescape: Torment*. *Planescape: Torment* takes place not in a single world or universe but in a collection of intersecting worlds, or multiverse. Moreover, the physical landscape, events, and people in this world respond directly to beliefs and ideas, especially those of the various factions in the planes, who organize themselves around a philosophical attitude toward the multiverse.

In the Nameless One's own dialogue, he defines the segments of this multiverse as "planes of the imagination, of thought and belief." This idea of a universe made of many intersecting worlds, also known as a multiverse, is what lends *Planescape* such power as allegory, earning it the title of "interactive inferno," in Barton's terms. A multiverse is a place where clashing viewpoints and belief systems are embodied physically, allowing intersections and portals between ideas as well as rooms and levels. The portals from plane to another open only when players possess specific keys, taking the form of unexpected objects like stones, junk, or a blood-soaked handkerchief. However, the in-game text in dialogues and descriptions suggests that sensory experiences and abstractions, like a musical tune or a thought, can also be portal keys. The philosophy behind this game blends a relativistic belief that perception shapes reality with a quest-based sense of urgent goals. There are many worlds in the planes, but each of these worlds presents goals and tasks that matter to the player and NPCs. Portals become increasingly important in *Planescape: Torment* as the player travels the planes, since the quests assigned by each faction take place in their own world, often requiring the player to be transported into another realm of dream, death, or the senses.

Practice

The lesson to be learned from this imaginative design is that the interpretative richness of a quest system can be increased if we see a book as a multiverse of many possible meanings rather than a universe of only one. When multiple worlds open up, multiple quests become possible—designers, readers, and players pursue different goals in a shared setting with many layers or "planes," depending on their viewpoints as readers. This abstract idea can become concrete through scripting portals from one location to another. In the Aurora Toolset, these portals can be built through

- a combination of a placeable visual effectf a glowing gate;
- the "CreateObject" function to make this effect appear;
- the "MoveTo" function to transport the player;
- setting a local variable to activate the portal;
- tagging waypoints for the location of the portal and its destination.

Combining portals and puzzles can make the relationship between configurative and intepretative play explicit. Dialing certain combinations, pressing certain plates, or rotating the concentric circles of a wheel could open portals associated with certain combinations of symbols in a complex quest narrative like *The Faerie Queen.* Perhaps some of these portals are associated with a religious interpretation of *The Faerie Queen,* opening up a doorway to a series of quests for holiness. Perhaps others are more focused on the poem's political allegory, sending the player on a series of battles with England's enemies.

Practice

Scripting Tutorial #3: Creating a Portal

1. From the menu above the palette, select the "paint waypoint" button. A waypoint is a marker of a specific location in the toolset, which can be given a unique name or "tag" and then referenced in scripts.

2. Under the "Waypoint" menu, select the plus sign to open up possible types of waypoints. Select "Waypoint" (a generic waypoint with no special traits); then single click on the area where you would like your portal to appear. A waypoint, in the form of a large yellow arrow with a blue flag, should show up at the location you clicked.

3. Left-click to select this waypoint; then right-click and pull the menu down to "Properties."

4. In the "Basic" tab, fill in the "Tag" box with a unique identifier for this waypoint, such as the location to which you want to

transport your player. This tag should be in all capital letters, such as "FORESTPORTAL." Click OK.

5. Place a trigger around this waypoint so that the portal will activate when the player walks into this area. Click the "Paint Triggers" button next to "paint waypoint." Press the plus sign next to the "Generic Trigger" menu. Select "New Generic." Triggers take the form of "Polygons" (many-sided geometric shapes, such as rectangles and squares), so you will need to click once at each point of the polygon and twice at the final point that closes the shape. You should see the trigger in the form of a light-blue polygon. Select it and give it a unique tag under the "Properties" menu.

6. Paint a second waypoint to designate the place where you want the portal to transport the player. This waypoint probably should be in a different area within the same module, such as a forest clearing outside of a dungeon. Tag this waypoint so that it can be referred to in the trigger script that will transport the player.

7. Now, decide how the portal will be activated and whether there are any conditions to entering it. Portals can be opened by pulling a lever, stepping on a rune plate, or using any placeable item in the game, such as an altar. For this example, place a rune plate on the ground near the waypoint. Select it, right-click its properties, and select the "Scripts" tab and the "OnUsed" handle. Click the "Edit" button and insert the following script:

```
void main( )
{
  object oPortalSpot = GetWaypointByTag("FORESTPORTAL");
  CreateObject(OBJECT_TYPE_PLACEABLE,"plc_portal",
   GetLocation(oPortalSpot), TRUE);
  SetLocalInt(GetObjectByTag("PORTALTRIGGER"), "READY", 1);
}
```

This script, adapted from Celowin's fifth scripting tutorial in the *NWN Lexicon,* causes the visual effect associated with the portal to appear as well as setting a local variable on the portal that signals it is ready.

8. Next, attach the following script, also adapted from Celowin's tutorial, to the portal itself:

```
void main()
{
```

Practice

```
   object oPC = GetEnteringObject();
   object oDest = GetWaypointByTag("FORESTCLEARING");
   int nReady = GetLocalInt(OBJECT_SELF, "READY");
   if ((nReady == 1) && (GetIsPC(oPC)))
      AssignCommand(oPC, JumpToLocation(GetLocation(oDest)));
}
```

This script retrieves the variable that set the trigger as "ready" when the player uses the rune plate. The "AssignCommand" function then transports the player to the location set by the waypoint tag.

Scripts Attached to NPCs

Scripting Alignment and Faction

Scripting can be used to convey multiple ethical implications if one designs quests that both respond to the player's alignment and cause this alignment to shift according to the choices that he makes in taking or completing them. In *Dungeons and Dragons* terminology, "alignment" refers to a player character's ethical stance. This alignment includes three possible values for morality (good, evil, or neutral) and three possible parameters for attitudes toward cosmic and social order (lawful, chaotic, or neutral). This yields nine possible ethical orientations that player characters may begin with when they create their character (or develop throughout their adventures).

The relevant function for this ethical meaning is "AdjustAlignment," described in the *Neverwinter Nights Lexicon* as

```
void AdjustAlignment(
    object oSubject,
    int nAlignment,
    int nShift
);
```

For example, if a designer wants to cause a player's alignment to shift toward evil by fifty points when she kills a particular innocent creature, you can put an "AdjustAlignment" function into the "OnDeath" handle of the creature. An example script would be

```
void main ( )
{
   object oPC = GetLastKiller();
   AdjustAlignment(oPC, ALIGNMENT_EVIL, 50);
}
```

"ALIGNMENT_EVIL" is a one of five constants representing the alignment possibilities in *Dungeons and Dragons*. These constants are "ALIGNMENT

EVIL," "ALIGNMENT_GOOD," and "ALIGNMENT_CHAOTIC," "ALIGNMENT_LAWFUL" and "ALIGNMENT_NEUTRAL."

Once the designer has set the alignment of a player, he can then cause certain quests to be available or unavailable based on this alignment, so that PCs who take a turn toward evil will be faced with increasingly greater opportunities for wickedness and vice versa. This requires that the module "get" a player's alignment and feed it back into another function, such as a "StartingConditional" attached to a dialogue node. The function to do this is "GetAlignmentGoodEvil" or "GetAlignmentLawChaos," which returns one of the five constants. Combined with an "if–then" statement, this function can be used to create quests that shift according to the player's previous ethical decisions, as in the following function:

```
{
    object oAlignment = GetAlignmentGoodEvil;

    if (oAlignment == "ALIGNMENT_GOOD")
        return TRUE;
}
```

The simplest way to apply such a function is in conjunction with dialogue, where NPCs will respond to the player with fear or respect, depending on his good or evil alignment and upon their own, if the function targets the NPC also. At the same time, other aspects of the world might change more subtly according to the player's moral stance. For example, certain doors might be blocked off or certain items might not be usable depending on the alignment of the player, moving a storyline in divergent directions or rewarding players for certain kinds of choices. For example, in the early RPG *Wizardry III: The Legacy of Llylgamyn,* certain doors on the first level of the dungeon would allow only an evil party to pass through them, while others would open only to a good party. If a good party attempted to enter an evil door, they would be magically transported out of the maze, requiring two separate parties to complete separate halves of the dungeon.

The association of alignment not only with individuals but with groups, or parties, reminds one that moral ideas often shape the allegiances that people form with each other. These associations can be modeled through functions that control the factions to which an NPC or PC belongs. Factions are groups of characters with similar goals and allegiances, such as guilds, gangs, tribes, and sects. The Aurora Toolset has a Faction Editor feature, which allows designers to use intersecting bar graphs to adjust varying degrees of friendliness and hostility between factions. Once these values have been set, functions can be used to alter the reputation that a PC or NPC has in relationship to a particular faction, using the "ChangeFaction" and "AdjustFactionReputation" functions. As the *Neverwinter Lexicon* explains, these two functions follow this pattern

```
void
AdjustFactionReputation(
    object oTargetCreature,
    object oMemberOfSourceFaction,
    int nAdjustment
)
```

and

```
void
ChangeFaction
(
    object oObjectToChangeFaction,
    object oMemberOfFactionToJoin
)
```

In addition to alignment and faction, designers can set local variables that measure moral or philosophical attributes associated with player characters' actions. For example, one can track the five knightly virtues associated with the pentacle on Sir Gawain's shield: courtesy, fellowship, generosity, purity (or chastity), and compassion (or piety). To set a variable for one such virtue, the scripter needs to first initialize it, ideally by attaching it somewhere where it can be retrieved when the module loads.

- Select the "edit" menu and drag it down to "module properties"; then press the "events" tab and select the "OnModuleLoad" handle.
- Then, press the "edit" button and place a script like the following into the window:

```
void main ()
{
  // Initialize five local variables to store the PC's five
  // virtues, so that they can be altered from other
  // scripts within the game.
  object oPC = GetPCSpeaker();
  string sCourtesy = "courtesy";
  string sFellowship = "fellowship";
  string sGenerosity = "generosity";
  string sChastity = "chastity";
  string sPiety = "piety";
  int nCourtesyValue = 3;
```

Practice

```
int nFellowshipValue = 3;
int nGenerosityValue = 3;
int nChastityValue = 3;
int nPietyValue = 3;
SetLocalInt(GetModule(), sCourtesy, nCourtesyValue);
SetLocalInt(GetModule(), sFellowship, nFellowshipValue);
SetLocalInt(GetModule(), sGenerosity, nGenerosityValue);
SetLocalInt(GetModule(), sChastity, nChastityValue);
SetLocalInt(GetModule(), sPiety, nPietyValue);
}
```

Scripts Attached to Objects

Puzzles and Interpretation in Quests

Designing and implementing a puzzle is one of the most effective ways to hone your scripting abilities, moving them past dialogue nodes and into the rule-based interactions at the heart of immersive games. In a quest whose aim is interpretation, a puzzle should ideally involve the rearrangement, or "configuration," of symbols, such as the symbolic objects that you created in Chapter 4. An interpretation of a book is a rearrangement of its symbols in a particular pattern of relationships.

For example, *Planescape: Torment* abounds in references to texts that are also puzzles, or puzzles that have to be arranged in different combinations to unlock hidden secrets. The Dodecahedron Puzzle box is an intricate Rubik's cube whose solution involves sliding panels and avoiding traps in order to unfold a text that must also be unfolded and interpreted. The Unbroken Circle of Zerthimon is another such puzzle with sliding, intricately interlocking wheels. These wheels both figuratively open parables of myth with allegorical meanings and physically slide open to reveal panels with spells whose function corresponds to the ideas in the stories. At first glance, it seems frustrating that the Infinity engine made it hard to implement these puzzles, which tend to be described in words. Solving them often involves selecting dialogue nodes, such as "open the box," rather than manipulating them physically as puzzles. Yet, in a way, these puzzles have been implemented in the overall design of the game. The manipulations of quest-solving and stat-grinding are in the service of unlocking the Nameless One's past as well as the complexities of the city of Sigil. It is no coincidence that the name "Sigil" is another word for "secret sign," implying that the entire city must be decoded.

Puzzles are a crucial component of early adventure games that feature quests, and it might be worth rethinking their role in today's quest games because of their potential relationship to interpretation. Some designers and players criticize puzzles because they slow down action with frustrating, pointless manipulations of levers and sliders. Yet such puzzles are poorly designed, in contrast to the best puzzles, which require a leap of insight in which players suddenly grasp an underlying pattern that was in front of them the whole time. In *The Puzzle Instinct,* Marcel Danesi calls this "insight thinking." While the insights required to solve a puzzle revolve around recognition of the formal patterns underlying the puzzle, these formal patterns could also entail insights about the game world, the human condition, or an emotion (27). Because of this potential in puzzles, Koster often blurs the line between puzzles and games when he exhorts designers to realize the expressive power of games. He writes: "We often discuss the desire of games to be art— / for them to be puzzles with more than one right answer, / puzzles that lend themselves to interpretation" (147). Koster is also blurring the line between physical reconfiguration and interpretation, a division that can be further bridged if literary texts are understood as puzzles that can also be reconfigured. For example, while Milorad Pavic's branching novel *The Dictionary of the Khazars* is often compared to a hypertext, Pavic compares its combinatorial interpretative possibilities to a Rubik's cube (13).

Practice

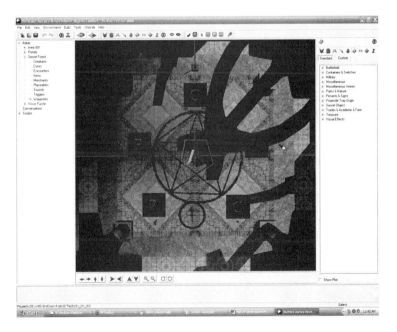

Figure 5.1. A puzzle in the Aurora Toolset.

Scripting a Puzzle

As players manipulate the symbols, such as runes and gems, within a puzzle, the state of the game world should change in ways that respond to these interpretative reconfigurations. With this in mind, the following tutorial teaches you how to implement and script a simple puzzle that involves Gawain manipulating objects and rune plates to explore the correspondences among the five pentads discussed by the author. This puzzle will allow players to explore the correspondences between the five virtues and the five senses by standing on each of five plates with the first letter of each virtue while holding the corresponding item. Once each plate is correctly activated in this way, the player can pull a lever to open a portal. The puzzle consists physically of five plates at each of the five points of the pentangle and a lever at the top (see Figure 5.1).

This puzzle is constructed using custom placeables from the Neverwinter Nights Community Expansion Pack, a collection of fan-made content highly useful in creating one's own tailor-made modules. Most "miscellaneous" items in the Aurora Toolset tend to appear within the game without their own three-dimensional models except for a generic gray bag, but the NWN modding community has used tools to construct a wider variety of items within the game. This means that the CEP provides a range of symbolic objects that can appear in the game to stand for each of the senses, such as

- a lantern (sight),
- a rose (smell),
- a harp (hearing),
- wine (taste), and
- a fan (touch).

To construct this puzzle or a similar one, place the rune plates around the circle in the appropriate places. Then, use conditional scripts (also known as if–then statements) to set up the actions that the player must perform to activate the plate.

1. For example, placing the following script in the "OnUsed" handle of the "F" rune plate associated with the harp will cause it to glow briefly when a player activates it while holding the harp in her inventory. The "SetLocalInt" function then sets a local integer which registers that this plate has been activated.

```
void main()
{
  object oPC = GetLastUsedBy ();
```

Practice

```
  if (GetItemPossessedBy (oPC, "FELLOWSHIPHARP") !=
  OBJECT_INVALID)
  {
    object oPlate = OBJECT_SELF;
    effect eCorrect =
      EffectVisualEffect(VFX_DUR_GLOW_LIGHT_YELLOW);
    ApplyEffectToObject(DURATION_TYPE_TEMPORARY, eCorrect,
      oPlate, 2.0);
    SetLocalInt(GetModule(), "HarpPlateActivated", 1);
  }
}
```

The same scripts can then be repeated for each of the other four plates, changing the tags of the required item in the conditional and the name of the local integer that activates them.

> 2.   Then, another script can be attached to the "OnUsed" handle of the lever to retrieve each of these local variables, opening a portal at the center of the pentacle only if each plate has been activated:

```
void main()
{
  int nRose = GetLocalInt (GetModule(), "RosePlateActivated");
  int nHarp = GetLocalInt (GetModule(), "HarpPlateActivated");
  int nLantern = GetLocalInt (GetModule(),
    "LanternPlateActivated");
  int nWine = GetLocalInt (GetModule(), "WinePlateActivated");
  int nFan = GetLocalInt (GetModule(), "FanPlateActivated");
  if (nRose == 1 && nHarp == 1 && nLantern == 1 && nWine == 1
    && nFan == 1)
  {
  object oPortalSpot = GetWaypointByTag("ROSEPORTAL");
    CreateObject(OBJECT_TYPE_PLACEABLE,"plc_portal",
      GetLocation(oPortalSpot), TRUE);
    SetLocalInt(GetObjectByTag("PENTPORTAL"), "READY", 1);
  }
}
```

The difficult move in this function is the retrieving of a variable by its name stored as a string, which is "HarpPlateActivated" rather than the "sHarp" name that it had when it was temporarily initialized as another variable. The string name is stored directly onto the module where it can be accessed in scripts like this, but the temporary variable "sHarp" works only within the scope of the function attached to the plate. However, once this variable has been retrieved as a string, the numerical value of this string cannot be tested directly. A function like "if "HarpPlateActivated" == 1" will return an error message about an "invalid operand" because 1 is an integer and "HarpPlate-Activated" is a string. To make this equality test work, we must pass the value named by the string to an integer with the initializiation statement

```
int nHarp = GetLocalInt (GetModule(), "HarpPlateActivated");
```

Because "nHarp" is a local integer within the scope of this function, the equality test "nHarp == 1" will compile correctly. Once all five local variables equal one, pulling on the lever will open the portal.

Scripting Exercise #1

Script a series of riddles and puzzles requiring the player to enact the correspondences around the five points of the pentangle. For example:

- King Arthur will give Gawain five keys, each of which will open one and only one of five chests.
- If the incorrect key is used, a trap is triggered.
- To mix things up, designers might include levers that must be pulled, pressure plates that must be stepped on, and actions that have to do with the four elements (e.g., setting something on fire or immersing it in water).
- Gawain may find the items in any order, which requires the designer to set one variable for each item found.
- Alternatively, the items must be found in a particular order, and King Arthur directs Gawain to the next item each time.

Scripting Exercise #2

To find the Green Chapel, the player must defeat five beasts in a series of five related "kill quests," with the added twist that some of the knightly virtues involved may require abstaining from killing by acting diplomatically or fleeing. These beasts represent the vices that will tempt the player as a knight, so he must utilize the weapons and armor of his virtues. As Sadowksi explains, quest narratives in medieval romances often represent the knight's struggle with his own animal impulses through a battle with monstrous beast. He writes:

> Amid manifold tests of physical endurance are also typically heroic struggles with various foes—animal, monstrous, or semi-human— which collectively typify the temptation of nature and the flesh in their different aspects. The hero's *psychomachia* to resist the onslaughts of the

fleshly powers involves 'wormez'—that is, the dragons (720), the ancient archenemy of man, the personification of the devil himself (Revelation 12:9) and also the 'wolues' (720), notorious for their rapacity, fury, and greediness, often said to represent the sin of avaritia, as well as lust and voluptuousness. (151-52)

To enact these ideas on the level of gameplay, the player may find the following instructions in riddle form, which tell him what "weapon" to use to defeat a given enemy, but there will be some ambiguity as to whether the weapon must be literally used or the virtue practiced as a form of metaphorical "defense" or "armor."

- "Only the Sword of Pure Mind can defeat the Dragon of Sin.
- Only the Helm of Compassion can protect you from the Raging Bull of Wrath. [Defeating this enemy means behaving compassionately toward him, perhaps by sparing the animal's life or adopting a defensive posture.]
- Only the Armor of Courtesy can quench the fires of the uncouth gibbering Giants.
- Only the Ring of Brotherly Love will stop the Boar of Hatred.
- Only the Shield of Beneficence can protect you from the Wolf of Malevolence."

Using the "encounter" palette in the Aurora Toolset combined with the "creature" palette, a designer can stage fights between the player and each of these monstrous opponents or groups of opponents. Many of the natural beasts, such as wolves and boars, can be placed only through the "creature" palette, whereas the supernatural ones, such as dragons or groups of giants, can be painted through the encounter system. To determine whether Gawain has fulfilled these kill quests, the designer can use either the built-in "plot wizard" of the toolset, or she may set local variables to keep track of the death of the monsters. The local variable solution may be more effective, since the plot wizard templates accommodate only standard kill quests and fetch quests, whereas the refusal to kill a boar can be registered only by a variable set for this purpose.

Scripting Exercise #3

Script the following "trial" from *Sir Gawain and the Green Knight,* which occurs primarily through conversation and the exchange of objects. Set up the scripts attached to conversation nodes so that each player has dialogue choices but must the following the rules of knightly courtesy to achieve an optimal outcome:

- He must remain courteous to the Lady of Hautdesert while avoiding sex.
- He must kiss the lady when she requests it.
- When offered the magical girdle,
  — he could take it, or
  — he could refuse to take it.
    * If he refuses to take it, does the Green Knight later
      • cut his head off,
      • congratulate him for achieving perfection, or
      • scold him for being too perfect, in a more subversive or humanistic reading?
    * If he does take it, does it protect him?

Notes

[1] One example of a collaborative classification scheme for quests in games is the Wikipedia article on the subject, found at http://en.wikipedia.org/wiki/Quest_%28gaming%29.

[2] Indeed, the etymological origins of quest in "questare" (Latin: to seek) implies that the search for something absent or hidden is fundamental to questing.

[3] While the influence of Gnosticism on video games is not as pervasive as postmodern novels, references to the Gnostics do appear in many video game quests, including the "Archons" of *King's Quest VIII* and the "Archon" of *Fable*. The 1980's game *Archon* featured a battle between monstrous black and white chess pieces, echoing Frye's description of the figures of quest romance with the opposing sides of chess as well as Philip K. Dick's description of reality as a "Gnostic computer chess game" (an idea that Dick derives in part from Campbell's notion of the hero's adversary as a "dark counterplayer") (Dick 241-43).

[4] Wardrip-Fruin is summarizing the explanations of the *Fable* writer James Leach, who comments of the short story that he wrote as the basis of *Fable*, "The reluctant hero, the call to arms, the mentor all appear in the traditional way."

Quests and Pedagogy

By deliberately merging the interpretative and gameplay functions performed by players, game design can be taught as a form of interpretative writing within literature classrooms. Such an assignment could involve transforming virtually any literary narrative into a quest, and any work that falls within the paradigmatic selection of quest narratives, running from ancient epic to post-modern novels, would be particularly amenable to this form of adaptation.

I have given one such assignment to my sophomore English literature class. I asked students to adapt Thomas Pynchon's postmodern novel *The Crying of Lot 49* into a quest game. *The Crying of Lot 49* is especially appropriate for this assignment because its main character, Oedipa Maas, herself embarks on a quest to discover the meaning of a possible conspiracy centered around the will of her late boyfriend. Oedipa gradually becomes drawn into a conspiracy surrounding an underground postal service called "W.A.S.T.E." that purports to allow communication between marginalized social groups. As she investigates the clues associated with this organization, including both physical items such as misprinted stamps as well as conversations with a bizarre cast of eccentric characters, she uncovers mysterious hints of a possible secret society called the Tristero. She travels across California, solving puzzles that gradually uncover this mystery. At the same time, she begins to doubt her own sanity, wondering if this supposed conspiracy may be a hoax or a hallucination.

The assignment to design an interpretative quest has two components: a six-page written paper combining features of a game design document and a traditional interpretative essay, as well as a small multimedia prototype of one part of the game. The design document in an English class integrates a formal description of gameplay with the interpretation of a literary text. Students create a context in which meaning can emerge by designing the components of the quest, including its spaces, NPCs, objects, and challenges. The design document should contain descriptions and analyses of these elements, including textual and contextual evidence explaining what they mean as well as reflection on how the students' own interpretative perspectives help to create this meaning.

Because of the role of space in shaping quests, adaptations of literary texts work best when the designer does not reproduce the events of the narrative in a strictly linear fashion but instead recreates spaces in which players can bring about some of these events and their meanings. Building on a fictional world already created by an author, the student translates these geographic features into a world of ideas that can be explored by players. This requires interpretative decisions, since a location such as the surrealist painting of Remedios Varo's tower described in *The Crying of Lot 49* could be read as

- an emblem of Oedipa's inescapable solipsism;
- a foreshadowing of her escape through the use of imagination;
- a range of intermediate possibilities.

Many of the most successful essays based their game concepts around spaces represented in Varo's art, since Pynchon prominently alludes to her painting "Embroidering Earth's Mantle" as a recurrent metaphor in the novel. This topic helped to generate game ideas because Varo's painting represents a dreamlike space conducive to a quest plot: a tower in which a group of captive girls weaves a tapestry that, paradoxically, contains the world. Moreover, the sequence of three paintings in the triptych that Pynchon alludes to suggests the structure of a journey in three stages (approaching the dreamlike world, imprisonment, and escape), which provides the potential outline for a quest.

Students produced three different analytical approaches to the thematic significance of these paintings and three different ways of enacting these interpretations in gameplay, all of them taking place within the metaphorical space of Varo's paintings. One student argued that the paintings suggest the mind's ability to escape the confines of socially constructed reality through the higher reality of the imagination—the etymological meaning of the "surreal" as practiced by Varo. A second student used the space of the Varo painting as the setting for a different game that takes the opposite interpretative stance, in which the weaving of the tapestry reflects Oedipa's solipsistic entrapment within a reality entirely created by her own mind. A third student named Annie Neugebauer synthesized these two interpretations, suggesting that her game design will reward players who remain open to both surrealistic and solipsistic views of the space of the Varo painting. In a highly nuanced thesis statement, this student writes, "If Oedipa could easily choose a side, she would then cease to touch the 'real world' that she so longs to find—creating the paradox that as long as Oedipa looks for 'reality,' or *life,* she lives in it; but as soon as she assumes she has found it, it ceases to exist for her" (Neugebauer). Neugebauer's thesis suggests one way in which visualizing *The Crying of Lot 49* spatially allowed a student to develop stylistically nuanced and argumentatively self-conscious writing that was flexibly open to the idea of interpretative indeterminacy.

Other teachers could benefit from this result by allowing students to design spaces that map the world of ideas onto simulated geographical space, including imagined and artistic spaces within the work of literature, such as Jane Eyre's ambiguously emblematic paintings or Achilles' encyclopedically engraved shield in *The Iliad.* Encouraging students to design these conceptual spaces as well as "actual" or "realistic" locations within literary narratives could also help accommodate literature from a variety of periods to the constraints of role-playing toolsets, which often feature fantastic medieval landscapes that lend themselves to allegory.

Despite the richly multivalent signifying potential of spatial allegories, students who are adapting literary works into interpretative quests need to be reminded that an awareness of labyrinthine indeterminacy should not become an excuse for an utter lack of interpretative commitment. In other words, students should design their spaces to balance openness and rule-based constraint, one of the recurrent features of level design advocated by Natkin. One example of the rationale for this pedagogical principle appears in students' readings of the end of *The Crying of Lot 49,* in which Oedipa confronts four "symmetrical" choices about the secret society she has been pursuing:

- it is real;
- it is a hallucination;
- it is a hoax;
- it is the hallucination of a hoax (Pynchon 171).

These choices resemble the paths through a labyrinth, each of which gives rise to further choices and multiple, disorienting endings. Thinking of *The Crying of Lot 49* as the basis for an adventure or role-playing game, in which players often explore labyrinths, led several students to embrace this indeterminacy as an opportunity for the exploration of multiple meanings rather than to become frustrated by it.

However, students sometimes tended to come to rest complacently in the image, of the labyrinth or to assert it dogmatically, often as a criticism of scholars who had developed rigorously sustained arguments about a particular interpretation. While these students were well-intentioned, they sometimes seemed to use the image of the labyrinth as an excuse to avoid crafting their own theses, as when one student wrote that "Through creating this game, I realize that the entire book, *The Crying of Lot 49,* was just a labyrinth itself!" This student's phrase "just a labyrinth" suggests that she is satisfied with multiple interpretative paths rather than a single interpretation. Yet her suggestion that "the entire" book can be understood in this way is itself a totalizing argument that contradicts her other idea: that multiple readers can take different paths through the text. Such a view sometimes resulted in a lack of interpretative focus, as students celebrated different readers' abilities to choose a path through the space of the quest without themselves committing to such a path. This tendency in some student essays serves as a reminder that simulated space is only one part of a well-designed quest, which must also pose goal-oriented and rule-based challenges to the player in order to produce an immersive game and allow the enactment of meaning.

Prototypes

The prototypes that students made combined aspects of their individual design documents to form playable games through which players would enact the students' interpretations of a portion of the novel. Students worked during four in-class game workshops and were instructed to meet two to three times out of class. The initial workshops were devoted primarily to planning and note-taking regarding the game concepts, while later workshops involved working with computers in the classroom to make the games.

There were four group projects in my class in which students used three different major software applications and a mixture of other programs. Students produced two small but functional role-playing quests made with the Aurora Toolset. By mastering the menus and buttons of such a toolset as well as a system of dragging and dropping objects, students were able to construct an explorable environment in a relatively short amount of time. A third group produced a web-based Alternate Reality Game made using Dreamweaver, Photoshop, and digital cameras. Another produced one part of a puzzle game in Macromedia Flash. This was the least successful project because Flash yields the least sophisticated results without expertise and significant time investment, which meant that large amounts of student work translated into a rough final product. If I had the opportunity to do this assignment again, I might exclusively use the Aurora Toolset because it yields visibly exciting end results that encourage students and because its "Plot Wizard" and journal system are built entirely around the idea of quests. Hence, I will focus primarily on the work of groups one and two, who used the Aurora Toolset.

Group one's prototype, called *Oedipa's Quest,* centered around the "dreaming children" episode in *The Crying of Lot 49,* in which Oedipa encounters a group of children warming themselves at an "imaginary fire," who tell her that they are "dreaming the gathering" (Pynchon 118). After they do not answer her questions satisfactorily, Oedipa, "to retaliate," stops "believing in them" (Pynchon 119). To allow players to act out this scene, the students used the Aurora Toolset to build a small city with a town square. In this square, they constructed a circle of runes to represent the hieroglyphic posthorns that the children have scrawled on the ground, along with an "imaginary fire" made of magical sparks (Pynchon 118). Around this fire they placed children and then scripted conversations for them, creating dialogue trees with multiple forking paths of possible interaction with the children. The students also gave the children invisibility spells so that they would disappear when attacked, thereby representing Oedipa's refusal to believe in them.

After this encounter, players could enter a tower that the students built in order to represent the environment of Remedios Varo's "Embroidering Earth's Mantle" painting. The students furnished this space with mysterious and arcane objects, and then they placed an old man in the tower to represent Genghis Cohen, the stamp collector whom Oedipa encounters just before she sits down to await "the crying of lot 49" and the book's indeterminate ending in the auction room. Again using dialogue trees, the group scripted a conversation in which Cohen asks Oedipa to interpret her encounter with the children and gives her three possible answers: "solipsism," "surrealism," and "there is no answer. The point is to keep searching for the truth." The first two answers result in a rebuke from Cohen because of the player's excessive certainty in the face of ambiguity, while the third response earns the player praise and encouragement to continue gaining knowledge by exploring further. Students were pleased with this final product, but they sometimes showed frustration when the toolset could not accommodate aspects of their design document, such as allowing players to fill in blanks rather than select multiple choice answers in conversation. In future classes, an introduction to the capabilities of the toolset before students write the document would help to circumvent these disappointments.

A second group used the Aurora Toolset to create the most extensive and functional prototype of the class, the humorously titled *Polar Inverarity's Overtly Symbolic Quest.* This prototype was highly creative and could actually be played as a game, in part because the students made excellent use of the Aurora Toolset's "plot wizard" to create quest objectives without having to master a scripting language. This group built their project around a series of "fetch quests," in which players retrieve an item and bring it to another nonplayer character for a reward or to advance further in the game. Players of this group's game had to acquire a key from Pierce Inverarity to open an armoire containing a page from *The Courier's Tragedy* (a book discovered by Oedipa in *The Crying of Lot 49*), which offers a clue to talk to a dreaming child from Chapter 5.

The child sends the player to talk to the drunken sailor, who asks the player to deliver a letter through the underground postal service or "W.A.S.T.E. system." After the player does this, the sailor gives the player a golden posthorn, which must be returned to Pierce Inverarity. Each of the nonplayer characters' dialogues gives some explanation of the significance of the player's tasks, which the student group elaborates on in the notes for their presentation. The students write, "Our focus was on polar opposites in the novel, with an extreme emphasis on sacred and profane images. This is reflected in our setting, characters, and humor." The students thus organized their project around the religious subtext of Pynchon's novel, as first analyzed by Edward Mendelson in "The Sacred, the Profane, and *The Crying of Lot 49.*" The game is filled with clever allusions to the novel, and (as its name suggests) strongly symbolic.

However, the relationship between meaning and action in the second group's game is not as well integrated as in *Oedipa's Quest,* in part because the students became a little too immersed in the whimsical humor of their game. Students created a world in which Pierce Inverarity has been transformed into a polar bear, and random creatures such as talking penguins periodically appear. Nevertheless, because the group also strove to be faithful to the details of Pynchon's text, they found that elements they originally intended to be humorous acquired meaning within the context of the quest. Indeed, Pynchon's idea of a "high magic to low puns" suggests that his own aesthetic draws its power from seemingly absurd jokes that reveal serious thematic implications upon a second look (Pynchon 129). Thus, the "polar" bear in the group's prototype led them to think about "polar" opposites running through the organization of their game, in which each object, character, and setting has its mirrored, symmetrical counterpart. Kimbrell summarizes these students' work in the write-up for their group:

> We split the geography into two separate but equal parts. Where one side has a very nice house, the other side has a slummy inn. One side has a nice garden with children and flowers; the other side contains ruins and skeletal remains. [. . .]The areas are separated by the river, water, a polar molecule. A single bridge connects the two, representing how sacred and profane are eternally linked within the novel's universe.

Chance puns on the word "polar" yield an organizational principle for the quest, in which the player must help an isolated, marginalized sailor to communicate through an underground postal box in the middle of town, thereby bridging the sacred and the profane both figuratively and literally.

In addition to this successful use of emblematic spaces, students wrote not only about the spaces of the quest but about its rules and challenges, in order to emphasize that a quest is a goal-oriented search for meaning rather than unfocused wandering through multiple interpretations. Classroom game design need not consist primarily of a set of rules that the instructor imposes upon a class in order to guide discussion; rather, students should be at least partially responsible for designing these rules if gaming is to fulfill the promise of interactivity. When students supported their ideas about gameplay with interpretative analyses of the book, they produced a context for meaning that was both creative and interpretative.

For example, Jason Kimbrell designed an action game about Pynchon's use of Jungian shadow archetypes. In this game, players would have not only standard combat moves but also an "interpret" move, akin to the "combo" or "finishing" moves in martial arts games. The interpret move would give characters the opportunity to experience sympathy for a demonized and shadowy Other, thereby humanizing an enemy instead of defeating it. Kimbrell writes:

> As enemies in the game, the Shadow will be portrayed as monsters. Oedipa has two options while fighting these creatures. She can kill them, like a normal action game, or she can 'interpret' them. Once she initiates the command, a quick cut-scene plays revealing the monster as a human being and Oedipa learns a special move specific to that monster. The downside to this is that interpretation has a high fail rate, which makes execution difficult. (Kimbrell 2006)

Kimbrell thus retained the challenge and violence of the typical "kill quest" in gameplay that required players to enact subtle, postmodern, and self-reflective ideas about tolerance for the demonized Other. His gameplay is metaintepretative, introducing interpretation as itself a move in the game, but one that is rendered not only as an abstract cognitive maneuver but as a difficult "combo move" in a well-designed martial arts combat game. Instructors uncomfortable with the violence of video games or who seek to encourage readings of bloody epics and romances through the more reflective lens of postcolonial or feminist theory could use this student's idea as a template for alternative approaches to *Beowulf,* the Arthurian legends, or any text that prominently features a protagonist challenged with slaying a monstrous Other.

Further inquiry into the theory and practice of quest design will allow literary scholars, games researchers, and game designers to find linkages between a tradition of games extending from *King's Quest* to *The Elder Scrolls IV: Oblivion,* as well as from Homer's *The Odyssey* to *The Crying of Lot 49.* As the academic study of games matures, the study of quests offers a possible bridge between games and narratives that can help us to progress beyond the divisive ludology versus narratology debate without losing sight of the venerable, implied questions about interpretative freedom, imagination, and the human search for meaning that made this debate so fierce in the first place.

Moreover, further research into the history and theory of quests can take its place among a variety of studies of particular game genres that emerge as new media researchers move past the first discipline-founding steps of game studies and into the specific inquiries that will bear the fruit of this discipline. The importance of studying quests specifically can only increase as MMORPGs and RPGs for the next-generation consoles boast of quest systems that contain thousands of side quests, often interlaced with an epic main quest whose dramatic sweep still corresponds to the ancient model of the hero's journey.

Because quests are also a structural paradigm that connects hundreds of literary works from myriad periods and genres, pedagogical applications of quests can potentially benefit humanities teachers in a broad range of educational situations. These applications could range from honors seminars introducing students to ancient epics, to thematic classes about the relationship between new media and literature, to single-author "major figures" courses on authors as diverse as Edmund Spenser and Thomas Pynchon. The most productive questions about quests may come from a design perspective, addressing the issue of how to relate theoretical understandings of quests to their enactment in gameplay. Since quests operate as a formal structure in narrative and an activity in games, the adaptation of narratives into games requires not just a theoretical consideration of interactivity but of the practical action that scholars, educators, and designers can themselves take in order to produce this interactivity. We should ask ourselves what technological skillsets might be required in order to produce meaningful action in games, and how we might use strategies derived from the literary tradition of quest games to create this action.

Strategies for Creative Quest Design

If adapting a narrative into a quest game can involve modifying game mechanics through scripting as well as actualizing the potential interactivity of a printed text, this potential for creative innovation within preexisting narratives and games raises the question of whether designers might use similar ideas to create their own quests. Would it be possible to create equally meaningful action without necessarily adapting a literary text like *Sir Gawain and the Green Knight*, *The Faerie Queen*, or *The Crying of Lot 49*? The answer is yes; what we gain from studying the history and theory of both quest games and quest narratives is actually a set of strategies for designing meaningful action. These strategies can but do not have to depend on a preexisting literary narrative. Rather, designers may use these techniques to intervene within the lore or mythos of a fictional world, including a world of their own invention.

Both these strategies and the practical skills associated with them can operate within a variety of contexts, whether the work is done by independent studios or by students studying game design as a form of creative writing. Modding teams like Dragonlance Adventures and Rogue Dao Studios are increasingly using the Aurora Toolset and NWN2 Toolset to build professionally polished modules with vast amounts of custom content, which can then be widely distributed. A similar commercial project, *The Witcher,* was produced by a Polish team using an overhauled version of the Aurora Toolset licensed from Bioware. Modding is, in effect, becoming a form of independent game design, with *Neverwinter Nights* modules competing in the most recent Independent Games Festival.

In order to use the material in this book within such contexts, the history and theory of quests can be distilled into four strategies for creative quest design.

1. Create a dream-like, surreal space that both immerses players in a world of ideas and offers a sense of challenge and progression between the starting point and the goal of a quest.

2. Design symbolic objects that both function within gameplay and reveal portions of a fragmented story, sometimes dispersed through the game world according to the principle of the "rod of seven parts."

3. Develop characters who serve crucial functions in giving, helping, or impeding quests. Supply them with sparse but memorable dialogue that motivates the player to embark on quests

but also offers some choice as to which tasks to accept and how
to perform them.

4. Script meaningful interactions that allow players to overcome
    challenges through strategic gameplay that also conveys ideas,
    such as the magic system of *Eternal Darkness* or the virtue sys-
    tem of the *Ultima* games.

Clive Barker and Quest Design in the Interactive Parallel Universe

To most fully realize these strategies for creating innovative quest games, we
should turn not only to the history of such games but to their future as well.
In the keynote address entitled "The Interactive Parallel Universe," given at
the 2007 Hollywood and Games Summit, novelist and game designer Clive
Barker insisted upon the potential of game design as an expressive medium
for creative artists of all types. Barker repeatedly paraphrased the poet and
mystic William Blake, whose character Los declares in the poem *Jerusalem*
that "I must Create a System or be Enslav'd by another man's" (152). Barker
gave his own gaming spin to this dictum, revising it to "create your own laws
or be enslaved by another man's," encouraging both designers and players to
break preconceived rules of the artistic status or potential of games in order
to reach "undreamed-of territories unique to the medium."

Barker epitomizes the potential for creative interplay between quest
games and quest narratives. He has executed both quest narratives and quest
games as well as exploring strategies for creating one on the basis of the other.
In an interview about his quest-based horror game *Undying*, Barker was specifically asked about the role of quests in games and narratives. Asked whether he still believed that quests were nonlinear and circular because of the
protagonist's progress from external to internal wisdom, Barker responded,
"I still believe that. I certainly believe that quests are clearly nonlinear narratives. There's also very plainly [. . .] the idea about the pursuit of knowledge,
which begins as outward knowledge but ends as inward knowledge. It's certainly something we talked about as far as this game is concerned" (Twelker).
Barker's definition of a quest as a "nonlinear narrative" is complex, since he
has written linear narratives, designed nonlinear quests in games, and helped
adapt one into the other. For example, he describes his novel *Imajica* as a
"spiritual quest story" and *Everville* as a "dream-quest" (*People Online*, Bacal).
These quest narratives are linear tales of characters voyaging through alternate
realities, yet the potential nonlinearity of their branching paths becomes actualized in the games related to these narratives.

Because of these artistic experiences, Barker offers useful reflections on
quests from the perspective of a storyteller and a designer. In addition to

Undying, he is now at work with the game company Codemasters to produce a horror game called *Jericho* about what Chris Marlowe of the *Hollywood Reporter Online* calls a "perilous quest to reach the innermost chamber of a mysterious place called Jericho, wherein lurks evil incarnate."

What makes this game design project both unusual and relevant to those designing their own quests or adapting a preexisting fictional world is that Barker is quite literally filling in the gaps of his own 1987 novel, *Weaveworld.* Jericho will require players to navigate through a labyrinthine city called Al-Khali, consisting of "walls within walls within walls" like Russian dolls (Marlowe). Yet, as Barker explains, his first fictionalized description of the vast swath of Saharan desert called the Rub' al-Khali, or "Empty Quarter," appeared in *Weaveworld.* Barker clarifies, "I've actually had the idea for this game [Jericho] for a long time. The Rub' al-Khali, which is where the game takes place, was in *Weaveworld,* but it occupies maybe 50 pages of that 800-page book, so I knew I'd have to go back to this place" (Semel). Indeed, the Rub' al-Khali as described in *Weaveworld* is a vast void surrounded by walls, with only the outlines of a paradise that would dimly appear and then disappear. While literary critics such as Wolfgang Iser have claimed that readers fill in the gaps of texts through their imagination, Barker goes further by suggesting that he himself can begin to fill in the gaps of a former text in a game format, using the game to allow players to explore various paths that the author did not take (Iser 1-45).

In addition to filling in the gaps of a former narrative spatially, Barker suggests that games can open up paths that had to be closed off while constructing the single linear narrative of a novel. As Daemon Hatfield's IGN article on *Jericho* explains, "Barker was drawn by a videogame's potential to allow the player to explore many paths in a story, rather than the one path viewers experience in a book or movie." Indeed, when describing the transformation of his self-described quest narrative of *Imajica* into a collectible card game in the style of *Magic: The Gathering,* Barker sees the ability to open up closed-off paths as a "glorious undoing" of his own work, a reversal of the novel's multiple possibilities into the final path of the completed book in which "the roads which I chose not to take in the book are once more available for the traveling." Barker views this process as a matter of reintroducing play into the narrative in all of its senses, including strategic calculation, chance, and spiritual celebration of creativity.

Questing in the Transmedia Multiverse

Multimedia artists like Clive Barker operate in a media landscape that is increasingly tending toward what Henry Jenkins has called "transmedia" creativity, in which multiple media like movies, games, and graphic novels converge to produce related storytelling or entertainment experiences. Geoffrey Long has theorized one application of this principle as "transmedia storytelling," which involves deliberately making use of the imaginative gaps created by plot holes in a story. These gaps can then be filled by telling other parts of the story in parallel media.

Extending this idea metaphorically, a game can become an alternate universe or parallel dimension to linear narrative mediums, allowing players to explore the implications of a mythology in idiosyncratic and personal ways. Barker eloquently expresses this relationship between interpretative and configurative play as well as between literature and gaming when he praises games for their "length," "complexity," and "elaboration of mythology." He explains, "Games are literary. A well-constructed game is a puzzle, a story, a philosophy. When people walk into a theater, the same movie plays for everyone. But games can reflect your personal tastes and shape themselves to you the way a novel does" (Semel). Quest games and quest narratives are powerful tools for artists working within the transmedia environment that Barker celebrates. Indeed, many classic quests games, like *The Bard's Tale III* and *Ultima Underworld II,* require players to voyage through multiple alternate dimensions that constitute not just a universe but a "multiverse." Quest design is not only a matter of adapting narrative material, but of exploring an "interactive parallel universe" that exists alongside the work of fiction, or a dreamworld alongside its waking reality. In seeking to realize the fullest future potential of quests in games and narratives, we may increasingly find ourselves questing within a transmedia multiverse.

This appendix discusses the NWN2 toolset, which was included with the role-playing game *Neverwinter Nights 2,* released in 2006. The NWN2 Toolset is a refinement and extension of the Aurora toolset rather than a radical break with it. Every exercise, theory, and tutorial in the main section of the book can be completed using the Aurora Toolset. At the same time, the NWN2 Toolset builds upon the Aurora Toolset, offering a few new features that reflect advances in technology as well as an interface refined by long years of development.

Because technologies progress quickly, it is worthwhile to know about the new features of the NWN2 toolset, both for practical purposes if one has access to it and for theoretical understanding of the technical resources underlying contemporary quest design. The relationship among all the components of the quest is made possible by the toolset that helps designers arrange these elements. Toolset interfaces and assets are shaped by the theoretical understandings of designers, which are in turn constrained by the form of the toolset.

Because of this interrelationship between technology and theory, the appendix follows the overall pattern of the book, discussing strategies for designing the spaces, objects, and challenges that produce meaningful action in quests. While the NWN2 toolset has new features, I am focusing only on those that are relevant to designing more sophisticated and expressive quests. These new features are:

- a shift from tile-based level design to terrain mapping and texturing;
- increasing customization of NPCs;
- a streamlined conversation editor that smooths the workflow of quest design by accepting input from parameters.

For the purposes of this appendix, I will reference a module I am building based on *The Faerie Queen* called "Redcrosse Knight's Quest." This is an extension of the *Faerie Queen* exercises throughout the main text.

Constructing an Area in the NWN2 Toolset

1. Select File – New – Area from the dropdown menu at the upper left hand side of the screen. Choose area type as "exterior." There is no need to select a particular landscape type, because exterior areas are built by shaping and texturing terrain with brushes rather than snapping together tiles.

2.   Press the Day/Night button and select the preferred lighting for your time of day. For example, in the Redcrosse Knight's battle with the dragon, I want the area to have an ominous, reddish tint, for which sunset lighting is perfect.

3.   Locate the "Blueprints" window at the right hand side of the screen. Detach it from the background of the toolset by left-clicking on the dots at the top of the window. Enlarge it by dragging any of its edges. (One of the virtues and difficulties of the NWN2 Toolset in comparison to its predecessor is the way that its workspace can be customized. This allows you to arrange windows in a pattern that best fits your own work habits, but it also means that you can sometimes lose track of a key window by hiding it or shrinking it down. If this happens, select View – Options – Windows; then press the Reset button and OK. Close and restart your toolset, and all of the windows will be back in their default positions.[1])

4.   Select "Placeables" from the "Blueprints" window, and press the "+" button to maximize the group of objects that suits your needs. For example, in the Redcrosse Knight's Quest module, I need to represent Una's parents' kingdom as laid waste by the dragon, so I will place many items, such as "ruins," a "broken tower," and "a burned barn." To place architecture in an exterior area, select "Building Props." Select a placeable by clicking on it. A "ghosted" (semitransparent) version of this object will appear on your cursor, and you can "paint" an instance of it down by clicking once.

       Important: To remove this object from your cursor after painting an instance of it, press "esc." Otherwise, you will paint many instances down because the placeable will be "stuck" to your cursor and will be painted each time you left-click.

5.   To raise land, lower land, or add water to your area, you need to select the "Terrain" tab, next to the "blueprints" tab at the bottom of the "Blueprints" window. This will bring up four buttons ("Terrain," "Texturing," "Grass," and "Water"). Press the "Terrain" button, and you will bring up eight buttons controlling eight brushes, of which the easiest three to master are "Raise," "Lower," and "Flatten." To use one of these brushes, left-click and hold on an area of terrain that you want to shape. The longer you hold, the more effect you will have on the land, through shaping a deeper hole or a higher hill. The three slid-

ers and boxes directly under the word "brush" allow you to adjust the shape of the "brush," indicated onscreen by a circle within circle. "Size" adjusts the overall diameter of the circles.

Creating NPCs in the NWN2 Toolset

1. Click on the "creature" button in the "Blueprints" window.
2. Right-click in the white space of this window and select "copy blueprint" from the drop-down menu. Select a creature of the type that you want to create, such as a "human" (or an "elf," since many characters in *The Faerie Queen* are elfin); then drag to "module." A new blueprint of the name "human" will appear in boldface at the end of the list of creatures in the category you have selected. Right-click this new blueprint and select "rename" to give it a unique identifier, such as "Una." Creating a creature by copying a blueprint and then modifying the creature's traits is a good practice, since creatures created from scratch tend to be missing many useful default features, such as standard scripts for responding to attacks.
3. In the "properties" window, click on the "appearance" line to select the racial form of your character, ranging from human to dragon to everything in between.
4. Each of the lines in this window allows you to customize one aspect of the NPC. You cannot modify individual body parts, though you can customize the face and facial hair by selecting various numbers in these lines. To change any feature of the NPC, left-click on the line associated with this trait, which will bring up a new menu or window that allows you to change aspects of the character. These lines are the equivalent of the tabs and boxes in the Aurora Toolset, updated to give the windows a more compressed appearance.

For the purposes of quests, the two most important features of these blueprints are the "conversation" window and the "inventory" window. NPCs often serve either as "quest givers" who initiate a task and then reward the player when it is completed or as "donors" who give an important item needed to complete the quest. These functions depend upon the objects that the NPCs have to give, either as rewards or as tools.

Moreover, the visual appearance of a character frequently identifies his or her role in the quest, and the easiest way to modify the "costume" of an NPC is to assign objects to his or her inventory. To do this in the NWN2

Toolset, click the "inventory" tab and then push the "edit" button. A new inventory window will open with three areas: a space that displays items in the NPC's inventory, a set of expandable list of all possible items within the game, and a set of slots on the right hand side of the screen. To assign items to an NPC, select them and drag them into the appropriate slots, which indicate the placement of items on various parts of the body, such as "head," "chest," and "right hand."

5.   The advantage of the NWN2 Toolset over its predecessor in NPC creation is the finely nuanced ability to tweak the appearance and features of the character, rather than choosing from a set of predefined appearances. This allows designers to create an NPC whose form fits his function in gameplay, as well as to adapt the details of a literary text with great accuracy. Dragging a tunic onto the "chest" of a human character can give him the appearance of nobility, and putting a golden circlet on his head can elevate a nobleman to the appearance of a king. Combining the "human, old, melancholy" soundset with great age and a very low constitution (as well as some severe ailments) allows designers to create Anfortas, the Fisher King of the Grail cycle, whose appearance and attributes will inspire a player to want to heal him.

Quest Workflow in the NWN2 Toolset

Quests in NWN2 are constructed in much the same way as in the Aurora Toolset, but there are some refinements in the journal, conversation editor, and scripting system that make the workflow a little more streamlined.

1.   The heart of the quest system is the journal editor, which you open by selecting "view," then "journal," then "module."
2.   Right-click on the node labeled "root" and drag the menu to "add category" to designate a category in the journal for a quest.
3.   In the "journal category" box at the bottom of the screen, fill in the "name" line with the title of your quest as you would like it to appear in the player's journal, such as "slay the dragon."
4.   Give the quest a priority ranging from "low" to "high," assign the amount of experience you would like the player to receive from completing the quest, and give the quest a unique tag.
5.   To fill in specific journal entries for each quest, right-click on the category node and select "add entry." Each entry will be

one thread in the network of quests that constitutes your module, either as a main quest that drives forward the storyline of the game or a side quest that grants players experience or items.

6. In the journal entry box at the bottom of the screen, add a number for the journal, preferably in increments of 10 or 20 in order to have room to add entries in between.

7. In the small square box at the right side of the screen, under the "editscreenref" button, fill in the text that should be in each journal entry at each stage in the quest.

8. When you have entered all the entries for each journal category, open the conversation editor by clicking on the "area contents" tab followed by the "conversations" tab. Click anywhere in the blank white space that appears below "conversations"; then drag the menu to "add." The new conversation will appear as "conversation1," and you can rename it by right-clicking on it and typing a unique name over the generic one.

9. Right-click on "root"; then drag to "add" to create a new conversation node, which is the first one that the NPC will speak when greeting the player. Right-click on this node and drag to "add" again in order to attach a player character's response. As in the Aurora Toolset, conversations consist of alternating nodes between PCs and NPCs. You create multiple possible PC responses by attaching several PC branches to the same NPC node. Moreover, you can attach nodes at different "levels" of a conversation to create larger branches that deal with radically different topics and minor forks that discuss nuances or variants of specific topics.

In terms of overall quest flow, three of the four tabs at the left bottom of the screen are extremely important: "conditions," "actions," and "node."

- "Conditions" regulates under what circumstances a conversation node will appear by applying various scripts that check for variables in the game state, such as whether a PC is carrying an object or whether a local integer has been set to a particular value. In terms of quest flow, the most important condition to check is whether the journal has updated to a certain stage. To attach a script that performs this function, click the conditions tab and the word "add" above the green box at the bottom of the screen. Then, under the "script" box, drag the menu down to "gc_journal_entry." Press the "refresh" button to the right of this box to bring up boxes for entering parameters to be passed to the script.

This ability to pass parameters into scripts is one of the most useful new features of the NWN2 Toolset, because it allows designers to "feed" certain values (such as numbers and tags) into scripts without having to rewrite or copy the scripts each time. In the case of the "gc_journal_entry" script, the two parameters required are "sQuestTag" (the tag that you assigned to the journal category of the quest) and "sCheck" (the number of the journal entry that must be reached before the conversation node fires). Similarly useful prewritten scripts include "gc_check_item," which checks for a particular item in the PC's inventory (or that of her party members) through the parameter "sItem" (the item tag). Fetch quests can be easily constructed by attaching this script to a node with the "conditions" tab. There is also a script specifically designed to check for the quest state that the PC or any party members have reached, differing from the "gc_journal_entry" script in that "<" or ">" signs can be used to check whether the quest state is any value greater than or less than a particular integer. Any script with a name beginning in "gc" can be used to check for a conditional that must return true before a conversation node will fire, if the appropriate parameters are entered.

- "Actions" determines what will occur after each conversation node fires, such as when an NPC gives the PC an item as a reward. Prewritten scripts for standard actions associated with conversation nodes have names beginning in "ga," such as "ga_give_item." This script is frequently used in the final "reward" stage of a quest to give an item indicated by the parameter "sTemplate," which consists of the item's blueprint ResRef.

- "Node" controls many aspects of a particular branch in the conversation related to NWN2's advanced system of displaying conversations in cinematic cut-scenes, such as what animation occurs as a PC speaks or the camera angle from which the conversation appears. For the purposes of quest flow, the box labeled "Quest" in the node properties is extremely useful, since it allows designers to specify a journal category and entry number that the journal will automatically be advanced to after the dialogue node fires.

10. Quest progress can be registered in the NWN2 Toolset through a combination of journal entries and conversation nodes with conditions, actions, and "Quest" settings that bump the quest forward to the next appropriate journal entry when the player has accomplished designated tasks. At the same time, many subquests can involve more sophisticated forms of quest progression that require setting local variables and a variety of other scripting functions. In addition to fetch quests and kill quests, NWN2 is particularly amenable to quests that involve activating a specified number of placeable items. In the official campaign, the player must activate five Iletharn statues to perform a ritual of purification that grants him special abilities, and the progress of this quest is tracked in the journal. Another quest asks players to activate nine statues beneath Castle Never and answer their riddles, with right and wrong answers either lessening or increasing the number of monsters.

Similar quests can be created fairly easily by attaching scripts to the "OnUsed" handle of a placeable object such as an altar or a statue. For example, one quest in my module involves the player as Redcrosse Knight trying to activate seven altars, each of which intones an evil chant and summons a monster to be defeated. These altars are placed at the end of each corridor in a dungeon in the shape of a monster with seven heads, alluding to the seven-headed beast of the biblical book of Revelations that Spenser associates with Roman Catholicism and idolatry. When all seven altars have been activated, the evil wizard Archimago appears in the center of the maze. A variable used as a "counter" tracks the number of altars out of the required seven that have been activated and updates the journal accordingly.

This counter must be set by retrieving the number of altars activated so far and adding one to them, programmed as "n = n + 1". A counter in the form of a local variable works well because setting a specific quest stage attached to each altar would require the player to find the altars in a particular linear sequence. A more flexible and nonlinear script would use a "switch-case" structure to test the number of altars activated and then provide the appropriate journal entry: "x out of 7 altars have been activated." The functions "CreateObject," "ApplyEffect," and "PlaySound" all add a level of dynamic responsiveness to the quest in addition to setting local variables and journal updates. The script for this quest should be placed in the "OnUsed" handle of each altar and read as follows:

```
void main ()
// Scripting a quest to activate seven altars
// If the player hasn't activated an altar yet, the local
// variable "numberofaltarsactivated"
// will return 0, which is what we want it to do.
{
  int nAltars = GetLocalInt (GetModule(),
   "numberofaltarsactivated");
  // Check if this altar has already been activated. If it
  // has not, activate it and update the journal.
  int nActivated = GetLocalInt (OBJECT_SELF,
   "alreadyactivated");
  if (nActivated == 0)
  {
    nAltars = nAltars + 1;
    // Check how many altars have been activated and update
    // the journal accordingly.  Spawn in a creature when
    // each altar is activated.
    // Now set the new value of nAltars as a local variable
    // so that the next script will know how many altars
    // have been activated.
    SetLocalInt (GetModule(), "numberofaltarsactivated",
     altars);

    object oPC = GetLastUsedBy();
    location lSpawn = GetLocation (oPC);
    switch (nAltars)
    {
      case 1:
      AddJournalQuestEntry("altars", 10, oPC);
      CreateObject (OBJECT_TYPE_CREATURE, "c_skeleton",
       lSpawn, TRUE);
      break;
      case 2:
      AddJournalQuestEntry("altars", 20, oPC);
      CreateObject (OBJECT_TYPE_CREATURE, "c_skeleton",
       lSpawn, TRUE);
```

```
   break;
   case 3:
   AddJournalQuestEntry("altars", 30, oPC);
   CreateObject (OBJECT_TYPE_CREATURE, "c_skeleton",
     lSpawn, TRUE);
   break;
   case 4:
   AddJournalQuestEntry("altars", 40, oPC);
   CreateObject (OBJECT_TYPE_CREATURE, "c_skeleton",
     lSpawn, TRUE);
   break;
   case 5:
   AddJournalQuestEntry("altars", 50, oPC);
   CreateObject (OBJECT_TYPE_CREATURE, "c_skeleton",
     lSpawn, TRUE);
   break;
   case 6:
   AddJournalQuestEntry("altars", 60, oPC);
   CreateObject (OBJECT_TYPE_CREATURE, "c_skeleton",
     lSpawn, TRUE);
   break;
   case 7:
   AddJournalQuestEntry("altars", 70, oPC);
   // Because all seven altars have been activated,
   // spawn in Archimago at the center of the dungeon.
   location larchimagotarget = GetLocation
     (GetWaypointByTag("archimagowaypoint"));
   CreateObject (OBJECT_TYPE_CREATURE, "archimago",
     larchimagotarget, FALSE);
   // Play an evil portal sound when Archimago is
   // summoned.
   PlaySound ("al_mg_portal4");
   break;
   }
// Now set a local variable to store the fact that this
// altar has been activated,
// so that the player can't keep activating it and
// getting more journal entries.
SetLocalInt (OBJECT_SELF, "alreadyactivated", 1);
// And apply a permanent red glow to the altar so that
// the player can tell which ones have been activated.
```

```
    effect eRedGlow = EffectVisualEffect
      (VFX_DUR_LIGHT_RED_10);
    ApplyEffectToObject (DURATION_TYPE_PERMANENT,
      eRedGlow, OBJECT_SELF);
    // Play the sound of magical chanting to alert the
    // player that the altar has been activated.
    PlaySound ("al_mg_chntmagic1");
  }
  // If the altar has already been activated, do nothing
  // and tell the player why.
  else
  {
    object oPC = GetLastUsedBy();
    SendMessageToPC(oPC,
      "This altar has already been activated.");
  }
}
```

Notes

[1] This tip comes from Gilthonym's "Don't Panic" tutorials.

Sir Gawain and the Green Knight
Books I and II

Translation by Paul Deane
Sir Gawain translation copyright © 1997-2000 Paul Deane. Available on the web at
Forgotten Ground Regained, http://www.alliteration.net. Reprinted by permission.

Historical Prologue

(1)

The siege and assault having ceased at Troy
as its blazing battlements blackened to ash,
the man who had planned and plotted that treason
had trial enough for the truest traitor!
Then Aeneas the prince and his honored line
plundered provinces and held in their power
nearly all the wealth of the western isles.
Thus Romulus swiftly arriving at Rome
sets up that city and in swelling pride
gives it his name, the name it now bears;
and in Tuscany Tirius raises up towns,
and in Lombardy Langoberde settles the land,
and far past the French coast Felix Brutus
founds Britain on broad hills, and so bright hopes
begin,
> where wonders, wars, misfortune
> and troubled times have been,
> where bliss and blind confusion
> have come and gone again.

(2)

From the founding of Britain by this brave prince,
bold men have bred there, burning for war,
stirring up turmoil through the turning years.
More wonders in the world have been witnessed here
than anywhere else from that age forward.
But of all who were crowned kings over Britain
the most honor was Arthur's, as old tales tell.
So I mean to make known a marvel on earth,
an astonishing sight, as some men would call it,
an extraordinary exploit among Arthur's wonders.

161

Listen to this lay for a little while
and as townsmen tell it, so this tale will trip
along,

       a story pinned in patterns
       steadfast, steady, strong:
       aligned in linking letters
       as folk have loved so long.

Book I: Christmas in Camelot

     (3)

One Christmas in Camelot King Arthur sat
at ease with his lords and loyal liegemen
arranged as brothers round the Round Table.
Their reckless jokes rang about that rich hall
till they turned from the table to the tournament field
and jousted like gentlemen with lances and laughs,
then trooped to court in a carolling crowd.
For the feast lasted a full fifteen days
of meals and merriment (as much as could fit.)
Such gay glee must gladden the ear --
by day what a din, and dancing by night!
The halls and chambers were heaped with happy
lords and ladies as high as you like!
There they were gathered with all the world's goodness:
knights as kind as Christ himself,
ladies as lovely as ever have lived,
and the noblest king our nation has known.
They were yet in the pride, in the prime of their youth,
and filled

       as full of heaven's blessing
       as the king had strength of will.
       And mighty men surpassing
       all were gathered on that hill.

     (4)

While the year was as young as New Years can be
the dais was prepared for a double feast.
The king and his company came in together
when mass had been chanted; and the chapel emptied
as clergy and commons alike cried out,
"Noel! Noel!" again and again.

And the lords ran around loaded with parcels,
palms extended to pass out presents,
or crowded together comparing gifts.
The ladies laughed when they lost at a game
(that the winner was willing, you may well believe!)
Round they milled in a merry mob till the meal was ready,
washed themselves well, and walked to their places
(the best for the best on seats raised above.)
Then Guinevere moved gaily among them,
took her place on the dais, which was dearly adorned
with sides of fine silk and a canopied ceiling
of sheer stuff: and behind her shimmering tapestries from far Tarsus,
embroidered, bedecked with bright gems
that the jewelers would pay a pretty price for
any day,

      but the finest gem in the field of sight
      looked back: her eyes were grey.
      That a lovelier's lived to delight
      the gaze - is a lie, I'd say!

    (5)

But Arthur would not eat till all were served.
He bubbled to the brim with boyish spirits:
liked his life light, and loathed the thought
of lazing for long or sitting still longer.
So his young blood boiled and his brain ran wild,
and in many ways moved him still more
as a point of honor never to eat
on a high holiday till he should have heard
a strange story of stirring adventures,
of mighty marvels to make the mind wonder,
of princes, prowess, or perilous deeds.
Or someone might come, seeking a knight
to join him in jousting, enjoying the risk
of laying their lives on the line like men
leaving to fortune the choice of her favor.
This was the king's custom at court,
the practice he followed at pleasant feasts held
in his hall;

      therefore with bold face
      he stood there straight and tall.
      As New Years proceeded apace
      he meant to have mirth with them all.

(6)

So he stood there stock-still, a king standing tall,
talking of courtly trifles before the high table.
By Guinevere sat Gawain the Good,
and Agravaine of the Heavy Hand on the other side:
knights of great worth, and nephews to the king.
Baldwin, the bishop, was above, by the head,
with Ywain, Urien's son, sitting across.
These sat at the dais and were served with due honor;
and many mighty men were seated on either side.
Then the first course came with a clamor of trumpets
whose banners billowed bright to the eye,
while kettledrums rolled and the cry of the pipes
wakened a wild, warbling music
whose touch made the heart tremble and skip.
Delicious dishes were rushed in, fine delicacies
fresh and plentiful, piled so high on so many platters
they had problems finding places to set down
their silver bowls of steaming soup: no spot
was clear.
       Each lord dug in with pleasure,
       and grabbed at what lay near:
       twelve platters piled past measure,
       bright wine, and foaming beer.

(7)

I need say no more how they served the food,
for what fool would fancy their feast was a famine?
But a new noise announced itself quickly enough
to grant the high lord leave to have dinner.
The music had finished but a moment before,
the first course just served, and set before the court,
when a horrible horseman hurtled through the doors,
his body as brawny as any can be,
so bull-necked, big-thighed, bulky and square,
so long-legged, large-limbed, looming so tall
I can hardly tell if he were half troll,
or merely as large as living man can be --
a handsome one too; as hearty a hulk as ever rode horse.
His back and chest were broad as a barrel,
but he slimmed at the waist, with a slender stomach,
and his face was well formed, with features sharp
and clean --

Men sat there gaping, gasping
at his strange, unearthly sheen,
as if a ghost were passing,
for every inch was green.

(8)

He was got up in green from head to heel:
a tunic worn tight, tucked to his ribs;
and a rich cloak cast over it, covered inside
with a fine fur lining, fitted and sewn
with ermine trim that stood out in contrast
from his hair where his hood lay folded flat;
and handsome hose of the same green hue
which clung to his calves, with clustered spurs
of bright gold; beneath them striped embroidered silk
above his bare shanks, for he rode shoeless.
His clothes were all kindled with a clear light like emeralds:
His belt buckles sparkled, and bright stones were set
in rich rows arranged up and down
himself and his saddle. Worked in the silk
were too many trifles to tell the half of:
embroidered birds, butterflies, and other things
in a gaudy glory of green and inlaid gold.
And the bit and bridle, the breastplate on the horse,
and all its tackle were trimmed with green enamel,
even the saddlestraps, the stirrups on which he stood,
and the bows of his saddle with its billowing skirts
which glimmered and glinted with green jewels.
The stallion that bore him was the best of its breed
it was plain,

a green horse great and strong,
that sidled, danced and strained,
but the bridle-braid led it along,
turning as it was trained.

(9)

He was a fine fellow fitted in green --
And the hair on his head and his horse's matched.
It fanned out freely enfolding his shoulders,
and his beard hung below as big as a bush,
all mixed with the marvelous mane on his head,
which was cut off in curls cascading to his elbows,
wrapping round the rest of him

like a king's cape clasped to his neck.
And the mane of his mount was much the same,
but curled up and combed in crisp knots,
in braids of bright gold thread and brilliant green
criss-crossed hair by hair.
And the tossing tail was twin to the mane,
for both were bound with bright green ribbons,
strung to the end with long strands of precious stones,
and turned back tight in a twisted knot
bright with tinkling bells of burnished gold.
No such horse on hoof had been seen in that hall,
nor horseman half so strange as their eyes now held
in sight.

      He looked a lightning flash,
      they say: he seemed so bright;
      and who would dare to clash
      in melee with such might?

      (10)

Yet he had on no hauberk, nor a helmet for his head,
neither neck-guard nor breastplate to break heavy blows,
neither shaft nor shield for the shock of combat.
But he held in one hand a sprig of holly
that bursts out greenest when branches are bare;
and his other hand hefted a huge and awful ax,
a broad battleax with a bit to tell (take it who can)
with a large head four feet long:
the green steel down the grain etched with gold,
its broad edge burnished and bright,
shaped razor-sharp to sheer through steel,
and held high on a heavy staff
which was bound at the base with iron bands
gracefully engraved in bright green patterns.
A strap was strung through the steel head, running
loop after loop down the length of the handle,
which was tied with tassels in abundance, attaching
by rich braids onto bright green buttons.
This rider reined in as he rode through the doors
direct to the high dais without a word,
giving no greeting, gazing down on them all.
His first word came when he stopped. "Where," he said,
"is the master of these men? I've a mind to see
his face and would fancy a chat with the fellow who wears
the crown."

To each lord he turned
and glancing up and down
he fixed each face to learn
which knight held most renown.

(11)

They stared at the stranger, stunned, a very long time.
For each man wondered what it might mean
that man and mount both shone a shade
as green as the grass, and greener even
than green enamel glows when gold makes it brighter.
All eyes were on him, and some edged closer,
wondering what in the world he would do.
They had seen enough strange sights to know how seldom they are real;
therefore they feared him for a phantom, a sending from the Unseen Realm.
So of all those noble knights, none dared answer
but sat there stupefied by the strength of his voice.
A silence fell filling that rich hall as if they'd all fainted
or suddenly slept: their voices just vanished
at their height.
             Some, I suppose, were not floored,
                but chose to be polite,
                letting their leader and lord
                be first to speak to that knight.

(12)

Arthur stood watching adventure advance
and answered quickly as honor bid, neither awed nor afraid,
saying, "Wanderer, know you are welcome here.
dismount, if you may; make merry as you wish,
and we may learn in a little while what you would like."
"So help me God who sits on high," he said, "No."
"It is not my purpose to pass any time in this place.
But I have been told that your reputation towers to heaven:
that your court and castle are accounted the finest,
your knights and their steeds as the sturdiest in steel,
the best, the boldest, the bravest on earth,
and as fitting foes in any fine sport.
True knighthood is known here, or so the tale runs,
which is why I have come calling today.
You may be sure by this branch that I bear
that I come in peace, with no plans for battle.
I have a hauberk at home, and a helmet too,

and other weapons I know well how to wield.
Yet as war is not my wish I am wearing soft silk,
but, if you are as bold as men believe you to be,
you will be glad to grant me the game that is mine
by right."
        Then Arthur said, "I swear,"
        "most courteous, noble knight,
        if you'd like to battle bare,
        you'll not fail to find a fight."

    (13)

"Never fear," he said, "I'm not fishing for a fight
with the beardless children on the benches all about.
If I were strapped on steel on a sturdy horse
no man here has might to match me.
No, I have come to this court for a bit of Christmas fun
fitting for Yuletide and New Years with such a fine crowd.
Who here in this house thinks he has what it takes,
has bold blood and a brash head,
and dares to stand his ground, giving stroke for stroke?
Here! I shall give him this gilded blade as my gift;
this heavy ax shall be his, to handle as he likes.
and I shall stand here bare of armor, and brave the first blow.
If anyone's tough enough to try out my game,
let him come here quickly and claim his weapon!
I give up all rights; he will get it for keeps.
I'll stand like a tree trunk -- he can strike at me once,
if you'll grant me the right to give as good as I get
in play.
        But later is soon enough,
        a full year and a day.
        Get up, if you think you're rough,
        let's see what you dare to say!"

    (14)

If at first he had stunned them, now they sat stone-still:
the whole hall, both high and low.
The mounted man moved in his saddle,
glared a red glance grimly about,
arched his bushy brows, all brilliant and green,
his beard waving as he waited for one man to rise,
to call or came forward. He coughed loudly,
stretched slowly, and straightened to speak.

"Hah! They call this King Arthur's house,
a living legend in land after land?
Where have your pride and your power gone,
your bragging boasts, your big words?
The glories and triumphs of the Round Table
have toppled at the touch of one man's words!
What? Fainting with fear, when no fight is offered?"
He let out a laugh so loud that Arthur winced
with shame; the blood shot to his flushed face
and churned

> with rage and raised a storm
> until their hearts all burned.
> All king in face and form,
> he reached that rider, turned,

(15)

and said, "Look here, by heaven! Have you lost your mind?
If you want to be mad, I will make you welcome!
Nobody I know is bowled over by your big words,
so help me God! Hand me that ax --
I will grant you the gift you beg me to give!"
He leaped lightly up and lifted it from his hand.
Then the man dismounted, moving proudly,
while Arthur held the ax, both hands on the haft,
hefted it sternly, considered his stroke.
That burly man bulked big and tall,
a head higher than anyone in the house.
He stood there hard-faced, stroking his beard,
impassively watching as he pulled off his coat,
no more moved or dismayed by his mighty swings
than anybody would be if somebody brought him a bottle
of wine.

> Gawain, sitting by the queen,
> could tell the king his mind:
> "Lord, hear well what I mean,
> and let this match be mine."

(16)

"Grant leave, good lord," said Gawain to the king,
"to stir from my seat and stand by your side;
that I might rise without rudeness from this table
without fear of offending your fair queen,
and come before your court as a counselor should.
It is plainly improper, as people know well,

to point this proposal at the prince himself.
Though you may be eager to act for yourself,
there are so many bold knights on the benches all about,
none more masterful in mind maybe than move move under heaven,
nor many built better for the field of battle.
Of all your men of war I am the weakest and least wise,
and my life little enough to lose, if you look at it clearly.
My only honor is that you are my uncle;
my only boast is that my body carries your blood.
Since this whole matter is such a mockery, it is not meant for you;
and I am first on the field: let this folly be mine.
If my claim is uncalled-for let the court judge; I will bear
the blame."

> They huddled hushed around
> and all advised the same:
> respect the royal crown,
> and give Gawain the game.

(17)

Then the king commanded him to rise and come forward,
and he stood quickly, walked with stately steps
to kneel before the king and claim his weapon.
Arthur handed it over and held up his hand
to give him God's blessing. With a glad smile
he charged him to be hardy in heart.
"Cousin, careful," he said, "cut him but once.
and if you teach him truly, I trust you will find
you can bear the blow that he brings you later."
Gawain went to the warrior, weapon in hand,
not the least bit bashful, as bold as can be.
Then the Green Knight said to Gawain,
"We should go over our agreement before we begin.
First, knight, I would know your name,
told truly as one I can trust."
"My name is Gawain," he said, "I give it in good faith,
as I will give you a blow and bear what comes after.
At this time in twelve months I will take a blow back
from what weapon you wish, but from no other knight
alive."

> The other answering spoke,
> "Sir Gawain: good. I derive
> great pleasure from the stroke
> your hardy hands will drive."

(18)

"Gad!" the Green Knight said. "Sir Gawain, I am glad
that your fist will fetch me the fun I hoped to find.
You have quickly retold in trustworthy words
a correct account of the contract I asked of the king,
save one stipulation that I must state: let it stand as your oath
that you will seek me yourself, and search anywhere
you feel I may be found to fetch back the same wages
I am paid today before this proud court."
"Where should I look?" Gawain asked, "Where do you live?"
"By Him that made me, your house is not known to me,
neither do I know you, knight, nor your court nor your name.
But teach me truly, tell me where to find you
and I shall work my wits out to win my way there.
I give my plain promise; I pledge you my word."
"That is enough for a New Year's pledge; you need say no more,"
-- So the green man answered gracious Gawain --
"If I'm telling the truth, why, when I've taken your tap,
and you've lopped me lovingly, you'll learn at once
of my house and my home and how I am named.
Then you can try my hospitality and be true to our compact.
Or I'll have no words to waste, which would be well for you:
you'd relax in this land, and not look for me further.
But stop!
   Take up the grim tool you need,
   and show me how you chop."
   "Gladly, sir," he said, "Indeed,"
   and gave the ax a strop.

(19)

The green knight got ready, feet firm on the ground;
leaned his head a little to let the cheek show,
and raised the rich riot of his hair
so the nape of his neck was naked and exposed.
Gawain held the ax high overhead,
his left foot set before him on the floor,
swung swiftly at the soft flesh
so the bit of the blade broke through the bones,
crashed through the clear fat and cut it in two,
and the brightly burnished edge bit into the earth.
The handsome head fell, hit the ground,
and rolled forward; they fended it off with their feet.

The red blood burst bright from the green body,
yet the fellow neither faltered nor fell
but stepped strongly out on sturdy thighs,
reached roughly right through their legs,
grabbed his graceful head and lifted it from the ground,
ran to his horse, caught hold of the reins,
stepped in the stirrup, strode into the saddle,
the head dangling by the hair from his hand,
and seated himself as firmly in the saddle
as if he were unhurt, though he sat on his horse without
a head.
       He swiveled his bulk about;
       the ugly stump still bled.
       They gaped in fear and doubt
       because of the words he said.

    (20)

For he held the head up evenly in his hand,
turned the face toward the top of the high table,
and the eyelids lifted and looked on them all
while the mouth moved, making these words:
"Gawain, get ready to go as you have promised,
Seek me out, sir; search till you find me
as sworn here in this hall where all these knights heard.
I charge you, come as you chose to the Green Chapel to get
as good as you gave -- you've got it coming
and will be paid promptly when another year has passed.
Many men know me as the Knight of the Green Chapel,
so search faithfully and you'll not fail to find me.
Come, or be called a faithless coward!"
He roared like a raging bull, turned the reins,
and drove for the door, still dangling the head,
while fire flashed from the horse's feet as if its hooves were flints.
Where he went no one knew,
nor could they name the country he came from nor his kin.
What then?
       The king and Gawain grinned
       and laughed at the Green Knight when
       they knew full well it had been
       a portent to their men.

    (21)

Though High King Arthur's heart was heavy with wonder
he let no sign of it be seen, but said aloud

with a king's courtesy to his lovely queen:
"Beloved lady, never let this dismay you.
It is good to get such games at Christmas,
light interludes, laughter and song,
or the whole court singing carols in chorus.
But truly, I can turn now to my table and feast;
as my word is good, I have witnessed a wonder."
He turned to Sir Gawain and tactfully said,
"Hang up your ax; it has cut all it can."
It was attached to a tapestry above the high table
for all men to marvel on who might see it there,
as a true token of a tale of wonder.
Then they sat in their seats to resume their feast,
Gawain and the king together, while good men served them
the rarest, dearest delicacies in double portions,
with whole batteries of the best foods, and the singing of bards.
The day finished, and their feast was filled with joy
and zest.

> Sir Gawain, have a care
> to keep your courage for the test,
> and do the deed you've dared.
> You've begun: now brave the rest.

Book II: Gawain's Journey

(Lines 491-784, sections 22-33)

(22)

This gift of adventure is what Arthur got
to bring in the year with the boasts he liked best.
Yet they said little, but sat, took their seats,
gorged with grim business heaped in their hands.
Gawain was glad when those games began,
but no one should wonder at the weighty ending.
Men's minds may grow merry when their drinks are mighty,
but a year paces past in unforeseen patterns:
The model seldom matches what is made.
So Yule raced by, and the year ran after,
each season passing in set sequence.
After Christmas comes the discomfort of Lent,
which tries the flesh with fish and simple food.
But then the world's weather wrestles with winter:
cold clings to the ground, but clouds rise,
releasing warm rain; rinsing showers

fall to the flat earth; flowers appear,
both field and forest are fringed with green.
Birds busy themselves building, and with brilliant song
celebrate summer, for soon each slope
will rush

> to bloom with blossoms set
> in lines luxuriant and lush,
> while noble notes form nets
> that fill the forest hush.

(23)

Then the summer season when the west breeze blows
and soft winds sigh on seed and stem.
How the green things glory in their urgent growth
when the dripping dew drops from the leaves,
waiting for the warm sun's welcome glance.
But then Fall flies in, and fills their hearts,
Bidding them be rich, ripe, and ready for winter.
The autumn drought drives up dust
that billows in clouds above the broad earth.
Wild winds whistle, wrestling the sun;
Leaves launch from each limb and land on the soil,
while the green grass fades to grey.
What rose at the first now ripens and rots
till the year has gathered its full yield of yesterdays.
In the way of the world, winter winds
Around

> til the Michaelmas moon
> brings frost to touch the ground.
> When Gawain remembers all too soon
> that he is duty bound.

(24)

Yet he lingered with Arthur past All Saints Eve
who set up a feast to send his knight off
with revelry rich as the Round Table offered.
Yet lordly knights and lovely ladies
gazing at Gawain anxious with grief
let nothing but laughter pass through their lips.
They made themselves merry for one man's sake.
Sad after supper he sought out his uncle,
spoke of his quest, and clearly proclaimed:
"My life's own liege lord, I ask now your leave.
What this matter means, and how much it costs

you know well enough: nothing worth words.
But soon after dawn I must search out onslaught
and meet the green man: may God be my guide."
Then the highest in that hall hastened together,
Iwain, and Erric, and many another –
Sir Dodinel de Sauvage, the Duke of Clarence,
Lancelot, and Lyonel, and Lucan the Good,
Sir Bors and Sir Bedivere (big men both)
And many proud lords, with Mador de la Port.
Thus the court collected and came near the king
to offer advice with anguished hearts.
So much secret sorrow swept through that hall
that one so good as Gawain must go forth doomed
to bear the brunt of a blow and let his own blade
rest.
    But Gawain said with cheerful face:
    "Why shrink back from the quest?
    Though fate bring glory or disgrace
    A man must meet the test."

   (25)

He rested till morning then rose to get ready,
asked early for his armor and they brought it all out,
arranging each piece on a rich, red rug
where the gear all glittered like a gallery of gold.
The strong knight stood there to take up his steel,
dearly dressed in a doublet of silk
and a hooded cloak cunningly made
with a lining of ermine layered inside.
His feet were fitted in fine steel shoes,
and his legs were sheathed in shining greaves
with kneeguards above them, burnished bright
and tied to his knees with tassels of gold --
Then cuisse-plates whose clever curves enclosed
his thick, hard thighs, and were bound there with thongs;
while the mesh of his mail-shirt with its rings of bright metal
richly quilted, wrapped him round,
and well-burnished braces on both of his arms,
gallant elbow-gear and gauntlets of steel,
and all the finest, fairest stuff to fit him
for his ride
    a surcoat richly made,
    his gold spurs worn with pride,

girt with a glistening blade,
a silk sash round his side.

(26)

When he got it all on his gear was splendid:
each loop and latch-hook lustrous with gold.
He left as he was, then listened to mass
offered in honor before the high altar,
came to the king and his court companions,
took loving leave of lords and ladies
in a crowd of kisses and hopes for Christ's care.
Gringolet was groomed and ready to go,
his gleaming saddle gaily fringed with gold
newly nailed there for this matter of note.
His striped bridle was bound with bright gold.
The pattern of the harness and the proud skirts,
of saddle-bow, caparison, crupper were all the same:
red arrayed with rich gold studs
that glinted and glittered like the glance of the sun.
Then he held up his helm and kissed it in haste:
It was stiffened with staples, padded with stuffing,
Sat high on his head, and buckled behind
where the neck-guard was graced with gleaming silk
bedecked and embroidered with the best gems.
There were birds on the seams of the broad silk bands:
painted parrots on a field of periwinkles,
turtledoves entwined with truelove blooms too thick
to be sewn by many women in seven winters'
care.

       Yet nothing half so dear
       brought color anywhere
       as the circlet's bright and clear
       diamonds in his hair.

(27)

When they brought him his shield, it was bright red gules,
painted with a pentacle of purest gold.
Holding the baldric, he hung it from his neck,
and the sign thus set suited him well.
Why the pentacle is proper to that noble prince
I must let you know, though I linger in the telling.
It is a sign that Solomon set long ago
to signify truth by a trustworthy token.

It is a figure with five fine points
and each line overlaps and locks with the others,
everywhere endless: the English, I hear,
most often call it the Endless Knot.
And so it fits this knight with his flashing armor,
who was faithful five ways and five times each.
All knew Gawain to be good as purified gold:
devoid of villainy, his virtues were a court's
delight.

> Thus he wore the five-point star
> on shield and surcoat in plain sight,
> his honor without stain or scar,
> a gentle, low-voiced knight.

(28)

First, he was found faultless in his five senses,
and his five fingers never failed him in any deed,
and all his faith in this world was in the five wounds
that Christ carried on the cross, as the Creed informs us.
No matter where he moved in melee or in battle
it was his fervent thought through thick or thin
that when he fought his courage came from the five joys
the high Queen of Heaven had of her child.
(And so the noble knight would never wear his shield
till her image had been painted on the inner half;
for when he saw her face his courage never failed.)
And a fifth five was found in Gawain:
bounty and brotherhood above all else;
courtesy and a clean heart (these were never crooked)
and the finest point, compassion -- these five virtues
marked him more than any man alive.
Now all these five fives were fastened round this knight
and each embraced the others in unbroken pattern
and met in five fixed points that never failed,
nor bunched together, nor split in pieces,
but ran on endlessly at every point --
where the figure failed, it found new beginnings.
Therefore the shield shone with the knot thus shaped,
gold royally arranged against red gules --
the noble pentacle as it is known by men
of lore.

> Now ready to go his way,
> he lifted his lance as if for war,

gave them all good day --
and left them there forevermore.

(29)

He set spurs to his steed and sprang on his way
so swiftly the sparks sprayed out behind him.
All that saw him so splendid sighed deep within
and whispered soft words one to another
in compassion for that prince: "By Christ, what a pity,
to lose such a leader, wh ose life is so noble!
There is hardly his equal anywhere on earth!
A wary approach would have been wiser;
better to have made such a man a duke --
such a brilliant leader; the best in the land.
Better by far than this foolish waste,
beheaded by an elf, and all for arrogant pride!
What kind of king would take such counsel
when his courtiers quarrel over Christmas games?
How the warm tears welled till all their eyes were wet
when that handsome lord left his home behind
that day,

> nor lingered on his road,
> but swiftly found his way.
> Through pathless realms he rode --
> so I heard the annal say.

(30)

So this rider rode through the realm of Britain,
Sir Gawain in God's service: and to him it was no game.
He would lie down alone with no one to lead,
nor find before him any food that he liked,
Nor any help but his horse over hill and wood,
Nor any man but his Maker to make conversation --
till he neared the neighborhood of North Wales,
held all the isles of Anglesey on his left
and reached the river where its headlands rose
high near Holyhead, and held on across
through the Forest of Wirral. Few or none lived there
whom God could love, or a good-hearted man.
And he asked often, of all whom he met
if they could give him news of a green knight
or how he could get to the Green Chapel.

And they all said no, never in their lives
had they seen someone who was such a shade
as green.

> The paths he would take were strange,
> with little cheer to glean,
> and his hopes would often change
> till that chapel could be seen.

(31)

He climbed past cliffs in unknown country,
a stranger faring far from his home.
At each stream and ford that he found in those lands
enemies lurked (unless his luck held) --
vicious, violent, hard to avoid.
In those mountains he met so many strange wonders
a tenth of the total could hardly be told.
He dared to fight dragons and warred with wolves,
or lurking woses, living wild on the crags,
or with bulls, or bears, or boars on occasion,
and trolls that hunted him across the high hills.
Only constant courage and the care of his God
could save him sometimes from certain death.
For if warfare was hard, winter was worse,
when the clouds shed water cold and clear
which froze in the air and fell as sleet.
He lay down half-dead, drenched in his armor,
too many times to bear: and on barren stone
where cold-running creeks came clattering down
and icecicles hardened high overhead.
Thus with peril and pain, in difficult plight,
he carried on alone till the Eve of Christmas
fell.

> Then lifting head he cried:
> "Good Mary, hear me well --
> and grant me grace to ride
> to realms where people dwell."

(32)

With sunrise his heart rose as he rode from the highlands
deep into woodland wild past belief.
There the high hills hemmed in a forest
of huge and hoary oaks -- hundreds together;

and heavy hazel and hawthorn thickets
with rags of rough moss wrapped round each limb --
while on the bare branches the huddled birds
were perched, piping pitifully in the cold.
Gawain passed them on Gringolet, going on
through marsh and mire, a man all alone
and worried. He wondered what he could do
to celebrate our Savior's service on the very night
he was born of a virgin to bear our sorrows.
And therefore sighing he said, "I beseech thee, Lord
and Mary, the mildest, dearest of mothers:
Help me to some haven where mass can be heard,
and matins tomorrow. I ask this meekly,
and in token now pray my Pater, my Ave,
my Creed.

> He continued on his way,
> confessing his misdeeds,
> and crossed himself to pray,
> "Christ's cross now grant me speed!"

(33)

He had signed himself scarcely three times
when he made out a moat and a mound in the wood --
a low hill with a lawn, through a lacework of branches
that grew from great oaks guarding a dike.
He had found there a castle fit for a lord,
placed in the open, a park all around it,
with bristling stakes in a strong stockade
that turned for two miles round groves of trees.
Sir Gawain saw one whole side of that stronghold
as it shimmered and shone through the shaking leaves.
He held his helm, with head bowed in thanks
to Jesus and Saint Julian, whose gentle grace
had cared for his needs and come to his aid.
"Safe lodging," he called, "I beseech of you yet!"
Then he goaded Gringolet with gilded heels
and choosing the chief roadway by sheer chance
he came quickly to the causeway's end
at last

> to drawbridge lifted tight
> to gateway shuttered fast.
> Such walls in granite might
> would shrug off wind or blast.

Christmas at a Strange Castle

(Lines 785-1125, sections 34-45)

(34)

He held back his horse where the bank halted
in a deep double ditch close dug to the wall,
which plunged in the pool impossibly deep --
and then its full, huge height heaved itself up
in tiers of tough stone straight to the top,
its battlements built in the best style,
its guard-towers rising in graceful rows
lined with loopholes covered and latched:
a barbican better than the best he knew.
He noticed behind it a high-roofed hall
tucked among towers, from whose clustered tips
buttresses sprang, and pinnacled spires
cunningly carved, and crafted with skill.
Chalk-white chimneys were checkered about
like radiance rising from rooftops and towers.
So many painted pinnacles stood round that place
or climbed from the castle's crenellated walls
that it seemed like a cutout clipped from paper.
As he sat there in saddle, it seemed very fine
if only he could enter the innermost court,
and win welcome there to worship in a house
so blessed.

> A porter came at call,
> more gracious than the best,
> who stood upon the wall
> and hailed that knight on quest.

(35)

"Good sir," said Gawain, "please grant me the favor
(if your lord allows) to lodge in this house."
"By Peter," said the porter, "be perfectly sure
that you, Lord, are welcome as long as you like!"
Then swift-paced the porter moved to approach him,
and others came with him to welcome their guest.
They dropped the great drawbridge, then drawing near proudly,
they bowed, their knees bent upon the bare earth
to one whom they welcomed as worthy of honor.
They granted him passage; the portals swung wide;
he called them to rise, and crossed the great bridge.

Men steadied his saddle: he slipped off his horse
and sturdy men came to lead it to stable.
Knights and their squires were the next to come,
delighted to lead the lord to the hall.
Hardly had he lifted his helm when many hands
were swift to receive it in courteous service --
and in the same way his sword was set by his shield.
He nobly acknowledged each of those knights,
proud men close-pressed to honor a prince.
Still strapped in bright steel, he strode to the hall
where a bonfire burned bright on the hearth.
Then the lord himself descended to see him,
moving to meet him with exquisite manners.
"You are welcome," he said, "to what this house holds,"
"everything is yours to use as you please
in this place."

    "God bless you," said Gawain then,
    "And Christ repay your grace."
    They met like joyful men
    in open-armed embrace.

(36)

Gazing on one who greeted him so well,
Gawain felt that fortress had a fine lord:
a man in his prime, massively made;
his beard all beaver-brown, glossy and broad;
stern, stalwart in stance on his sturdy thighs,
his face bold as fire, a fair-spoken man --
who certainly seemed well-suited, he judged,
to rule there as master of excellent men.
The lord led him in, and ordered at once
that someone be sent to serve in his chamber.
Then the household staff hurried to obey
and brought him to a bedroom, brightly arranged
with gold-trimmed curtains of the clearest silk
and fine-crafted coverlets, beautiful quilts
with bright fur above and embroidered edges.
There were rings of red gold on rope-drawn drapes,
tight-hung tapestries from Tarsus and Tolouse;
and similar fabrics were set underfoot.
As they talked with him gaily, they took off his garments,
removing his byrnie and his bright armor.
Then rich robes were brought as the servants rushed in

a choice from the best to change for his own.
As soon as he picked one and pulled it in place,
a fine-fitting kilt with swirling folds,
it seemed to them all that suddenly light
shone round his shape in the shades of spring,
beautiful, bright about all his limbs.
Christ never had such a handsome knight,
they thought:

>   Wherever men appear,
>   surely Gawain ought
>   to reign without a peer
>   in fields where fierce men fought.

(37)

Before the chimney where charcoal glowed a chair
lined with fine fabric was found for Sir Gawain,
sumptuous with cushions on a quilted seat.
And then a rich robe was thrown around him
of brilliant, gaily embroidered silk
filled out with fur: the finest of pelts,
and every bit ermine, even the hood.
Thus he sat, relaxed and in lavish splendor,
till he felt far better in the fire's warmth.
Then they took a table, laid it on trestles,
and covered it with clean and clear white cloth,
saltcellars, napkins, and a silver service.
He washed as he wished and went to his meal.
Then the table was set in suitable style
with soups of all kinds, seasoned superbly
in double-sized servings; plus assorted fish,
some breaded and baked, some broiled on the coals,
some simmered, some set in savory stews;
each subtly spiced with sauces that pleased him.
Exclaiming he kept on calling it a feast,
but all of them answered with equal courtesy
and said,

>   "Take penance while you can;
>   tomorrow you'll be fed!"
>   He made a merry man --
>   the wine went to his head.

(38)

Then queries and questions carefully framed
on private matters were put to that prince.

So he spoke of his court, in courteous words,
as that which highborn Arthur held as his own,
who ruled the Round Table as its regal king --
and their guest, he told them, was Gawain himself,
come to them at Christmas as his course unfolded.
On learning whom luck had brought him the lord
laughed out loud for sheer heart's delight.
Within that moat every man was eager to move,
and pressed forward promptly to enter the presence
of "that paragon of prowess and of perfect manners,
whose virtues and person are constantly praised:
of all men on earth most worthy of honor!"
Each man of them, murmuring, remarked to his fellows,
"Now we shall see courtesy cleverly displayed
among faultless feats of fine conversation!
We will learn untaught how to talk nobly
when we face such a fine father of breeding!
God has graced us indeed, with a grand blessing,
to grant us the guest that Gawain will make
when we sit and sing glad songs of Christ's
new birth.

      The meaning of his mannered ways
      will show what words are worth --
      and teach us terms to play
      the game of lovers' mirth."

(39)

When the dinner was done, and their darling rose,
it was nearly dark, for night was approaching.
The chapels were opened as the chaplains came
with bells ringing richly, right as they should
for vesper devotions on the verge of Christmas.
The lord now led the way, his lady beside him;
she paced along prettily and entered her pew.
When Gawain came gliding in with a glad heart,
the lord latched on to him and led him to his seat,
glad-handing Gawain, greeting him by name,
and said he was the most welcome guest in the world.
After hearty hugs and heartfelt thanks,
they sat soberly together till the service ended.
As the lady had been longing to look on the knight,
she emerged to meet him, her maidens about her.
In form she was fairest: in figure and face,
complexion, comportment surpassing all others,

and to Gawain not even Guinevere could equal her grace.
She steered through the chancel to strengthen his welcome.
Another lady led her by the left hand
who was obviously older: an elderly matron
whom the household held in the highest honor.
But in looks the two ladies were obviously unlike:
one active and young, one yellow with age.
On the first a flush rose, ruddy and fair;
on the other, rough wrinkles on rugged cheeks
. On the first one, clear pearls displayed on a kerchief
shone from her breast and her bare throat
whiter than snow on the winter hills.
The other one's kerchief covered her neck,
and bright veils billowed round her black chin,
while silk framed her forehead, which was fretted round
with lacework linked in delicate loops.
Nothing was bare about her but her black brows,
over eyes and nose over naked lips,
and those made a sorry sight, bleary and sour.
She was, God knows! A lady of grace
and pride --
        but her body was short and thick;
        her buttocks big and wide.
        A tastier plum to pick
        was the beauty by her side.

                    (40)

Meeting her gracious, light-hearted gaze
he took the lord's leave and approached the ladies.
He greeted the elder with a grand bow,
and wrapping the lovelier in a light embrace,
he planted a pretty kiss with extravagant praise.
They offered their acquaintance, and he asked at once
to be their faithful servant if it seemed fitting.
They took him between them and led him off, talking,
to a chimneyed chamber; and they charged the servants
to speed out for spices, and not to be sparing,
but to bring back each time the best of the wine.
The lord kept leaping about in delight,
bid them make merry as much as they could,
then hauled off his hood and hung it on a spear,
urging them to earn it as a signal honor
for the merriest man among them that Christmas.
"By my word! I shall work to win with the rest

against all this company, to keep it myself!"
Thus the lord made it lively with laughter and jokes
to gladden Sir Gawain with the joy that games
incite.

>   Time passed; the twilight fled;
>   the servants kindled light.
>   Then Gawain sought his bed,
>   and bade them all good night.

(41)

In the morning when men remember the birth
of our dear Lord to die for our destiny's sake,
all men on earth grow merry at heart.
So it was that delicacies filled out their day:
At breakfast and banquet the best of the food
was spread out in splendor by spirited men.
The old, ancient woman had honor of place,
with the lord, I believe, politely beside her.
Gawain and the gracious lady were both given seats
in the middle, where the meal was measured out first,
and afterward to everyone all through the hall,
served in due sequence, as it seemed proper.
They had food, they had fun, they were filled with joy:
too much for tongue to tell of with ease,
and a struggle, at least, to state it in full.
But this I give you: that Gawain and the gracious lady
were perfect companions in their place together,
and such pleasantries passed in their private speech
(which was fine and fair; also free from sin)
that no princely sport could possibly surpass
their game.

>   Then trumpets, drums to measure
>   tunes that pipes proclaim:
>   as each man took his pleasure,
>   and those two did the same.

(42)

One fun-filled day followed another,
with a third day thrust into the thick of it.
Saint John's day was generous with jubilant song:
the last day like it left to them there.
The guests would be going in the grey morning,
so they were up to all hours over their wine,
kept calling for dances and caroling round,

and left their leavetaking till late in the night
that would soon send them off by separate ways.
'Good day,' began Gawain, but grabbing him his host
pulled him aside privately by a pleasant fire,
laid it on at length and lavishly thanked him
for granting him such grace and gladness of heart
as to honor his house on this high season
and fill up his fortress with the finest manners.
'As long as I live, sir, my life will be better
to have had Gawain as my guest at God's own feast.'
'God help me,' said Gawain, 'may He grant you better:
for any such honor is only your due.
I am simply your servant, one who seeks to please you,
oath-bound to honor all men, be they high
or low.'

> And though the lord takes pains
> to urge him not to go,
> Sir Gawain still explains
> his answer must be no.

(43)

"But Gawain," that good man graciously asked,
"Has some dark deed driven you forth,
that you rushed from the royal court? Must you now ride alone
when holiday feasts are not wholly done?"
"Sir," he responded, "you have spoken truly:,
"I had to depart on a high and a hasty matter.
For I myself am summoned to seek out a place,
though I wonder where in the world to find it.
I'd not fail to near it by New Year's morning
for all the land in Britain -- by the love of God!
I have come with questions that require answers --
so tell me the truth: has any tale reached you
of the Green Chapel, or on what ground it stands,
or about its guardian, a green-skinned knight?
For I have set myself, by most solemn pledge,
to meet this man, though it may go hard.
But now the New Year is nearly complete,
and if the Lord allows it, I'll look upon him
more gladly -- by God's Son! -- than on any good thing.
Therefore sir, as you see, I must set out now
for I doubt that three days will do for this business
and I'd far rather die than be doomed to fail."
Then the lord answered, laughing, "You must linger now!"

"You will get to your goal in good enough time,
and can give up guessing on what ground it lies,
and can lie abed as late as you wish,
and finally set forth the first of the year,
yet make it there with morning still mostly left
that day --

      spend till New Years as you please,
      then rise and ride that way;
      We'll guide you there with ease --
      it's not two miles away."

(44)

Then gaiety filled Gawain, and he gladly laughed.
"I must earnestly offer my uttermost thanks!
With my goal at hand, I can grant your wish,
dwell here a while, and do as you bid me."
"Sit down," said his host, seizing his arm.
"Come, let's delight in the ladies' presence!"
Thus they made a pleasant party apart by themselves.
The lord let out laughs as loud and as merry
as a madman, maybe, whose mind was far gone.
He called to his company, crying aloud,
"You have sworn to serve me however seems best;
will you act to honor this oath here and now?"
"Certainly, sir," he said in reply.
"While your walls ward me your will is supreme."
He returned: "You are tired, and have traveled far.
We all have been wakeful, nor are you well-rested,
nor fed quite as fully, I fear, as should be.
You must lie in late, and lounge at your ease
past morning mass, and make it to breakfast
whenever you wish. My wife will eat with you
and keep you company till I come again.
You stay,

      but I myself will ride
      hunting at break of day."
      Then Gawain bowed with pride
      and promised to obey.

(45)

"Look," said the lord - "Let us now bargain:
What I get in the wood I will give to you,
and charge in exchange whatever chance may deal you.
Friend, here's how to do it: we'll hold to our word

regardless who gains or gives up the most."
"By God!" Gawain answered, "I grant what you ask;
just give me the game -- I will gladly play it!"
"Then let's down this drink, and our deal is made!"
said the lord of that land, and they laughed together.
So these lords and ladies relaxed as they drank
and played gallant games while it gave them pleasure.
Then in French fashion, with many fine words,
they made their excuses with murmured farewells,
and pretty pecks planted on either cheek.
Then bright burning torches were born by the servants
who led them at last to lie down softly
in bed.

> Before they reached the door,
> what promises they said!
> And how that country's lord
> made fun times fly ahead!

The Faerie Queen

Book One, Cantos XI and XII

Edited with notes by George Armstrong Wauchope, M.A., Ph.D.
Professor of English in the South Carolina College

CANTO XI

> The knight with that old Dragon fights
>   two dayes incessantly;
> The third him overthrowes, and gayns
>   most glorious victory.

I

High time now gan it wex for Una faire
  To thinke of those her captive Parents deare,
  And their forwasted kingdome to repaire:
  Whereto whenas they now approched neare,
  With hartie wordes her knight she gan to cheare,   5
  And in her modest manner thus bespake;
  Deare knight, as deare as ever knight was deare,
  That all these sorrowes suffer for my sake,
High heaven behold the tedious toyle ye for me take.

II

Now are we come unto my native soyle,   10
  And to the place where all our perils dwell;
  Here haunts that feend, and does his dayly spoyle;
  Therefore henceforth be at your keeping well,°
  And ever ready for your foeman fell.
  The sparke of noble courage now awake,   15
  And strive your excellent selfe to excell:
  That shall ye evermore renowmed make,
Above all knights on earth that batteill undertake.

III

And pointing forth, Lo yonder is (said she)°
  The brasen towre in which my parents deare   20
  For dread of that huge feend emprisond be,
  Whom I from far, see on the walles appeare,
  Whose sight my feeble soule doth greatly cheare:

And on the top of all I do espye
  The watchman wayting tydings glad to heare,   25
  That O my parents might I happily
Unto you bring, to ease you of your misery.

IV

With that they heard a roaring hideous sound,
  That all the ayre with terrour filled wide,
  And seemd uneath° to shake the stedfast ground.   30
  Eftsoones that dreadful Dragon° they espide,
  Where stretcht he lay upon the sunny side,°
  Of a great hill, himselfe like a great hill.
  But all so soone as he from far descride
  Those glistring armes, that heaven with light did fill,   35
He rousd himselfe full blith, and hastned them untill.

V

Then bad the knight his Lady yede aloofe,
  And to an hill her selfe withdraw aside:
  From whence she might behold that battailles proof,
  And eke be safe from daunger far descryde: 40
  She him obayd, and turnd a little wyde.
  Now O thou sacred muse,° most learned Dame,
  Faire ympe of Phoebus and his aged bride,
  The Nourse of time and everlasting fame,
That warlike hands ennoblest with immortall name;   45

VI

O gently come into my feeble brest
  Come gently, but not with that mighty rage,
  Wherewith the martiall troupes thou doest infest,
  And harts of great Heroës doest enrage,
  That nought their kindled courage may aswage,   50
  Soone as thy dreadfull trompe begins to sownd,
  The God of warre with his fiers equipage
  Thou doest awake, sleepe never he so sownd,
All scared nations doest with horrour sterne astownd.

VII

Faire Goddesse, lay that furious fit aside,   55
  Till I of warres° and bloody Mars do sing,
  And Briton fields with Sarazin bloud bedyde,

Twixt that great Faery Queene, and Paynim king,
That with their horrour heaven and earth did ring;
A worke of labour long and endlesse prayse: 60
But now a while let downe that haughtie string°
And to my tunes thy second tenor rayse,
That I this man of God his godly armes may blaze.

        VIII

By this the dreadfull Beast drew nigh to hand,
  Halfe flying, and halfe footing in his haste,   65
  That with his largenesse measured much land,
  And made wide shadow under his huge wast,
  As mountaine doth the valley overcast.
  Approching nigh, he reared high afore
  His body monstrous, horrible, and vaste,   70
  Which to increase his wondrous greatnesse more,
Was swoln with wrath, and poyson, and with bloudy gore.

        IX

And over, all with brasen scales was armd,
  Like plated coate of steele, so couched neare,
  That nought mote perce, ne might his corse be harmd   75
  With dint of sword, nor push of pointed speare;
  Which, as an Eagle, seeing pray appeare,
  His aery plumes doth rouze, full rudely dight;
  So shaked he, that horrour was to heare,
  For as the clashing of an Armour bright,   80
Such noyse his rouzed scales did send unto the knight.

        X

His flaggy wings when forth he did display,
  Were like two sayles, in which the hollow wynd
  Is gathered full, and worketh speedy way:
  And eke the pennes, that did his pineons bynd,   85
  Were like mayne-yards, with flying canvas lynd;
  With which whenas him list the ayre to beat,
  And there by force unwonted passage find,
  The cloudes before him fled for terrour great,
And all the heavens stood still amazed with his threat.   90

        XI

His huge long tayle wound up in hundred foldes,
  Does overspred his long bras-scaly backe,
  Whose wreathed boughts when ever he unfoldes,

And thicke entangled knots adown does slacke,
Bespotted as with shields of red and blacke,   95
It sweepeth all the land behind him farre,
And of three furlongs does but litle lacke;
And at the point two stings in-fixed arre,
Both deadly sharpe, that sharpest steele exceeden farre.

XII

But stings and sharpest steele did far exceed   100
  The sharpnesse of his cruell rending clawes;
Dead was it sure, as sure as death in deed,
  What ever thing does touch his ravenous pawes,
  Or what within his reach he ever drawes.
But his most hideous head my toung to tell   105
Does tremble: for his deepe devouring jawes
  Wide gaped, like the griesly mouth of hell,
Through which into his darke abisse all ravin fell.

XIII

And that more wondrous was, in either jaw
  Threeranckes of yron teeth enraunged were,   110
  In which yet trickling blood, and gobbets raw
Of late devoured bodies did appeare,
  That sight thereof bred cold congealed feare:
Which to increase, and as atonce to kill,
  A cloud of smoothering smoke and sulphure seare,   115
  Out of his stinking gorge forth steemed still,
That all the ayre about with smoke and stench did fill.

XIV

His blazing eyes, like two bright shining shields,
  Did burne with wrath, and sparkled living fyre:
As two broad Beacons,° set in open fields,   120
  Send forth their flames far off to every shyre,
  And warning give, that enemies conspyre
With fire and sword the region to invade;
  So flam'd his eyne with rage and rancorous yre:
  But farre within, as in a hollow glade,   125
Those glaring lampes were set, that made a dreadfull shade.

XV

So dreadfully he towards him did pas,
  Forelifting up aloft his speckled brest,
  And often bounding on the brused gras,

As for great joyance of his newcome guest.   130
  Eftsoones he gan advance his haughtie crest,
  As chauffed Bore his bristles doth upreare,
  And shoke his scales to battell ready drest;
  That made the Redcrosse knight nigh quake for feare,
As bidding bold defiance to his foeman neare.   135

XVI

The knight gan fairely couch his steadie speare,
  And fiercely ran at him with rigorous might:
  The pointed steele arriving rudely theare,
  His harder hide would neither perce, nor bight,
  But glauncing by forth passed forward right;   140
  Yet sore amoved with so puissaunt push,
  The wrathfull beast about him turned light,
  And him so rudely passing by, did brush
With his long tayle, that horse and man to ground did rush.

XVII

Both horse and man up lightly rose againe,   145
  And fresh encounter towards him addrest:
  But th'idle stroke yet backe recoyld in vaine,
  And found no place his deadly point to rest.
  Exceeding rage enflam'd the furious beast,
  To be avenged of so great despight;   150
  For never felt his imperceable brest
  So wondrous force, from hand of living wight;
Yet had he prov'd the powre of many a puissant knight.

XVIII

Then with his waving wings displayed wyde,
  Himselfe up high he lifted from the ground,   155
  And with strong flight did forcibly divide
  The yielding aire, which nigh too feeble found
  Her flitting parts,° and element unsound,
  To beare so great a weight: he cutting way
  With his broad sayles, about him soared round: 160
  At last low stouping° with unweldie sway,
Snatcht up both horse and man, to beare them quite away.

XIX

Long he them bore above the subject plaine,
  So far as Ewghen bow a shaft may send,
  Till struggling strong did him at last constraine   165

To let them downe before his flightes end:
As hagard hauke,° presuming to contend
With hardie fowle, above his hable might,°
His wearie pounces all in vaine doth spend
To trusse the pray too heavy for his flight;   170
Which comming downe to ground, does free it selfe by fight.

XX

He so disseized° of his gryping grosse,
  The knight his thrillant speare again assayd
  In his bras-plated body to embosse,
  And three mens strength unto the stroke he layd;   175
  Wherewith the stiffe beame quaked, as affrayd,
  And glauncing from his scaly necke, did glyde
  Close under his left wing, then broad displayd:
  The percing steele there wrought a wound full wyde,
That with the uncouth smart the Monster lowdly cryde.   180

XXI

He cryde, as raging seas are wont to rore,
  When wintry storme his wrathfull wreck does threat
  The roaring billowes beat the ragged shore,
  As they the earth would shoulder from her seat,
  And greedy gulfe does gape,° as he would eat   185
  His neighbour element in his revenge:
  Then gin the blustring brethren° boldly threat
  To move the world from off his steadfast henge,
And boystrous battell make, each other to avenge.

XXII

The steely head stucke fast still in his flesh,   190
  Till with his cruell clawes he snatcht the wood,
  And quite a sunder broke. Forth flowed fresh
  A gushing river of blacke goarie blood,
  That drowned all the land, whereon he stood;
  The streame thereof would drive a water-mill: 195
  Trebly augmented was his furious mood
  With bitter sence of his deepe rooted ill,
That flames of fire he threw forth from his large nosethrill.

XXIII

His hideous tayle then hurled he about,
  And therewith all enwrapt the nimble thyes   200
  Of his froth-fomy steed, whose courage stout

Striving to loose the knot that fast him tyes,
  Himselfe in streighter bandes too rash implyes,
  That to the ground he is perforce constraynd
  To throw his rider: who can quickly ryse   205
  From off the earth, with durty blood distaynd,
For that reprochfull fall right fowly he disdaynd.

XXIV

And fiercely tooke his trenchand blade in hand,
  With which he stroke so furious and so fell,
  That nothing seemd the puissaunce could withstand: 210
  Upon his crest the hardned yron fell,
  But his more hardned crest was armd so well,
  That deeper dint therein it would not make;
  Yet so extremely did the buffe him quell,
  That from thenceforth he shund the like to take,   215
But when he saw them come, he did them still forsake.

XXV

The knight was wroth to see his stroke beguyld,
  And smote againe with more outrageous might;
  But backe againe the sparckling steele recoyld,
  And left not any marke, where it did light,   220
  As if in Adamant rocke it had bene pight.
  The beast impatient of his smarting wound,
  And of so fierce and forcible despight,
  Thought with his wings to stye above the ground;
But his late wounded wing unserviceable found.   225

XXVI

Then full of griefe and anguish vehement,
  He lowdly brayd, that like was never heard,
  And from his wide devouring oven° sent
  A flake of fire, that, flashing in his beard,
  Him all amazd, and almost made affeard: 230
  The scorching flame sore swinged all his face,
  And through his armour all his body seard,
  That he could not endure so cruell cace,
But thought his armes to leave, and helmet to unlace.

XXVII

Not that great Champion° of the antique world,   235
  Whom famous Poetes verse so much doth vaunt,
  And hath for twelve huge labours high extold,

So many furies and sharpe fits did haunt,
  When him the poysond garment did enchaunt,
  With Centaures bloud and bloudie verses charm'd;   240
  As did this knight twelve thousand dolours daunt,
  Whom fyrie steele now burnt, that earst him arm'd,
That erst him goodly arm'd, now most of all him harm'd.

XXVIII

Faint, wearie, sore, emboyled, grieved, brent°
  With heat, toyle, wounds, armes, smart, and inward fire,   245
  That never man such mischiefes did torment;
  Death better were, death did he oft desire,
  But death will never come, when needes require.
  Whom so dismayd when that his foe beheld,
  He cast to suffer him no more respire,   250
  But gan his sturdy sterne about to weld,
And him so strongly stroke, that to the ground him feld.

XXIX

It fortuned, (as faire it then befell,)
  Behind his backe unweeting, where he stood,
  Of auncient time there was a springing well,   255
  From which fast trickled forth a silver flood,
  Full of great vertues, and for med'cine good.
  Whylome, before that cursed Dragon got
  That happy land, and all with innocent blood
  Defyld those sacred waves, it rightly hot   260
The well of life,° ne yet his vertues had forgot.

XXX

For unto life the dead it could restore,
  And guilt of sinfull crimes cleane wash away,
  Those that with sicknesse were infected sore
  It could recure, and aged long decay   265
  Renew, as one were borne that very day.
  Both Silo° this, and Jordan did excell,
  And th' English Bath,° and eke the German Spau;
  Ne can Cephise,° nor Hebrus match this well:
Into the same the knight back overthrowen, fell.   270

XXXI

Now gan the golden Phoebus for to steepe
  His fierie face in billowes of the west,
  And his faint steedes watred in Ocean deepe,

Whiles from their journall labours they did rest,
  When that infernall Monster, having kest   275
  His wearie foe into that living well,
  Can high advance his broad discoloured brest
  Above his wonted pitch, with countenance fell,
And clapt his yron wings, as victor he did dwell.

XXXII

Which when his pensive Ladie saw from farre,   280
  Great woe and sorrow did her soule assay,
  As weening that the sad end of the warre,
  And gan to highest God entirely pray,
  That feared chance from her to turne away;
  With folded hands and knees full lowly bent,   285
  All night she watcht, ne once adowne would lay
  Her daintie limbs in her sad dreriment,
But praying still did wake, and waking did lament.

XXXIII

The morrow next gan early to appeare,
  That Titan rose to runne his daily race;   290
  But early ere the morrow next gan reare
  Out of the sea faire Titans deawy face,
  Up rose the gentle virgin from her place,
  And looked all about, if she might spy
  Her loved knight to move° his manly pace: 295
  For she had great doubt of his safety,
Since late she saw him fall before his enemy.

XXXIV

At last she saw, where he upstarted brave
  Out of the well, wherein he drenched lay:
  As Eagle° fresh out of the Ocean wave,   300
  Where he hath left his plumes all hoary gray,
  And deckt himselfe with feathers youthly gay,
  Like Eyas hauke up mounts unto the skies,
  His newly budded pineons to assay,
  And marveiles at himselfe, still as he flies: 305
So new this new-borne knight to battell new did rise.

XXXV

Whom when the damned feend so fresh did spy,
  No wonder if he wondred at the sight,
  And doubted, whether his late enemy

It were, or other new supplied knight.   310
  He, now to prove his late renewed might,
  High brandishing his bright deaw-burning blade,°
  Upon his crested scalpe so sore did smite,
  That to the scull a yawning wound it made;
The deadly dint his dulled senses all dismaid.   315

XXXVI

I wote not, whether the revenging steele
  Were hardned with that holy water dew,
  Wherein he fell, or sharper edge did feele,
  Or his baptized hands now greater grew;
  Or other secret vertue did ensew;   320
  Else never could the force of fleshly arme,
  Ne molten mettall in his blood embrew°;
  For till that stownd could never wight him harme,
By subtilty, nor slight, nor might, nor mighty charme.

XXXVII

The cruell wound enraged him so sore,   325
  That loud he yelded for exceeding paine;
  As hundred ramping Lyons seem'd to rore,
  Whom ravenous hunger did thereto constraine:
  Then gan he tosse aloft his stretched traine,
  And therewith scourge the buxome aire so sore,   330
  That to his force to yeelden it was faine;
  Ne ought his sturdy strokes might stand afore,
That high trees overthrew, and rocks in peeces tore.

XXXVIII

The same advauncing high above his head,
  With sharpe intended sting° so rude him smot,   335
  That to the earth him drove, as stricken dead,
  Ne living wight would have him life behot:
  The mortall sting his angry needle shot
  Quite through his shield, and in his shoulder seasd,
  Where fast it stucke, ne would there out be got: 340
  The griefe thereof him wondrous sore diseasd,
Ne might his ranckling paine with patience be appeasd.

XXXIX

But yet more mindfull of his honour deare,
  Then of the grievous smart, which him did wring,
  From loathed soile he can him lightly reare,   345

And strove to loose the far infixed sting:
  Which when in vaine he tryde with struggeling,
  Inflam'd with wrath, his raging blade he heft,
  And strooke so strongly, that the knotty string
  Of his huge taile he quite a sunder cleft,   350
Five joints thereof he hewd, and but the stump him left.

XL

Hart cannot thinke, what outrage, and what cryes,
  With foule enfouldred smoake and flashing fire,
  The hell-bred beast threw forth unto the skyes,
  That all was covered with darkenesse dire: 355
  Then fraught with rancour, and engorged ire,
  He cast at once him to avenge for all,
  And gathering up himselfe out of the mire,
  With his uneven wings did fiercely fall,
Upon his sunne-bright shield, and gript it fast withall.   360

XLI

Much was the man encombred with his hold,
  In feare to lose his weapon in his paw,
  Ne wist yet, how his talaunts to unfold;
  For harder was from Cerberus greedy jaw
  To plucke a bone, then from his cruell claw   365
  To reave by strength the griped gage° away:
  Thrise he assayd it from his foot to draw,
  And thrise in vaine to draw it did assay,
It booted nought to thinke to robbe him of his pray.

XLII

Tho when he saw no power might prevaile,   370
  His trustie sword he cald to his last aid,
  Wherewith he fiercely did his foe assaile,
  And double blowes about him stoutly laid,
  That glauncing fire out of the yron plaid;
  As sparckles from the Andvile use to fly,   375
  When heavy hammers on the wedge are swaid;
  Therewith at last he forst him to unty
One of his grasping feete, him to defend thereby.

XLIII

The other foot, fast fixed on his shield,
  Whenas no strength, nor stroks mote him constraine   380
  To loose, ne yet the warlike pledge to yield,

He smot thereat with all his might and maine,
That nought so wondrous puissaunce might sustaine;
Upon the joint the lucky steele did light,
And made such way, that hewd it quite in twaine;   385
The paw yett missed not his minisht might,°
But hong still on the shield, as it at first was pight.

XLIV

For griefe thereof and divelish despight,°
  From his infernall fournace forth he threw
  Huge flames, that dimmed all the heavens light,   390
  Enrold in duskish smoke and brimstone blew:
  As burning Aetna from his boyling stew
  Doth belch out flames, and rockes in peeces broke,
  And ragged ribs of mountains molten new,
  Enwrapt in coleblacke clouds and filthy smoke,   395
That all the land with stench, and heaven with horror choke.

XLV

The heate whereof, and harmefull pestilence
  So sore him noyd, that forst him to retire
  A little backward for his best defence,
  To save his body from the scorching fire,   400
  Which he from hellish entrailes did expire.
  It chaunst (eternall God that chaunce did guide,)
  As he recoiled backward, in the mire
  His nigh forwearied feeble feet did slide,
And downe he fell, with dread of shame sore terrifide.   405

XLVI

There grew a goodly tree° him faire beside,
  Loaden with fruit and apples rosie red,
  As they in pure vermilion had beene dide,
  Whereof great vertues over all were red°:
  For happy life to all which thereon fed,   410
  And life eke everlasting did befall:
  Great God it planted in that blessed sted
  With his Almighty hand, and did it call
The tree of life, the crime of our first fathers fall.°

XLVII

In all the world like was not to be found,   415
  Save in that soile, where all good things did grow,
  And freely sprong out of the fruitfull ground,

As incorrupted Nature did them sow,
Till that dread Dragon all did overthrow.
Another like faire tree eke grew thereby,   420
Whereof whoso did eat, eftsoones did know
Both good and ill: O mornefull memory:
That tree through one mans fault hath doen us all to dy.

XLVIII

From that first tree forth flowd, as from a well,
A trickling streame of Balme, most soveraine   425
And dainty deare, which on the ground, still fell,
And overflowed all the fertile plaine,
As it had deawed bene with timely raine:
Life and long health that gratious ointment gave,
And deadly wounds could heale and reare againe   430
The senselesse corse appointed for the grave.
Into that same he fell: which did from death him save.

XLIX

For nigh thereto the ever damned beast
Durst not approch, for he was deadly made,°
And all that life preserved did detest: 435
Yet he is oft adventur'd to invade.
By this the drouping day-light gan to fade,
And yield his roome to sad succeeding night,
Who with her sable mantle gan to shade
The face of earth, and wayes of living wight,   440
And high her burning torch set up in heaven bright.

L

When gentle Una saw the second fall
Of her deare knight, who wearie of long fight,
And faint through losse of blood, mov'd not at all,
But lay, as in a dreame of deepe delight,   445
Besmeard with pretious Balme, whose vertuous might
Did heale his wounds, and scorching heat alay,
Againe she stricken was with sore affright,
And for his safetie gan devoutly pray,
And watch the noyous night, and wait for joyous day.   450

LI

The joyous day gan early to appeare,
And faire Aurora from the deawy bed
Of aged Tithone gan herselfe to reare

With rosy cheekes, for shame as blushing red;
Her golden locks for haste were loosely shed   455
About her eares, when Una her did marke
Clymbe to her charet, all with flowers spred;
From heaven high to chase the chearelesse darke,
With merry note her loud salutes the mounting larke.

LII

Then freshly up arose the doughtie knight,   460
All healed of his hurts and woundes wide,
And did himselfe to battell ready dight;
Whose early foe awaiting him beside
To have devourd, so soone as day he spyde,
When now he saw himselfe so freshly reare,   465
As if late fight had nought him damnifyde,
He woxe dismayd, and gan his fate to feare;
Nathlesse with wonted rage he him advaunced neare.

LIII

And in his first encounter, gaping wide,°
He thought attonce him to have swallowd quight,   470
And rusht upon him with outragious pride;
Who him r'encountring fierce, as hauke in flight
Perforce rebutted backe. The weapon bright
Taking advantage of his open jaw,
Ran through his mouth with so importune might,   475
That deepe emperst his darksome hollow maw,
And back retyrd,° his life blood forth with all did draw.

LIV

So downe he fell, and forth his life did breath,
That vanisht into smoke and cloudes swift;
So downe he fell, that th' earth him underneath   480
Did grone, as feeble so great load to lift;
So downe he fell, as an huge rockie clift,
Whose false foundation waves have washt away,
With dreadfull poyse is from the mayneland rift,
And rolling downe, great Neptune doth dismay;   485
So downe he fell, and like an heaped mountaine lay.

LV

The knight himselfe even trembled at his fall,
So huge and horrible a masse it seem'd,
And his deare Ladie, that beheld it all,

 Durst not approch for dread, which she misdeem'd;°   490
 But yet at last, whenas the direfull feend
 She saw not stirre, off-shaking vaine affright,
 She nigher drew, and saw that joyous end:
  Then God she praysd, and thankt her faithfull knight,
That had atchieved so great a conquest by his might.   495

   * * * * *

CANTO XII

  Faire Una to the Redcrosse knight,
   betrouthed is with joy:
  Though false Duessa it to barre
   her false sleights doe imploy.

       I

BEHOLD I see the haven nigh at hand,
 To which I meane my wearie course to bend;
 Vere the maine shete,° and beare up with the land,
 The which afore is fairely to be kend,
 And seemeth safe from storms that may offend;   5
 There this faire virgin wearie of her way
 Must landed be, now at her journeyes end:
  There eke my feeble barke a while may stay
Till merry wind and weather call her thence away.

       II

Scarsely had Phoebus in the glooming East   10
 Yet harnessed his firie-footed teeme,
 Ne reard above the earth his flaming creast;
 When the last deadly smoke aloft did steeme
 That signe of last outbreathed life did seeme
 Unto the watchman on the castle wall,   15
 Who thereby dead that balefull Beast did deeme,
  And to his Lord and Ladie lowd gan call,
To tell how he had seene the Dragons fatall fall.

       III

Uprose with hastie joy, and feeble speed
 That aged Sire, the Lord of all that land,   20
 And looked forth, to weet if true indeede
 Those tydings were, as he did understand,
 Which whenas true by tryall he out found,

He bad to open wyde his brazen gate,
  Which long time had bene shut, and out of hond°   25
  Proclaymed joy and peace through all his state;
For dead now was their foe which them forrayed late.

IV

Then gan triumphant Trompets sound on hie,
  That sent to heaven the ecchoed report
  Of their new joy, and happie victorie   30
  Gainst him, that had them long opprest with tort,
  And fast imprisoned in sieged fort.
  Then all the people, as in solemne feast,
  To him assembled with one full consort,
  Rejoycing at the fall of that great beast,   35
From whose eternall bondage now they were releast.

V

Forth came that auncient Lord and aged Queene,
  Arayd in antique robes downe to the ground,
  And sad habiliments right well beseene;
  A noble crew about them waited round   40
  Of sage and sober Peres, all gravely gownd;
  Whom farre before did march a goodly band
  Of tall young men,° all hable armes to sownd,
  But now they laurell braunches bore in hand;
Glad signe of victorie and peace in all their land.   45

VI

Unto that doughtie Conquerour they came,
  And him before themselves prostrating low,
  Their Lord and Patrone loud did him proclame,
  And at his feet their laurell boughes did throw.
  Soone after them all dauncing on a row   50
  The comely virgins came, with girlands dight,
  As fresh as flowres in medow greene do grow,
  When morning deaw upon their leaves doth light:
And in their hands sweet Timbrels all upheld on hight.

VII

And them before, the fry of children young   55
  Their wanton sports and childish mirth did play,
  And to the Maydens° sounding tymbrels sung,
  In well attuned notes, a joyous lay,

And made delightfull musicke all the way,
 Untill they came, where that faire virgin stood;   60
 As faire Diana in fresh sommers day,
 Beholds her Nymphes enraung'd in shadie wood,
Some wrestle, some do run, some bathe in christall flood:

VIII

So she beheld those maydens meriment
 With chearefull vew; who when to her they came,   65
 Themselves to ground with gracious humblesse bent,
 And her ador'd by honorable name,
 Lifting to heaven her everlasting fame:
 Then on her head they set a girland greene,
 And crowned her twixt earnest and twixt game;   70
 Who in her self-resemblance well beseene,°
Did seeme such, as she was, a goodly maiden Queene.

IX

And after, all the raskall many° ran,
 Heaped together in rude rablement,
 To see the face of that victorious man: 75
 Whom all admired, as from heaven sent,
 And gazd upon with gaping wonderment.
 But when they came where that dead Dragon lay,
 Stretcht on the ground in monstrous large extent,
 The sight with idle feare did them dismay,   80
Ne durst approch him nigh, to touch, or once assay.

X

Some feard, and fled; some feard and well it faynd;
 One that would wiser seeme then all the rest,
 Warnd him not touch, for yet perhaps remaynd
 Some lingring life within his hollow brest,   85
 Or in his wombe might lurke some hidden nest
 Of many Dragonets, his fruitfull seed;
 Another said, that in his eyes did rest
 Yet sparckling fire, and bad thereof take heed;
Another said, he saw him move his eyes indeed.   90

XI

One mother, when as her foolehardie chyld
 Did come too neare, and with his talants play,
 Halfe dead through feare, her little babe revyld,

And to her gossips gan in counsell say;
  How can I tell, but that his talants may   95
  Yet scratch my sonne, or rend his tender hand?
  So diversly themselves in vaine they fray;
  Whiles some more bold, to measure him nigh stand,
To prove how many acres he did spread of land.

XII

Thus flocked all the folke him round about,   100
  The whiles that hoarie king, with all his traine,
  Being arrived where that champion stout
  After his foes defeasance did remaine,
  Him goodly greetes, and faire does entertaine
  With princely gifts of yvorie and gold,   105
  And thousand thankes him yeelds for all his paine.
  Then when his daughter deare he does behold,
Her dearely doth imbrace, and kisseth manifold.

XIII

And after to his Pallace he them brings,
  With shaumes, and trompets, and with Clarions sweet;   110
  And all the way the joyous people sings,
  And with their garments strowes the paved street:
  Whence mounting up, they find purveyance meet
  Of all that royall Princes court became,
  And all the floore was underneath their feet   115
  Bespred with costly scarlot of great name,°
On which they lowly sit, and fitting purpose frame.°

XIV

What needs me tell their feast and goodly guize,°
  In which was nothing riotous nor vaine?
  What needs of dainty dishes to devize,   120
  Of comely services, or courtly trayne?
  My narrow leaves cannot in them containe
  The large discourse of royall Princes state.
  Yet was their manner then but bare and plaine:
  For th' antique world excesse and pride did hate;   125
Such proud luxurious pompe is swollen up but late.

XV

Then when with meates and drinkes of every kinde
  Their fervent appetites they quenched had,
  That auncient Lord gan fit occasion finde,

   Of straunge adventures, and of perils sad,   130
    Which in his travell him befallen had,
    For to demaund of his renowmed guest:
    Who then with utt'rance grave, and count'nance sad,
    From point to point, as is before exprest,
Discourst his voyage long, according his request.   135

            XVI

Great pleasures mixt with pittiful regard,
   That godly King and Queene did passionate,
   Whiles they his pittifull adventures heard,
   That oft they did lament his lucklesse state,
   And often blame the too importune fate,   140
   That heaped on him so many wrathfull wreakes:
   For never gentle knight, as he of late,
   So tossed was in fortunes cruell freakes;
And all the while salt teares bedeawd the hearers cheaks.

           XVII

Then sayd the royall Pere in sober wise;   145
   Deare Sonne, great beene the evils which ye bore
   From first to last in your late enterprise,
   That I note whether prayse, or pitty more:
   For never living man, I weene, so sore
   In sea of deadly daungers was distrest;   150
   But since now safe ye seised have the shore,
   And well arrived are, (high God be blest)
Let us devize of ease and everlasting rest.

          XVIII

Ah, dearest Lord, said then that doughty knight,
   Of ease or rest I may not yet devize,   155
   For by the faith, which I to armes have plight,
   I bounden am streight after this emprize,
   As that your daughter can ye well advize,
   Backe to returne to that great Faerie Queene,
   And her to serve six yeares in warlike wize,   160
   Gainst that proud Paynim king° that workes her teene
Therefore I ought crave pardon, till I there have beene.

          XIX

Unhappie falles that hard necessitie,
   (Quoth he) the troubler of my happie peace,
   And vowed foe of my felicitie;   165

Ne I against the same can justly preace:
But since that band ye cannot now release,
Nor doen undo°; (for vowes may not be vaine,)
Soone as the terme of those six yeares shall cease,
Ye then shall hither backe returne againe,   170
The marriage to accomplish vowd betwixt you twain.

XX

Which for my part I covet to performe,
In sort as° through the world I did proclame,
That whoso kild that monster most deforme,
And him in hardy battaile overcame,   175
Should have mine onely daughter to his Dame,
And of my kingdome heyre apparaunt bee:
Therefore since now to thee perteines the same,
By dew desert of noble chevalree,
Both daughter and eke kingdome, lo, I yield to thee.   180

XXI

Then forth he called that his daughter faire,
The fairest Un' his onely daughter deare,
His onely daughter, and his onely heyre;
Who forth proceeding with sad sober cheare,
As bright as doth the morning starre appeare   185
Out of the East, with flaming lockes bedight,
To tell that dawning day is drawing neare,
And to the world does bring long wished light:
So faire and fresh that Lady shewd her selfe in sight.

XXII

So faire and fresh, as freshest flowre in May;   190
For she had layd her mournefull stole aside,
And widow-like sad wimple throwne away,
Wherewith her heavenly beautie she did hide,
Whiles on her wearie journey she did ride;
And on her now a garment she did weare,   195
All lilly white, withoutten spot, or pride,
That seemd like silke and silver woven neare,
But neither silke nor silver therein did appeare.

XXIII

The blazing brightnesse of her beauties beame,
And glorious light of her sunshyny face,   200
To tell, were as to strive against the streame;

My ragged rimes are all too rude and bace,
  Her heavenly lineaments for to enchace.
  Ne wonder; for her owne deare loved knight,
  All were she° dayly with himselfe in place,   205
  Did wonder much at her celestiall sight:
Oft had he seene her faire, but never so faire dight.

XXIV

So fairely dight, when she in presence came,
  She to her Sire made humble reverence,
  And bowed low, that her right well became,   210
  And added grace unto her excellence:
  Who with great wisedome and grave eloquence
  Thus gan to say. But eare he thus had said,
  With flying speede, and seeming great pretence
  Came running in, much like a man dismaid,   215
A Messenger with letters, which his message said.

XXV

All in the open hall amazed stood
  At suddeinnesse of that unwarie sight,
  And wondred at his breathlesse hastie mood.
  But he for nought would stay his passage right,   220
  Till fast before the king he did alight;
  Where falling flat, great humblesse he did make,
  And kist the ground, whereon his foot was pight;
  Then to his hands that writ he did betake,
Which he disclosing, red thus, as the paper spake.   225

XXVI

To thee, most mighty king of Eden faire,
  Her greeting sends in these sad lines addrest,
  The wofull daughter, and forsaken heire
  Of that great Emperour of all the West;
  And bids thee be advized for the best,   230
  Ere thou thy daughter linck in holy band
  Of wedlocke to that new unknowen guest:
  For he already plighted his right hand
Unto another love, and to another land.

XXVII

To me sad mayd, or rather widow sad,   235
  He was affiaunced long time before,
  And sacred pledges he both gave, and had,

False erraunt knight, infamous, and forswore:
Witnesse the burning Altars, which he swore,
And guiltie heavens of his bold perjury,   240
Which though he hath polluted oft of yore,
Yet I to them for judgement just do fly,
And them conjure t'avenge this shamefull injury.

XXVIII

Therefore since mine he is, or free or bond,
Or false or trew, or living or else dead,   245
Withhold, O soveraine Prince, your hasty hond
From knitting league with him, I you aread;
Ne weene my right with strength adowne to tread,
Through weaknesse of my widowhed, or woe;
For truth is strong her rightfull cause to plead,   250
And shall find friends, if need requireth soe.
So bids thee well to fare, Thy neither friend, nor foe, *Fidessa*.

XXIX

When he these bitter byting wordes had red,
The tydings straunge did him abashed make,
That still he sate long time astonished,   255
As in great muse, ne word to creature spake.
At last his solemne silence thus he brake,
With doubtfull eyes fast fixed on his guest;
Redoubted knight, that for mine onely sake
Thy life and honour late adventurest,   260
Let nought be hid from me, that ought to be exprest.

XXX

What meane these bloody vowes, and idle threats,
Throwne out from womanish impatient mind?
What heavens? what altars? what enraged heates
Here heaped up with termes of love unkind,   265
My conscience cleare with guilty bands would bind?
High God be witnesse, that I guiltlesse ame.
But if your selfe, Sir knight, ye faultie find,
Or wrapped be in loves of former Dame,
With crime do not it cover, but disclose the same.   270

XXXI

To whom the Redcrosse knight this answere sent
My Lord, my King, be nought hereat dismayd,
Till well ye wote by grave intendiment,

What woman, and wherefere doth me upbrayd
  With breach of love, and loyalty betrayd.   275
  It was in my mishaps, as hitherward
  I lately traveild, that unwares I strayd
  Out of my way, through perils straunge and hard;
That day should faile me, ere I had them all declard.

XXXII

There did I find, or rather I was found   280
  Of this false woman, that Fidessa hight,
  Fidessa hight the falsest Dame on ground,
  Most false Duessa, royall richly dight,
  That easy was to invegle weaker sight:
  Who by her wicked arts, and wylie skill,   285
  Too false and strong for earthly skill or might,
  Unwares me wrought unto her wicked will,
And to my foe betrayd, when least I feared ill.

XXXIII

Then stepped forth the goodly royall Mayd,
  And on the ground her selfe prostrating low,   290
  With sober countenaunce thus to him sayd;
  O pardon me, my soveraigne Lord, to show
  The secret treasons, which of late I know
  To have bene wroght by that false sorceresse.
  She onely she it is, that earst did throw   295
  This gentle knight into so great distresse,
That death him did awaite in dayly wretchednesse.

XXXIV

And now it seemes, that she suborned hath
  This craftie messenger with letters vaine,
  To worke new woe and unprovided scath,   300
  By breaking of the band betwixt us twaine;
  Wherein she used hath the practicke paine
  Of this false footman, clokt with simplenesse,
  Whom if ye please for to discover plaine,
  Ye shall him Archimago find, I ghesse,   305
The falsest man alive; who tries shall find no lesse.

XXXV

The king was greatly moved at her speach,
  And, all with suddein indignation fraight,

Bad on that Messenger rude hands to reach.
Eftsoones the Gard, which on his state did wait,   310
Attacht that faitor false, and bound him strait:
Who seeming sorely chauffed at his band,
As chained Beare, whom cruell dogs do bait,°
With idle force did faine them to withstand,
And often semblaunce made to scape out of their hand.   315

XXXVI

But they him layd full low in dungeon deepe,
  And bound him hand and foote with yron chains
  And with continual watch did warely keepe:
  Who then would thinke, that by his subtile trains
  He could escape fowle death or deadly paines?   320
  Thus when that princes wrath was pacifide,
  He gan renew the late forbidden bains,
  And to the knight his daughter dear he tyde,
With sacred rites and vowes for ever to abyde.

XXXVII

His owne two hands the holy knots did knit,   325
  That none but death for ever can devide;
  His owne two hands, for such a turne most fit,
  The housling fire° did kindle and provide,
  And holy water thereon sprinckled wide;
  At which the bushy Teade a groome did light,   330
  And sacred lamp in secret chamber hide,
  Where it should not be quenched day nor night,
For feare of evill fates, but burnen ever bright.

XXXVIII

Then gan they sprinckle all the posts with wine,
  And made great feast to solemnize that day;   335
  They all perfumde with frankencense divine,
  And precious odours fetcht from far away,
  That all the house did sweat with great aray:
  And all the while sweete Musicke did apply
  Her curious skill, the warbling notes to play,   340
  To drive away the dull Melancholy;
The whiles one sung a song of love and jollity.

XXXIX

During the which there was an heavenly noise
  Heard sound through all the Pallace pleasantly,
  Like as it had bene many an Angels voice   345
  Singing before th' eternall Majesty,
  In their trinall triplicities° on hye;
  Yet wist no creature whence that heavenly sweet
  Proceeded, yet eachone felt secretly
  Himselfe thereby reft of his sences meet,   350
And ravished with rare impression in his sprite.

XL

Great joy was made that day of young and old,
  And solemne feast proclaimd throughout the land,
  That their exceeding merth may not be told:
  Suffice it heare by signes to understand   355
  The usuall joyes at knitting of loves band.
  Thrise happy man the knight himselfe did hold,
  Possessed of his Ladies hart and hand,
  And ever, when his eye did her behold,
His heart did seeme to melt in pleasures manifold.   360

XLI

Her joyous presence, and sweet company
  In full content he there did long enjoy;
  Ne wicked envie, ne vile gealosy,
  His deare delights were able to annoy:
  Yet swimming in that sea of blissfull joy,   365
  He nought forgot how he whilome had sworne,
  In case he could that monstrous beast destroy,
  Unto his Faerie Queene backe to returne;
The which he shortly did, and Una left to mourne.

XLII

Now strike your sailes ye jolly Mariners,   370
  For we be come unto a quiet rode,
  Where we must land some of our passengers,
  And light this wearie vessell of her lode.
  Here she a while may make her safe abode,
  Till she repaired have her tackles spent,°   375
  And wants supplide. And then againe abroad
  On the long voyage whereto she is bent:
Well may she speede and fairely finish her intent.

Notes to *The Faerie Queen*, Cantos XI and XII

CANTO XI

I. *The Plot*: The Redcross Knight reaches the Brazen Tower in which Una's parents, the King and Queen of Eden, are besieged by the Dragon. The monster is described. The first day's fight is described, in which the Knight is borne through the air in the Dragon's claws, wounds him under the wing with his lance, but is scorched by the flames from the monster's mouth. The Knight is healed by a bath in the Well of Life. On the second day the Knight gives the Dragon several sword-wounds, but is stung by the monster's tail and forced to retreat by the flames. That night he is refreshed and healed by the balm from the Tree of Life. On the third day he slays the Dragon by a thrust into his vitals.

II. *The Allegory*: 1. Mankind has been deprived of Eden by Sin or Satan (Dragon). The Christian overcomes the devil by means of the whole armor of God (shield of faith, helmet of salvation, sword of the Spirit, etc.). The soul is strengthened by the ordinances of religion: baptism, regeneration, etc.

2. There is a hint of the long and desperate struggle between Reformed England (St. George) and the Church of Rome, in which the power of the Pope and the King of Spain was broken in England, the Netherlands, and other parts of Europe. Some may see a remoter allusion to the delivery of Ireland from the same tyranny.

13. BE AT YOUR KEEPING WELL, be well on your guard.

iii. This stanza is not found in the edition of 1590.

30. AND SEEMD UNEATH, etc., and seemed to shake the steadfast ground (so that it became) unstable. Church and Nares take *uneath* to mean "beneath" or "underneath"; Kitchin conjectures "almost."

31. THAT DREADFUL DRAGON, symbolical of Satan. Spenser here imitates the combat between St. George and the Dragon in the *Seven Champions of Christendom*, i.

32. This description of the dragon watching the tower from the sunny hillside is justly admired for its picturesqueness, power, and suggestiveness. The language is extremely simple, but the effect is awe-inspiring. It has been compared with Turner's great painting of the Dragon of the Hesperides.

42. O THOU SACRED MUSE, Clio, the Muse of History, whom Spenser calls the daughter of Phoebus (Apollo) and Mnemosyne (Memory).

56. TILL I OF WARRES, etc. Spenser is here supposed to refer to his plan to continue the *Faerie Queene* and treat of the wars of the English with Philip II ("Paynim King") and the Spanish ("Sarazin").

61. LET DOWNE THAT HAUGHTIE STRING, etc., cease that high-pitched strain and sing a second (or tenor) to my (lower) tune.

120. AS TWO BROAD BEACONS. Kitchin thinks this passage is a reminiscence of the beacon-fires of July 29, 1588, which signaled the arrival of the Armada off the Cornish coast.

158. HER FLITTING PARTS, her shifting parts; referring to the instability of the air.

161. LOW STOUPING, swooping low (to the ground); a term in falconry.

167. HAGARD HAUKE, a wild, untamed falcon.

168. ABOVE HIS HABLE MIGHT, beyond the strength of which he is capable.

172. HE SO DISSEIZED, etc., i.e. the dragon being thus dispossessed of his rough grip. The construction is nominative absolute.

185. AND GREEDY GULFE DOES GAPE, etc., i.e. the greedy waters gape as if they would devour the land.

187. THE BLUSTRING BRETHREN, the winds.

228. HIS WIDE DEVOURING OVEN, the furnace of his maw, or belly.

235. THAT GREAT CHAMPION, Hercules. The charmed garment steeped in the blood of the Centaur Nessus, whom Hercules had slain, was given him by his wife Dejanira in order to win back his love. Instead of acting as a philter, the poison-robe burned the flesh from his body. Ovid's *Metamorphoses*, ix, 105.

xxviii. Observe the correspondence between the adjectives in l. 244 and the nouns in l. 245. The sense is: "He was so faint," etc.

261. THE WELL OF LIFE. This incident is borrowed from *Bevis of Hampton*. The allegory is based on *John*, iv, 14, and *Revelation*, xxii, 1.

267. SILO, the healing Pool of Siloam, *John*, ix, 7. Jordan, by bathing in which Naaman was healed of leprosy, *II Kings*, v, 10.

268. BATH, in Somersetshire, a town famous from the earliest times for its medicinal baths. SPAU, a town in Belgium noted for its healthful waters, now a generic name for German watering-places.

269. CEPHISE, the river Cephissus in Boeotia whose waters possessed the power of bleaching the fleece of sheep. Cf. *Isaiah*, i, 18. HEBRUS, a river in Thrace, here mentioned because it awaked to music the head and lyre of the dead Orpheus, as he floated down its stream. Ovid's *Metamorphoses*, xi, 50.

295. TO MOVE, moving. This is a French idiom.

300. AS EAGLE FRESH OUT OF THE OCEAN WAVE, etc. There was an ancient belief, that once in ten years the eagle would soar into the empyrean, and plunging thence into the sea, would molt his plumage and renew his youth with a fresh supply of feathers.

312. HIS BRIGHT DEAW-BURNING BLADE, his bright blade flashing with the "holy water dew" in which it had been hardened (l. 317).

322. NE MOLTEN METTALL IN HIS BLOOD EMBREW, i.e. nor sword bathe itself in his (the dragon's) blood.

335. WITH SHARPE INTENDED STING, with sharp, outstretched sting.

366. THE GRIPED GAGE, the pledge (shield) seized (by the dragon).

386. MISSED NOT HIS MINISHT MIGHT, felt not the loss of its diminished strength; i.e. though cut off, the paw still held to the shield.

xliv. In comparing the fire-spewing dragon to a volcano, Spenser follows Vergil's *Aeneid*, iii, 571, and Tasso's *Jerusalem Delivered*, iv, 8.

406. A GOODLY TREE. Cf. *Genesis*, ii, 9, and *Revelation*, xxii, 2.

409. OVER ALL WERE RED, everywhere were spoken of.

414. Cf. *Genesis*, iii, 2. Adam and Eve were expelled from the garden lest they should eat and live forever.

434. DEADLY MADE, a creature of death, i.e. hell-born.

469. An imitation of an incident in the *Seven Champions* in which a winged serpent attempts to swallow St. George; i, 1.

477. AND BACK RETYRD, and as it was withdrawn. A Gallicism.

490. WHICH SHE MISDEEM'D, in which she was mistaken. Una feared that the dragon was not dead.

CANTO XII

I. *The Plot*: The death of the dragon is announced by the watchman on the tower of the city, and Una's parents, the King and Queen, accompanied by a great throng, come forth rejoicing at their deliverance. The Knight and Una are conducted with great honors into the palace. On the eve of their betrothal, Archimago suddenly appears as Duessa's messenger and claims the Knight. Their wicked attempt is frustrated, and the pair are happily betrothed. After a long time spent in Una's society, the Knight sets out to engage in the further service of the Faerie Queene.

II. *The Allegory*: Holiness, by conquering the devil, frees the whole human race from the tyranny of sin. It is embarrassed by the unexpected appearance of the consequences of its past sins, but makes a manly confession. In spite of hypocritical intrigues (Archimago) and false slanders (Duessa), Holiness is united to Truth, thus forming a perfect character. The champion of the church militant responds cheerfully to the calls of duty and honor.

2. Reformed England, having destroyed the brutal power of Rome, is firmly united to the truth in spite of the intrigues of the Pope to win it back to allegiance. It then goes forth against the King of Spain in obedience to the command of Queen Elizabeth.

3. VERE THE MAINE SHETE, shift the mainsail, BEARE UP WITH THE LAND, direct the ship toward land.

25. OUT OF HOND, at once.

43. OF TALL YOUNG MEN. An allusion to Queen Elizabeth's Pensioners, a band of the tallest and handsomest young men, of the best families and fortunes, that could be found (Warton). ALL HABLE ARMES TO SOWND, all proper to wield arms.

57. TO THE MAYDENS, to the accompaniment of the maidens' timbrels.

71. IN HER SELF-RESEMBLANCE WELL BESEENE, looking well in her resemblance to her proper self, i.e. a king's daughter.

73. THE RASKALL MANY, the crowd of common people.

116. OF GREAT NAME, of great celebrity, i.e. value.

117. FITTING PURPOSE FRAME, held fitting conversation.

xiv. Kitchin and Percival think this whole passage a clever compliment to the parsimony of the Queen's court.

161. THAT PROUD PAYNIM KING, probably a reference to Philip of Spain.

168. NOR DOEN UNDO, nor undo what has been done.

173. IN SORT AS, even as.

205. ALL WERE SHE, although she had been. IN PLACE, in various places.

313. BAIT. In Spenser's time bear-baiting was a favorite pastime of the people and received royal patronage.

328. THE HOUSLING FIRE, the sacramental fire. Spenser seems here to have in mind, not the Christian *housel* or Eucharist, but the Roman marriage rites with their symbolic fire and water.

347. TRINALL TRIPLICITIES, the threefold three orders of the celestial hierarchy according to the scholastic theologians. They were as follows: (1) Seraphim, Cherubim, Thrones; (2) Dominations, Virtues, Powers; (3) Princedoms, Archangels, and Angels. Cf. Dante's *Paradiso*, xxviii, Tasso's *Jerusalem Delivered*, xviii, 96, and Milton's *Paradise Lost*, v, 748.

375. HER TACKLES SPENT, her worn-out rigging.

Aarseth, Espen. "Allegories of Space: The Question of Spatiality in Computer Games." In Markku Eskelinen, Raine Koskimaa (Ed). *Cybertext Yearbook 2000*: University of Jyväskylä, Jyväskylä, Finland.

—. *Cybertext: Perspectives on Ergodic Literature*. Baltimore: Johns Hopkins UP, 1997.

—. "Quest Games as Post-Narrative Discourse." *Narrative across Media*: *The Languages of Storytelling*. Ed. Marie-Laure Ryan. Lincoln: U of Nebraska P, 2004. 361-76.

Abrams, M. H., Ed. *The Norton Anthology of English Literature*. New York: W. W. Norton, 2001.

Addams, Shay. *The Official Book of Ultima*. Greensboro, North Carolina: Compute, 1992.

Aspyr. *Dreamfall: The Longest Journey*. [Microsoft Xbox] Austin, TX: Aspyr, 2006.

Atari. *Neverwinter Nights 2*. [PC] New York: Atari, 2006.

Atkins, Barry. *More Than a Game*: *The Computer Game as Fictional Form*. Manchester: Manchester UP, 2003.

Auden, W. H. "The Quest Hero." *Texas Quarterly* IV (Winter 1961) 81-93.

Bacal, Simon. "Lord of Illusions: A Fable of Death and Resurrection." *Sci-Fi Entertainment* 1.5 (February 1995).

Barker, Clive. Introduction. *Clive Barker's Imajica Rulebook*. New York: HarperPrism, 1997.

—. "The Interactive Parallel Universe." Hollywood and Games Summit. Los Angeles. June 2007.

—. *People Online* Appearance. Transcript of online appearance, July 30 1998.

Barton, Matt. "The Early History of Computer Role-Playing Games Part I: The Early Years (1980–1983)." Feb 23 2007. http://www.gamasutra.com/features/20070223a/barton_01.shtml Apr 15 2007.

—. "The History of Computer Role-Playing Games Part II: The Golden Years (1985–1993)." Feb 23 2007 http://www.gamasutra.com/features/20070223b/barton_01.shtml Apr 15 2007.

—. "The History of Computer Role-Playing Games Part III: The Platinum and Modern Ages (1994–2004)." February 23 2007. http://www.gamasutra.com/features/20070411/barton_01.shtml Jun 22 2007

Barwood, Hal. "Writing Before the Words—Narrative Design." Game Developers' Conference. San Francisco. March 2007.

Bateman, Chris. *21ˢᵗ Century Game Design.* Hingham, Massachussetts: Charles River Media, 2005.

Bethesda. *Call of Cthulhu.* [Microsoft Xbox] Rockville, MD: Bethesda, 2005.

—. *The Elder Scrolls III: Morrowind.* [Microsoft Xbox and PC] Rockville, MD: Bethesda, 2002.

—. *The Elder Scrolls IV: Oblivion.* [Microsoft Xbox 360] Rockville, MD: Bethesda, 2006.

Blake, William. *Jerusalem. The Complete Poetry and Prose of William Blake.* Ed. David Erdman. Berkeley: U of California P, 1982. 144–259.

Blizzard. *World of Warcraft.* [PC] Irvine, CA: Blizzard, 2006.

Bogost, Ian. *Unit Operations: An Approach to Videogame Criticism.* Cambridge, MA: 2006.

Bolter, Jay, and Richard Grusin. *Remediation: Understanding New Media.* London: MIT P, 1999.

Campanella, Eric. "Eric Campanella on the Symbol of Torment." Jul 30 2003. http://crap.planescape-torment.org/threads/eric_symbol.htm Aug 27 2007.

Campbell, Joseph. *The Masks of God: Creative Mythology.* 1968. New York: Penguin, 1976.

—. *The Hero with a Thousand Faces.* 1949. Princeton, NJ: Princeton UP, 1973.

Celowin. Scripting Tutorials I-IX. *NWN Lexicon.* Compiled HTML File. http://nwvault.ign.com/View.php?view=Other.Detail&id=736

Crawford, Chris. *Chris Crawford on Interactive Storytelling.* Berkeley: New Riders, 2005.

Danesi, Marcel. *The Puzzle Instinct: The Meaning of Puzzles in Human Life.* Bloomington: Indiana UP, 2002.

Davis, Erik. *TechGnosis: Myth, Magic, and Mysticism in the Age of Information.* New York: Harmony, 2004.

Dawson, Tom. "A Beginner's Guide, Lesson 4—Anatomy of a Quest, part 1." http://cs.elderscrolls.com/constwiki/index.php/A_beginner%27s_guide%2C_lesson_4__Anatomy_of_a_quest%2C_part_1

—. "A Beginner's Guide, Lesson 5—Anatomy of a Quest, part 2." http://cs.elderscrolls.com/constwiki/index.php/A_beginner%27s_guide%2C_lesson_5_-_Anatomy_of_a_quest%2C_part_2

Demaria, Rusel. *High Score! The Illustrated History of Video Games.* Emeryville, California: McGraw Hill/Osborne, 2004.

Dick, Philip K. "If You Find This World Bad, You Should See Some of the Others." *The Shifting Realities of Philip K. Dick*. Ed. Lawrence Sutin. New York: Pantheon, 1995. 259-80.

Dunniway, Troy. "Using the Hero's Journey in Games." Nov 27 2000. http://www.gamasutra.com/features/20001127/dunniway_01.htm Feb 10 2007.

de Troyes, Chrétien. *Arthurian Romances*. Trans. William Kibler. London: Penguin, 1991.

Dyack, Denis. "Creating Universes: Blog # 10." Jul 6 2006. http://blogs.ign.com/silicon-knights/p3 Aug 27 2007.

Electronic Arts. *Clive Barker's* Undying. [PC] Redwood City, California: Electronic Arts, 2001.

Emigh, David. *The Quest*. Champaign-Urbana: Icarus Games, 1984.

Erickson, Daniel. "A Craftsman's Guide to Nonlinear Dialogue." Game Developers' Conference. San Francisco. March 2007.

Erickson, Wayne. *Mapping the Faerie Queen: Quest Structures and the World of the Poem*. New York: Garland, 1996.

Fisher, Adrian. *Secrets of the Maze: An Interactive Guide to the World's Most Amazing Mazes*. Hauppage, New York: Barron's Educational Series, 1987.

Frasca, Gonzalo. "Ludologists Love Stories, Too: Notes from a Debate That Never Took Place." Level Up Conference 2003. http://ludology.org/articles/Frasca_LevelUp2003.pdf. October 26 2006.

Freeman, R. Austin "The Art of the Detective Story." *The Art of the Mystery Story: A Collection of Critical Essays*. Ed. Howard Haycraft. New York: Biblo and Tannen, 1976. 7-17.

Frye, Northrop. *Anatomy of Criticism: Four Essays*. Princeton, N.J.: Princeton UP, 1957.

Gaider, David. "Setting Variables." Neverwinter Nights: For Builders. http://nwn.bioware.com/builders/sctutorial1.html

Gee, James Paul. *What Video Games Have to Teach Us About Learning and Literacy*. New York: Palgrave MacMillan, 2004.

Gilthonym. *Don't Panic: The Hitchiker's Guide to the Neverwinter Nights 2 Toolset*. http://nwvault.ign.com/View.php?view=NWN2Tutorials.Detail&id=14. Jun 22 2007.

Glassner, Andrew. *Interactive Storytelling: Techniques for 21ˢᵗ Century Fiction*. Natick, MA: A K Peters, 2004.

Guardiola, Emmanuel. *Écrire pour le jeu: techniques scenaristiques du jeu informatique et vidéo*. Paris: Dixit, 2000.

Gygax, Gary. *Master of the Game: Principles and Techniques for Becoming an Expert Role-Playing Game Master*. New York: Perigee, 1989.

Hatfield, Daemon. "Clive Barker Summoning New Game." IGN. Jul 18 2006 http://pc.ign.com/articles/719/719433pl.html Aug 31 2007.

Hite, Kenneth. "Narrative Structure and Creative Tension in *Call of Cthulhu*." *Second Person: Role-Playing and Story in Games and Playable Media*. Eds. Pat Harrigan and Noah Wardrip-Fruin. Cambridge: MIT P, 2007.

Interplay. *Planescape: Torment*. [PC] Irvine, California: Interplay, 1999.

Iser, Wolfgang. "Indeterminacy and the Reader's Response in Prose Fiction." *Aspects of Narrative: Selected Papers from the English Institute*. Ed. J. Hillis Miller. New York: Columbia UP, 1971.

Jenkins, Henry. "Game Design as Narrative Architecture." *First Person: New Media as Story, Performance, and Game*. Eds. Noah Wardrip-Fruin and Pat Harrigan. Cambridge: MIT P, 2004.

Jerz, Dennis G. "Somewhere Nearby is Colossal Cave: Examining Will Crowther's Original 'Adventure' in Code and in Kentucky." *Digital Humanities Quarterly* 1:2 (Summer 2007). http://www.digitalhumanities.org/dhq/

Juul, Jesper. *Half-Real: Video Games between Real Rules and Fictional Worlds*. Cambridge: MIT P, 2005.

Kaplan, Jeff. "Questing in *World of Warcraft*: Interview with Jeff Kaplan." *World of Warcraft Insider*. http://blizzard.com/wow/insider/insider19interview.shtml June 20 2006.

Kelly 2, R. V. *Massively Multiplayer Online Role-Playing Games: The People, the Addiction, and the Playing Experience*. Jefferson, North Carolina: McFarland & Company, 2004.

Kimbrell, Jason. "Write-Up of Group One's Work." Student paper, 2006.

—. "Quest Structures and Shadows in *The Crying of Lot 49*." Student paper, 2006.

King, Brad, and John Borland. *Dungeons and Dreamers: The Rise of Computer Game Culture from Geek to Chic*. New York: McGraw-Hill, 2003.

Koster, Ralph. *A Theory of Fun for Game Design*. Scotsdale, Arizona: Paraglyph, 2005.

Long, Geoffrey. "Transmedia Storytelling." ACM SIGGRAPH Symposium on Digital Games. Boston. July 2006.

Mackay, Daniel. *The Fantasy Role-Playing Game: A New Performing Art*. Jefferson: McFarland & Company, 2001.

Marlowe, Chris. "Barker Hears Call, Creates 'Jericho' Game." *Hollywood Reporter*. 18 July 2006. http://www.clivebarker.info/ints06.html

Matarasso, P. M., Trans. *The Quest of the Holy Grail*. New York: Penguin, 1969.

Mendelson, Edward. "The Sacred, the Profane, and *The Crying of Lot 49*." *Pynchon: A Collection of Critical Essays*. Edward Mendelson, Ed. Englewood Cliffs, NJ: Prentice-Hall, 1978. 97-111.

Merriman, Iskander, *et al.* "A Simple Quest." *Neverwinter Nights Lexicon*. Compiled HTML file.

McGann, Jerome. *Radiant Textuality: Literature after the World Wide Web*. New York: Palgrave Macmillan, 2001.

Microsoft. *Fable: The Lost Chapters*. [Microsoft Xbox] Redmond, WA: Microsoft, 2005.

Milton, John. *Paradise Lost. The Complete Poetry of John Milton*. Ed. John T. Shawcross. 249-517.

Mona, Erik. "From the Basement to the Basic Set: The Early Years of *Dungeons & Dragons*." Cambridge: MIT P, 2007.

Montfort, Nick. *Twisty Little Passages: An Approach to Interactive Fiction*. Cambridge: MIT P, 2003.

Natkin, Stéphane. *Video Games & Interactive Media: A Glimpse at New Digital Entertainment*. Wellesley, MA: A K Peters, 2006.

Neugebauer, Annie. "Quest of Life." Student paper, 2006.

Neverwinter Nights Lexicon. Ed. Jasperre *et al.* Compiled HTML File. 2004. http://nwvault.ign.com/View.php?view=Other.Detail&id=736

Niesz, Anthony J., and Norman N. Holland. "Interactive Fiction." *Critical Inquiry* 11 (1984): 110–29.

Nintendo. *Eternal Darkness: Sanity's Requiem*. [Nintendo Gamecube] Kyoto: Nintendo, 2002.

Novak, Jeannie. *Game Development Essentials: An Introduction*. New York: Thomson, 2005.

Origin Systems. *Ultima IV: Quest of the Avatar*. [PC] Austin, TX: Origin Systems, 1985.

Pavic, Milorad. *Dictionary of the Khazars: A Lexicon Novel in 100,000 Words*. Trans. Christina Pribicevic-Zoric. New York: Knopf, 1988.

Pinsky, Robert. "The Muse in the Machine: Or, the Poetics of Zork." *New York Times* March 19, 1995. pp. 3, 26–27.

Propp, Vladimir. 1928. *Morphology of the Folktale.* Austin: U of Texas P, 1973.

Pynchon, Thomas. *The Crying of Lot 49.* 1964. New York: Harper & Row, 1990.

Pyrhönen, Heta. *Murder from an Academic Angle: An Introduction to the Study of Detective Narrative.* Columbia, SC: Camden House, 1994.

Robinett, Warren. "Adventure as a Video Game: Adventure for the Atari 2600." *The Game Design Reader: A Rules of Play Anthology.* Eds. Katie Salen and Eric Zimmerman. Cambridge: MIT P, 2006.

Rollings, Andrew, and Ernest Adams. *Andrew Rollings and Ernest Adams on Game Design.* Indianapolis: New Riders, 2003.

—. *Fundamentals of Game Design.* New Jersey: Prentice Hall, 2007.

Ryan, Marie-Laure. *Narrative as Virtual Reality: Immersion and Interactivity in Literature and Electronic Media.* Baltimore: Johns Hopkins UP, 2001.

Sadowski, Piotr. *The Knight on His Quest: Symbolic Patterns of Transition in Sir Gawain and the Green Knight.* Newark: U of Delaware P, 1996.

Salen, Katie, and Eric Zimmerman. *Rules of Play: Game Design Fundamentals.* MIT P: Cambridge, 2004.

Schick, Lawrence. *Heroic Worlds: A History and Guide to Role-Playing Games.* Buffalo: Prometheus, 1991.

Skydiver. "Making a Quest for Morrowind: A Very, Very, Very Basic Guide." http://www.themcnews.com/Quest_tut.pdf October 6 2007

Semel, Paul. "Gory Days." *Complex.* February/March 2007. http://www.clivebarker.info/ints07.html

Spenser, Edward. *The Faerie Queen.* Ed. Thomas P. Roche. New York: Penguin, 1987.

Tosca, Susana. "The Quest Problem in Computer Games." *Proceedings of the First International Conference on Technologies for Interactive Digital Storytelling and Entertainment TIDSE '03.* Ed. Stefan Göbel et al. Darmstadt: Fraunhofer IRB Verlag 2003. http://www.it-c.dk/people/tosca/quest.htm. April 7 2006.

Tronstad, Ragnhild. "Semiotic and Nonsemiotic MUD Performance." COSIGN. Amsterdam. 10-12 September 2001. http://www.cosignconference.org/cosign2001/papers/Tronstad.pdf. April 7 2006.

Truffaut, Francois. *Hitchcock.* New York: Simon and Schuster, 1985.

Twelker, Eric. "Crossing Over: Master of Horror Discusses *Undying*." Dec 2000 http://www.svenlib.sandy.ru/clivebarker/inter%5C00amazon.htm Aug 30 2007.

Vogler, Christopher. *The Writer's Journey: Mythic Structures for Writers*. Studio City: M. Wiese Productions, 1998.

Von Eschenbach, Wolfram. *Parzival*. Trans. Helen Mustard and Charles Passage. New York: Vintage, 1961.

Walker, Jill. "A Network of Quests in *World of Warcraft*." *Second Person: Role-Playing and Story in Games and Playable Media*. Ed. Pat Harrigan and Noah Wardrip-Fruin. Cambridge: MIT P, 2007.

Wallis, James. "Making Games That Make Stories." *Second Person: Role-Playing and Story in Games and Playable Media*. Cambridge: MIT P, 2007. 69-80.

Wardrip-Fruin, Noah, and Pat Harrigan, eds. *First Person: New Media as Story, Performance, and Game*. Cambridge: MIT P , 2004.

—. *Second Person: Role-Playing and Story in Games and Playable Media*. Cambridge: MIT P, 2007.

—. "Writing *Fable*, Part One." http://grandtextauto.gatech.edu/2004/09/13/writing-fable-1/#comments

Wesp, Edward M. "The Past as Present: Virtual Histories and Historical Fictions." *Modern Language Association*. Washington, D.C. December 28 2005.

Williams, Roberta. *The King's Quest Collection*. pdf manual and documentation for *King's Quest Collection* on DVD-ROM

Zimmerman, Eric. "Narrative, Interactivity, Play, and Games: Four Naughty Concepts in Need of Discipline." *First Person: New Media as Story, Performance, and Game*. Eds. Noah Wardrip-Fruin and Pat Harrigan. Cambridge: MIT P, 2004.